What others say about
America's Steadfast Dream

"If out of the abundance of the heart man speaketh and writeth, then I believe that E. Merrill Root must be a noble soul."

Elder Ezra Taft Benson
Former U.S. Secretary of Agriculture

"Merrill Root says more worth saying, with more wisdom and beauty and just plain goodness, than almost anyone I ever heard of. He is a great man who makes us all even prouder that, like him, we too are Americans."

Walter Brennan
Three-time Academy Award Winner

"Professor E. Merrill Root's gentle manner conceals an inner fire that has forged a great poet-patriot."

Devin A. Garrity
President, Devin-Adair Publishers

"A new book by E. Merrill Root! I know the poet, the philosopher, and the person — and I love them all. If Root wrote it, I want it."

Clarence E. Manion
Former Dean, Notre Dame Law School

"Professor Root is someone very special. He is a great man who loves our country and understands its people and purpose. He is the Poet Laureate of the real America that is simple and decent and good."

Hon. George C. Wallace
Governor of Alabama

AMERICA'S STEADFAST DREAM

E. MERRILL ROOT

WESTERN ISLANDS

PUBLISHERS

BOSTON   LOS ANGELES

The twenty-five chapters of this book originally appeared as essays in *American Opinion* magazine over a period of ten years. They are reproduced here by permission of the copyright holder, Robert Welch, Inc.

The hardbound edition of *America's Steadfast Dream* was published by Western Islands in 1971. This paperbound reprinting contains every word that appeared in the original hardbound edition.

Introduction, Foreword, and Afterword © 1971 by Western Islands. Paperbound edition issued November 1974.

Published by Western Islands, Belmont, Massachusetts 02178

Standard Book Number 88279-117-6

Manufactured in the United States of America.

To

Scott Stanley Jr.,
once my student and
always my friend.

Introduction

I HAVE been long familiar with the
writings and poetry of Professor E. Merrill Root, and I have
read every poem, article and essay in this
book with delight, with deep emotion, with keen
joy, and profound appreciation of a mind that is
increasingly rare in this dull and sterile
and intellectually bankrupt era.

Professor Root's voice is the voice of the majestic
and wonder-creating past, and, I hope, of a
future Renaissance. It is the voice of eternal
youth, and the awestruck voice of youth.
He is constantly elated over the beauties of the
world, as at a new discoverance, the new morning
of creation. He is everlastingly moved when
contemplating how the world is charged with the grandeur
of God. He sees, not only with the eyes of an
admirer of beauty, the understanding of an
intellectual man, but with the eyes of wisdom.
Wisdom, when combined with the clarity and ecstasy of youth,
is a God-given gift, and Professor Root possesses it.

His essays equal Emerson's in profundity and truth,
and he is the heir of Thoreau. There is much
in his poetry which reminds one of Thomas Hardy and
William Blake, with sometimes an overtone of
Browning. And there are lines that equal Shakespeare. As a
Briton, I am given more to understatement than to

overstatement, and when I say it is my opinion
that Professor Root's essays, in particular, are literary
gems I mean it with all sincerity, and
with all my heart.

Were E. Merrill Root an insane and screaming "Liberal,"
a traitor to the God and the country he
so reveres, he would be among the most famous
literary figures in America, the Poet Laureate —
and we surely need a sane one! His poetry
can be understood, for it has the mercurial
brightness of pure water, and his essays appeal to all that
is noble in man. For these reasons, I am
sure, he is as yet known only to a smaller circle
of admirers of his genius. But, who knows? There is always
tomorrow, and a hope for America in tomorrow,
and honor for great men.

TAYLOR CALDWELL
Buffalo, New York

Acknowledgements

I OWE deep gratitude to Scott Stanley Jr., my editor and friend, who encouraged me to write these essays for the pages of *American Opinion*. Intuitively he saw that, in our mortal struggle with collectivism, we need to speak to the soul and for the Inner Kingdom; and that there are thousands and thousands who are waiting for such a word. Amazingly, he would suggest to me just the topic on which I wanted to write, even before I had known it myself. That faculty, among many others, makes him unique and great.

I wish to thank, also, Marian Probert Welch. In her beautifully gracious wisdom and her unfailing insight, she is one of the great women I have known. I owe her much.

To Taylor Caldwell, who wrote such world-masterpieces as *A Pillar Of Iron* and *Great Lion Of God*, and who did me the honor to write my Introduction, my humble thanks!

I cannot thank enough Mrs. Kennedy Smith Sr., of Pittsburgh, Pennsylvania. Mother of brilliant sons and daughters, a woman brilliant in herself, she devoted a year of wise and patient work to the reading, selection, and arrangement of these essays. If they become not separate essays but a book, hers the credit and the praise.

I thank Lee Clark, who, in her charm, her generous appreciation, her abiding faith, made it a delight to deliver manuscripts.

I must thank also the great conservatives, G.K. Chesterton, Hilaire Belloc, C.S. Lewis, and others, who wrote proud work so that I can humbly review it. I hope that my words may serve their name and fame, and help their work to reach even more thousands.

To the many friends who have written me and criticized me, whom I cannot mention by their too numerous individual names, my thanks.

To my wife, Dorothy MacNab Root, for her patient typing, her careful reading and criticism, her unfailing inspiration, and her revelation of the Feminine Woman, my more than thanks.

And finally I wish to thank Robert Welch, our greatest champion of less government, more responsibility, and a better world, and one of our greatest champions against the collectivist conspiracy. He is not only far-sighted and inexorable against that conspiracy, he is also wide-souled and generous in his appreciation of religion, philosophy, and art — and all the grace notes of conservatism. I admire him, I revere him, and I acknowledge my debt to him.

E. MERRILL ROOT
Kennebunkport, Maine

Table Of Contents

Preserve Thy Integrity

In The Beginning Was The Word

Foreword

IT IS an almost frightening thing to reread what you have written, sometimes years before, and to face it after it has gone out into the world and become an individual in its own right. It may daunt you; sometimes it may inspire you; always it reveals you to yourself. So it has been for me, with the book you are about to read.

This volume is a collection of chapters, written over nearly a decade, as essays in AMERICAN OPINION. They are united by one underlying philosophy and one dominant mood.

I here try to make coherent and affirmative a certain philosophy, an American philosophy, and to do so in terms of art. That philosophy is conservative, in the sense that it would conserve and affirm certain elements of life that I believe are supreme in value and fundamental in position. In a way, I try to be a conservationist of the inner life, as the conservationist we usually think of is the conservationist of the outer world. Like that other conservationist, I wish to preserve the earth from erosion and depletion; the purity of our waters from contamination; the glory of our forests that "are lovely, dark and deep" from the axes of the ignorant. I would conserve the values in the inner life which correspond to these values in the outer life. I would be an ecologist of the soul.

More and more as my life has matured, I have realized that by fundamental nature I am a conservative. I have realized that I wish to preserve the roots of life whence grow the blossoms and the fruits of life, and that I have become a genuine radical — *i.e.*, one who works with the roots of life, laboring to set them more firmly and to nourish them more richly. I applaud fruitful change that comes from an enhancement and intensification of last things that maintain their continuity with first things. But, as I see it, such change must be growth from within, so that you and I and our nation become ever more clearly, more richly, more truly, what we always *are*, potentially in principle. Man is ever seeking novelty; God is forever and ever making things new. He does not make the seasons, nor the rose, nor the Labrador retriever, nor the lover nor the poet, *novel —*

He makes them new. And because they are new in terms of their fundamental being, they are vitally old; as tomorrow's sunrise will be the newest of dawns and also the oldest of dawns, since it shone upon the Birthday of Creation. Such is my deepest belief. It was mine even before I fully knew it; it has grown increasingly mine with all the changes and experiences of my life. As I live geographically in America, so I live, psychographically, in this faith.

This philosophy is the dynamic within all that you read here. It is the true I, as much mine as the flesh that adorns (if I may venture such a word) my bones. In every various topic that I treat, this one central philosophy is there. I try to make it live with imagination, art, humor, parable; but it is the philosophy that is to me the important thing. In presenting it, I make no pretence of tolerance. I make no pretence of "seeing all sides" (in the sense of affirming all sides). I know what I believe; I know what I don't believe. I say so — and let the icicles fall where they may.

By the nature of my philosophy and myself, I have to reject and deplore certain political and social systems. I abhor Communism, Socialism, and that half-and-half neuter thing known as "Liberalism." I regard them as enemies of God and enslavers of man. I say so, without fear or favor. I am not impartial about them, though I think the evidence against them is objective; and it is because of that objective evidence that I cannot be impartial. No good doctor is impartial to tetanus; no good jeweler is impartial before paste and pearl, or diamond and glass.

But at the same time I am not partial to what is today called Capitalism. Recently, Cleon Skousen wrote a revealing book called *The Naked Capitalist*. It explores what AMERICAN OPINION, through the articles of Gary Allen and others, has more and more been exploring — the strange underworld of international finance-capitalism, where *Insiders* of the Establishment seek to use masks of Socialism and "Liberalism" and even Communism, to secure (they think) their own wealth, and to increase (they hope) their own power. An exploration of the deracinated secularism that accompanies modern Capitalism, the smartness and neon light of it, its cynical and negative license that is supposed to be liberty, is long overdue. I applaud it. I do not equate what is today called Capitalism with what is genuinely conservative. I believe that those who truly believe in the free market, in private property, in every man under his own vine and fig tree, will agree.

At any rate, my chief interest and my central emphasis here is not the political and social battle between Capitalism and Communism. The social and the political are, to me, the surface of things, not the center of things. I do not believe in economic determinism, whether of Karl Marx or of Jeremy Bentham, or of anybody else. I am interested in the weather of the mind and the climate of the soul, and I believe that we can do something about them. And I believe that only as the mind is straight and the soul is healthy can we have a social *order* and a political *Republic*. So, if any of you read further, you will find, again and again and again, that I am concerned with philosophy, with religion, with art, as the fundamental things. I seek to see them as they are; I seek to see them in terms of orthodoxy, which means straight thinking. I do not claim any "right" to this point of view; I express it because I think it is right; and I feel a deep responsibility to express it. And I have no more tolerance for its denial and negation than Elijah did for the priests of Baal.

I am here deeply interested in youth. For many years I was a teacher. I found youth vivid and congenial; I never "taught down" to youth, for I felt that we were sharing the great adventure of mind and soul, seeking truth, seeking reality, and that in such an adventure the few more years or the few less years were unimportant. Goethe at eighty-three died young, in the right sense; Keats, at twenty-six, died old, in the right sense. So here I speak to youth as I think youth would have me, without any button on my rapier, saying starkly what I think, criticizing what I do not like, but with a deep belief in and a reverence for the integrity of youth. Yet I am interested equally in maturity and the wisdom of age, as the Chinese were while China was still free and sane. I am interested, as you will see if you consent to read, in the family as an organic and integral unit, where the many, or the several, are made one. I am interested in seeing the living center of things – first God, and then the family, and then our country.

I also wish to encourage what may be called a Renaissance of Wonder, a renewal of the world with the elixir of poetry. If somehow, even for a vital minority, we can initiate that Renaissance of Wonder, we may again find happiness in this temporal earthly interlude that we call life. For we shall again find meaning in our pilgrimage and zest in our journey.

. One thing that I hope to make clear is this: I do not regard affluence, or a high standard of living, or material wealth, as sufficient reasons *in themselves* for upholding an economic or social system. Sometimes such things can be impediments to the clarity of our vision or the audacity of our action. Remember what the Roman legions called their necessary baggage. They spoke of such things as *impedimenta*. From the same root we get the word impediments. But to the legions, *impedimenta* made their advance possible and their attack formidable. So it should be with us. Our affluence and our wealth should not be impediments, but *impedimenta.* We need the *impedimenta*, and it is one of the curses of Communism that it gives many men, indeed most men, no necessary *impedimenta*. But we must never let our *impedimenta* become impediments!

I would define this book as an attempt to see our goal — neither a utopia nor a myopia — in the mind, the spirit, the soul. Carl Jung named one of his finest books, *Modern Man In Search Of A Soul.* That, not in terms of psychology in itself, but of philosophy in itself, is my search too; I think modern man's greatest need is to find his soul, and that is what I am seeking. I hope you will share the search.

As a part of my clearest belief and my deepest intent I try to show, I wish to reveal, that conservatism does not uphold a *status quo*, or state in which things stand, but that its center is a *potentia qua* (another Latin phrase which we ought to incorporate into English), or power from which things flow.

I wish, also, to define the difference between conformity and confirmation. I show, in the following pages, that the "Establishment" is the "Liberal" collectivist Establishment; that the mass conformity today is conformity to loose, slack, and flaccid ideas, to the easy assumptions and unexamined premises of the Left, to the absurd. And, as Socrates told us long ago, the unexamined life is not worth living. The conservative, on the contrary, seeks not conformity to, but confirmation by — confirmation by the logic of the mind, the experience of the soul, the reality of the laws of Nature. George Orwell knew this and said it well: The basic freedom (his Winston Smith wrote) is the freedom to say that two plus two are four.

And I would define the mood of this volume as one of zest and joy. If anyone supposes that conservatism is sourpuss negation, here the bars are down and the clover field is waiting; come with me and run in the green grass and lie laughing in the pink clover of God, come and walk or stand quietly and smile to yourself or romp until you are weary and can throw yourself on the green bed of the meadow and breathe the sweetness of God's earth. For I believe that until you know the glory of God, you cannot enjoy Him forever; nor can you long (or really) enjoy anything else. Consider:

Poor A.E. Housman seems to have had no faith at all. Consequently he wrote, in anguish: "I, a stranger and afraid / In a world I never made." Housman could fashion fine lyrics. But if he *had* made the world, I fear it would have been a bleak one, with too many lads twitching out their lives kicking heels at the end of a rope. No, the Maker of the world was He who created the dodo (beak with a faint excuse of bird); the tiger . . . and the lamb; Pascal and Pasteur and the peacock; and Shakespeare, who could create the tragedy of Lear and the romance of the Forest of Arden, where jolly voices sing:

> This carol they began that hour,
> With a hey, and a ho, and a hey nonino,
> How that life was but a flower.

Of course we are all "strangers" here, for our home lies elsewhere than on this earth; but we do not need to be "afraid," for *He* made the world and He has overcome the world. The tragedy of our hour is that — modern man has forgotten His joy. But I have known it, and can assure you it is real. I hope that what I write will prove it.

In *Sartor Resartus*, Thomas Carlyle said that the true spiritual life of man begins with an "Everlasting No" and should continue until it also embraces an "Everlasting Yes." The Everlasting No is the soul's ultimatum to falsity, to ugliness, to evil; these it challenges with a great refusal. "The Everlasting No had said: 'Behold, thou art fatherless, outcast, and the universe is mine [*the Devil's*]'; to which my whole Me now made answer: '*I* am not thine, but Free, and forever hate thee!'" But more than this, the Everlasting Yes transcends this negative nobility; it says Yes to truth, to beauty, to good. In it, we affirm that which is excellent; and we truly live — for good, and in God. Then, "The mad primeval Discord is hushed; the rudely-jumbled conflicting elements bind themselves into separate Firmaments: deep silent rock-foundations are built beneath; and the skyey vault with its everlasting Luminaries above: instead of a dark wasteful Chaos, we have a blooming, fertile, heaven-encompassed World."

I hope that what I write may be a new statement of that Everlasting No, that Everlasting Yes; for I believe that they are necessary for life in every age, and possible for life even in this age. At least I try to say this in the pages that follow.

And so let this foreword conclude with the words of the Mediaeval mystic, Angelus Silesius: "Friend, it is e'en enough. Wouldst thou more? Then thyself become the book, become the reading!"

Enter The Search For The Soul

Frontiers Of Self-Reliance

SURELY you have noticed the recent renewal of distaste for the American Frontier. By frequent statement and by pervading innuendo, the American Frontier is supposed to be a vestigial relic that is responsible, like an infected appendix, for the alleged "sickness" and the recurring "violence" in America today. Mixed up with this, as a recurrent motif, is an attack on self-reliance and a surrender to reliance upon "society." And, oddly stirred into this mélange of modernity and illogic, there is an almost hysterical assertion that the "frontier" is completely done for and about to be embalmed.

In *Huckleberry Finn* the delightfully nauseous "King," in his bumbling maudlin way, refers to funeral obsequies as "funeral orgies." And "funeral orgies" is the term for what we have been witnessing in these sad ludicrous days of the latest "Liberal" binge — "funeral orgies" over the grave of the frontier, and over the corpse of the self-reliant American who inhabited that frontier.

In these orgies we are of course receiving the solicitude of many famous morticians. All speak of a dead frontier and the coffined man of self-reliance. And all remind me of the undertaker in *Huckleberry Finn* — "He was the softest, glidingest, stealthiest man I ever see; and there warn't no more smile to him than there is to a ham." The Kept Press, the Kept TV, the Kept Politicians are all there. Their theme is: *The frontier is dead. The self-reliant man is dead. Long live the society-dependent man!*

I

I SUPPOSE they do this because they are so afraid that Americans

1

will see that we live on a vaster and more terrible frontier than ever and that this frontier demands we rely upon ourselves more than ever before.

Today's frontier is not only in the West. It is in the East and North as well; it is in the heartland of "civilization," and nowhere is it more obvious than in the Nation's Capital. The terrors of the frontier are no longer on the wild edge of the country, but in our cities. It is a frontier where disarmed and brow-beaten Marshal Dillons are forbidden to enforce the law, except against good citizens who try to defend themselves, and where outlaws, professional badmen, and brash characters who love to shoot up the town are regarded by the Liberal Establishment as innocent victims of "underprivilege," who deserve Welfare at best and a psychiatrist at worst. It is a frontier where you don't drive a bus in certain sections at night unless you have the deathwish; where your business lies always under the threat of arson; and where to walk the street at night is to invite mugging, rape, or murder.

Our cities are like the old frontier before the coming of order and law, before the Wyatt Earps or the Marshal Dillons. In this frontier mere survival, not to speak of fruitful labor and a home under one's own vine and figtree, depends as always upon self-reliance. We are on the frontier today, and we all live dangerously.

You pay your taxes, of course, and one supposed benefit is civil security. Your great right, as a citizen, is civil security. But you do not get it. When this happened on the Western frontier, the only chance, first of survival and then of civilization, lay in the man himself, the self-reliant man. And so today, in an age when we have been lulled by the lie that "Washington can do it!" — or "You can depend on society!" — we again face the eternal fact that, outside intelligence and courage in the individual soul, there *is* no security.

Nor is there any chance of building the wild new frontier into an ordered, livable, and fruitful society except by the intelligence, courage, energy, and will of self-reliant men. Washington — or New York under a mayor like John Lindsay — can never rid us of our slums, our rats, our "poverty," our monstrously styled "ghettos." Only the wit and the hard work and will of individual men, black men and white men, can from wreck and sediment create a fairer world. The great words of Chesterton are eternally valid. In "The Ballad Of The White Horse," Our Lady tells King Alfred, as She tells brave men always:

I tell you naught for your comfort,
Yea, naught for your desire,
Save that the sky grows darker yet
And the sea rises higher.

The flabby generations, fed on the pap and treacle of "Liberalism," expect the easy answer and live in the syntax of the passive voice. They expect all to be done for them; they want to do nothing for themselves — and others. They don't want to be free men, but *freedmen*. And that is why nothing is done for real to help our cities, and all that is falsely done *undoes*. But slums will be made homes, and work will be found for willing men, and a fairer world will be created, when men awake from the collective somnambulism and resolve to be — and become — self-reliant.

On the old frontier there were no subsidies, no governmental cushions, no social air-conditioning. You faced the flood or the drought, the wolves amid the sheep or the cougars among the cattle, the wind and the snow and the sand, the failure of the crops or the fire in the night, as a man should. It was your responsibility. No one gave you a right to a living; you made a living or you accepted your dying. Your neighbors would help you, but they could not take your burdens wholly upon themselves. You had to take, like Ulysses' men in Tennyson's poem, the thunder or the sunshine with a frolic welcome.

And, the self-reliant man of the old frontier did just that — he accepted the thunder or the sunshine with a frolic welcome — and he built from both the greatness which is America. He made his own house, he made his own living — and he made his own happiness. Instead of being "bored" like the children of suburbia with affluence everywhere except in their own souls, he found always some new thing to do, to build, to invent, to create, to see and to know.

But today "Liberals" make fun of that sort of life, that sort of man, and they try to ridicule such men while they can . . . and crush such self-reliance when they must.

II

ONE mode of anti-frontier and anti-self-reliance propaganda is contemporary hysteria about gun control — a part of the materialistic determinism of the hour. To the superficial minds of "Liberals," collectivists, Marxians, *et al.*, instruments are supposed to act upon man, and men (no longer self-reliant) merely to be acted upon; to them, murder lies in the gun and not in the soul of man. So they think that to deprive men of guns would prevent man from murder!

What the Power Boys — the *Insiders* — behind the gun controls really want, of course, is not to control guns but to control us. They want registration so that they can confiscate; they want to confiscate so that they will have power and we shall be powerless — even as we live today upon a wild frontier demanding ever more self-reliance.

On the old frontier, men had to rely upon themselves and had to be armed until there were sound laws and until law-enforcement officers could enforce the laws. Today laws against thieves, muggers, thugs, rapists, arsonists, looters, murderers (thanks largely to the "Liberal" majority on the Supreme Court) are diluted almost to the point of abolition; the Marshal Dillons of the world, thanks to the same Court, are disarmed or emasculated, they are told to respect the "rights" of thieves, muggers, thugs, rapists, arsonists, looters, murderers, above the right of good citizens to be secure from such felons.

Good citizens, deprived of the processes of the law or the protection of the police, are supposed to accept their lot as the passive happy victims of "the unfortunate," sheep to be sheared or fed to the wolves bleating about the loveliness of it all. It is "violence" if good citizens defend themselves; it is not "violence" but "protest" if they or their property are assaulted. So gun controls are the order of the day — gun controls that will disarm men of good will, but will not disarm the Mafia, the mobs out on a spree, the wolves on the prowl, the men of ill will.

This is a part of the "Liberal" sentimentality that does not see sin, evil, violence, as realities *in the soul of man*. To the "Liberal," all we need is dialogue, discussion, compromise, co-existence, under-standing — always in favor of the vicious and never in defense of the victim. The sentimental "Liberal," fearful of self-reliant man, believes this to be a good thing; the cynical Power Boys pretend to believe it, and use it for their own ends.

Gun control is the new Prohibition. It will not work, as Prohibition did not work. But meanwhile it will be tried, as a sentimental cure-all, a new usurpation of the rights of a once thoroughly self-reliant people, another step on the march to 1984. It is only a symptom of our modern disease, but it is well worth examining at a little more length. And, as I recently made a trip to the land of Sentimentalia, and brought back a published account of gun controls there, I hope you will permit me to offer it as evidence speaking to our condition:

"A few hundred of the several hundred million citizens of Sentimentalia have in recent years been shot by criminals. The Congress of that land, led by Senators Tom Prodd and Jokey Hidings, and egged on by the President, responded with a law to first register, and eventually confiscate, all the wicked instruments known as 'guns.' The law was passed amid tears of joy.

"But, alas, when guns continued to be used by the happy thugs thus freed from the fear of being shot by self-reliant citizens, the Prohibitionists claimed that this meant that *knives* needed to be forbidden . . . and *then* violence and murders would end. They already had laws against switchblades (quietly evaded); but now they claimed that any sort of knife was lethal; so they sent out teams of bureaucrats to register pocket-knives, letter openers, and straight-edged razors, and to register and license the owners of paring-knives and butcher-knives, and steak-knives and ice-picks . . . so nobody was supposed to be murdered any more. Some conforming, society-hypnotized housewives even came marching into police stations with aprons full of knives, and sang 'You Shall Overcome' as they dumped them in heaps . . . presumably to be melted into plowshares. (Nobody was ever sure of this, and the cynical even suggested that they found their way to the underprivileged, for after all the underprivileged needed knives.)

"Even so, murders continued in Sentimentalia, and sporadic violence, so the Prohibitionists announced that it was because the controls hadn't gone far enough. After all, murders were often committed with baseball bats, hammers, axes, hatchets, *etc., etc.,* and how could you have a non-violent world until you did away with baseball bats, hammers, axes, and hatchets, *etc., etc.* Thereupon carpenters, bowed with a sense of guilt, paraded into public squares with hatchets and hammers by the gross, and dumped them before the melting pots. But houses were no longer built, and baseball ceased to be much of a game, and Paul Bunyon went for the tall timber and was never seen again because, as a self-reliant man, he wouldn't register his axe.

"When murders still continued, the Prohibitionists found a wicked book called the Hebrew Bible, and discovered that Jael had killed the sleeping Sisera with a nail or a tent-peg, and Samson had slain a thousand with the jawbone of an ass — and so they registered and licensed all tent-pegs and nails, and searched out and confiscated the jawbone of every last ass. And when murders still took place, the Prohibitionists found that they were sometimes committed with women's stockings, so now no woman was allowed to appear with stockings unless her legs were examined full length to assure that she had a license sewed onto her nylons, and eventually they decided that women had no constitutional right to stockings anyway, and should keep them in a public repository while not wearing them, and call for them when needed. And the police went around stripping nylons off women's legs, and everybody was sure that this was the end of murder.

"Next some 'Liberal' read a play by William Shakespeare and found that Othello murdered Desdemona with a pillow, so all pillows had to be licensed. Often the Prohibitionists came breaking into homes at night, and snatched pillows from under sleepy heads for failure to produce a license. When murders still continued, 'Liberals' discovered that desperate men used fingernails and teeth, and now going to extremes they extracted all teeth and abolished all fingernails. But even this wasn't enough. They discovered that murders had been committed by kicking; so you had to have a license for a pair of shoes, and you had to register every pair of feet, and some large, brutal-looking feet were amputated.

"By this time, people were so fed up with controls that they took out after the sentimentalists and the Power Boys with fists and fingers and frozen snowballs and rocks. Senators Prodd and Hidings and even the President took refuge in bomb-shelters and managed to survive; but on the other side of their trauma they armed themselves with *guns.*"

Such is the account of something rotten in the State of Sentimentalia. But "Liberals" never learn, and the Prohibitionists still suppose that murder is in the gun and not in the soul of man!

III

OF COURSE, the Liberal Establishment employs many techniques to maintain its power. Particularly does it work to delude youth into conformity to its silly "radical" ideas. The technique is to uphold the wrong "frontier" and to infect youth with a false caricature of "self-reliance." The Kept Press, and the Kept TV especially, present favorably only that youth which has gone off at tangents to reality, into a new conformity to nonsense. This they applaud by exaggerating it.

By selecting the wrong examples, and parading every lie-in or love-in, and glorifying hippies and the invasion of a college president's office for use as a latrine, and magnifying the numbers present and the violence done at a "rally," our system of mass communications buncoes youth into supposing it is the crown of life to scorn "suburbia," to run away from home, to hide behind beards, to experiment with LSD and "pot," to make themselves disgusting with sloppy dress, and to substitute group conformity for self-reliance.

Or, largely by the mis-emphasis of certain magazines and TV programs, youth is channelled into the so-called "ghettos" to lift the "victims" there into the suburbia which they themselves have fled in disgust. Nothing, indeed, is more symptomatic of our modern lack of logic than our consciousness of the futility of mere material affluence in itself, and at the same time our pathetic belief that the salvation of the "poor" is to lift them into affluence!

If our young rebels from the suburbs were truly self-reliant they would not flee suburbia but would redeem its affluence into a new dimension of being. They would not abandon the excellent beginning of spacious and gracious homes, with their possibilities or actualities of fine music, valid painting, and great books; rather they would use these noble possibilities in suburbia to lift suburbia nearer to Heaven.

The "advantaged" youths of our suburbs are given a chance to study the sky, and they should find the fixed stars therein and guide themselves thereby. They should use the foundation of suburbia to expand and heighten their lives, to deepen themselves into wisdom, to purge themselves into holiness, to transcend what may seem the outer "discipline" of parents into a far sterner *self*-discipline of their own inner life — to pass beyond the code-laws of society to the far more drastic codes of inner law, to learn what Nietzsche meant by his words "Clear shall thine eye tell me, not free *from* what but free *for* what"; to follow our Lord Don Quixote as Knight Errant on the white roads of the world seeking "to right wrongs and win glory"; to realize the poetry of being and the clarity of Reason, to find the joy of loneliness and the romance of a White Unicorn, to enter the search for the soul that is modern man's great need and goal. . . .

That, of course, would be the way for the young to transcend and conquer their parents! So they might find those parents, bewildered, delighted, challenged, conquered, following the footsteps of their children into the Kingdom of Heaven. But instead young people too often go howling off after drugs that destroy their minds and dull their legitimate senses, sexuality that rusts the magic of sex, musicians who caricature and ruin music, looting or murder for "kicks," baby-talk instead of the passion of Zarathustra, group or gang conformity that makes the conformity of suburbia seem individualism — and so they slide down the slope of being as they devolve toward the ring-tailed baboon.

What youth subconsciously wants is — the frontier. What youth desires in its heart is — self-reliance. And without the culture-distorters and the brainwashing by the culture-distorters, youth might find it. But, to do so, our youths must self-reliantly face the reality of our contemporary frontier.

Young people must step out of the air-conditioning and the social cushioning that make Flower Children suppose that somehow they will still be fed, and protected, and sheltered without their own effort; they need harsh drastic reality — hunger, thirst, wounds, weather without central-heating or air-conditioning, food that they earn or raise, cyclones and floods, work. (If no one plows or sows, how shall anyone eat? If no one builds how shall anyone have shelter?) They need to experience the war that comes from the eternal conflict of good with evil, blood and sweat and tears, animals to love and take care of, children to raise, knowledge to hunger after as a lion hungers for his prey, the saints and the poets and the heroes for images, the mystics who are the astronauts of the transcendent dimensions that are not of space and time.

The trouble with the rebellion of youth is that it too often is old stuff, space-age stuff; few, few even know that the day after tomorrow (if it is to be at all) will not be the age of space but the age of the psyche. *That* is the frontier of our day — and it demands the self-reliant man.

IV

THE LEFT tells us that the frontier is over. But the frontier is with us as never before! There is (positively speaking, creatively and affirmatively speaking) the frontier of the psyche, of the Inner Kingdom, of the unexplored land of psychography, of the Passage to India of the soul. There are great and fascinating expanses to be explored ... not in *ex*tension but in *in*tention. Only the self-reliant can do it successfully . . . or at all; for only they have the courage and zest. Freud hurled a few stones into the darkness, and churned the darkness into greater darkness. But there is not only darkness— there are high Sierras, snow-crowned mountain peaks, fertile valleys, geysers and primeval forests of redwood — all, all are there. The daring and the lonely and the free stand on the edge of that frontier and even cross into the dark side of their own moon.

In that inner land, they will, by self-reliance, find sustenance and freedom and a new life in worlds unrealized. But they must be self-reliant. There are no giants from a Ford Foundation there, no government subsidies; no psychic security guaranteed from the outside; no civil-rights. And there are mythical monsters there — the chimera, Medusa, the Furies — the dark side of your subconscious, the lusts and envies — and there are the men on this side who hate the new frontier and will do their worst to harm you, because you will not conform to their old style world of relativism, materialism, collectivism, secularism. You will, for a long time, be lonely there. You will live in the unspoiled grandeur of the wilderness. You will find a new home, you will find bread to eat you knew not of, you will leave circumstances and enter introstance. You will be the new pioneers. You will live dangerously.

But fortunately there will be not only a necessary defense, of our self-reliant selves, there will be possible creation by our affirmative selves. If you find the reality of the subjective world you will find as never before the reality of the objective world. When you find your own soul you will see the outer world come alive; you will know objectively the form and shape, the tint and texture and solidarity and substance, of mountain and tree and flower and weed, of water (formless and multiform), of earthquake and of serene calm under the noon, of the firm abiding integrity of God's objective universe. You will know the objective reality of Natural Law.

You will exult in simple objective things, so much better than "affluence." No sane man can call Vincent van Gogh a "square"; but he was one of the world's great conservationists. He loved the simple objective things of his not affluent life — his hat, his table, his pipe, his chair, his bed; and so he painted them, through love, into beauty. Of such a painting, the fine critic, Robert Goldwater, said: "But beyond the problems of design is the utter seriousness with which the painter regarded such familar objects, a respect so profound as almost to transform them into living beings."

That reverence for simple things, for the simple objectivity of things, is the very spirit of the frontier. It is to that that we must return with a new intensity. The subjective-sick, the fashionable "Liberals" yielding to whim and brittle rationalistic sentimentality, the pseudo-sophisticated bored with the bread that feeds them or the sky over them, are taking the old dead road of the decadents of every culture in decay. But the new men, the conservatives, see the flowers of the field more resplendent than Solomon in all his glory; they thank God for cold water to the thirsty mouth; they see the terrible splendor of the lightning; they know the mystery and miracle of the bed that gives you sleep — and wakening.

Edna St. Vincent Millay said it with greatness: "Feed the grape and bean/ To the vintner and monger;/ I will lie down lean/ With my thirst and my hunger." That is the spirit of the self-reliant who by their very nature dwell ever on the frontier which is the horizon of life.

"Liberals" dwell ever in the dead yesterday that men forgot to bury. Because they are dead, they think the frontier is dead. Because they have surrendered their self-reliance to society, they think that there are no more self-reliant men. But *we* say with Don Quixote, "The road is always better than the inn," and with Miguel de Unamuno, "God deny you peace — and give you glory."

In Search Of A Real Man

IT is paradoxical, ironic, but true, that in this man-centered age of social-democracy man is practically extinct. Today one doesn't even dare say, "Be a man!" Too few will know what you mean. It is valid, therefore, in an age of the denial of man, to discuss the rediscovery of man, and that is what I wish to do. How may we rediscover what it is to be a man?

We praise anything best when we can say that, affirming its own nature, it has outwardly become what its inner essence means it to be. The best praise of a Toledo blade is to say, "That is a sword!" The best praise of the winner of the Kentucky Derby is to say, "That is a horse!" The best praise of Rodin is to say of the stone touched by his chisel, "That is a statue!" The crown of praise is to say that something has accomplished explicitly its implicit destiny; has outwardly fulfilled its intrinsic being; has become as existence what it means as essence.

So with man. It is as I wrote in *Shoulder The Sky,* a volume of my poems:

> Deep in the marble of myself I know
> A prisoned statue waits. O dream and deed
> Yet unaccomplished! Take Thy chisel, strike
> Stone into statue, free me from myself
> Until Thy sculpture makes me what I am!

For all things and creatures, and for man especially, life may be defined as an opportunity to become in time what we mean in eternity. That philosophy is our beam across today's airways darkened with fog — a philosophy previously unstated and unnamed, which I here christen *essentialism.*

Essentialism means that to understand man we must not confine ourselves to an observation of his outward existence, but must also discover his inner essence. Only so can we know what it means to be a man. By essentialism we may begin, even in this day of the

11

social-democratic lumping of man into mass, a resurrection from the graves in which we lie — existentialism, pragmatism, relativism, social-democracy . . . those various tombs all full of the querulous and petulant dead who still suppose they are alive. Let us, then, begin our resurrection by asking: What does it mean to be a man?

I

IN ESSENCE, and in contradiction to existence as seen by the Freudian and the Marxist, man when truly man is not passive like a victim but active like a protagonist.

The Freudians believe that we are not really free because, being only the flotsam and jetsam on dark irrational tides, we never think by reason nor choose by will. Consciousness (to them) is the rationalizer, the adjuster, of the blind desires and blear drives of the libido; will is a futile, tossed, froth of illusion on the irresistible waters of subconscious desire. So man is never the strong ship skillfully steered over dangerous seas by the compass of reason and the captain of will. Man is the slave of psychological compulsion.

The Marxists, also, tell us that we are not free: Man can never really think or will because there are no ideas, only "ideologies"; no free art, philosophy, or religion, only shadows cast by economic solids, material facts, and the dialectic of history; no men, only clicking dummies automated by social systems. Man is the slave of economic determinism.

The resurrection of man means, first, that we must break the chains and slavery of such defeatist philosophies, such conformities and surrenders, and become again free men and proud swimmers, striking out for a new destiny. To be a man means that we live by the affirmation: "I *am* — therefore I think, therefore I will. No matter what my surroundings, my environment, my social conditioning, I am large, I contain multitudes, I am potent. Like even an acorn fallen into a meager cup of earth on a boulder's top, I have life and destiny within me: I affirm my introstance against all circumstances. I grow; I thrust my roots down into earth and my crown up toward the sun; I split the rock. I am a man — for I live, I grow, I will, I *am!*"

II

THE SOCIAL-DEMOCRATS abolish man by claiming that he is "privileged" but never responsible, that he has "rights" but never duties, that he is to be a recipient of change but never an architect of growth. He is to be "done to" and "done for" (in several senses); but he is never to *do*. He is to be an amoeba thrusting pseudopodia into the milk of human kindness, or the good chameleon adopting — his not to reason why, his but to adjust — the colors of social conformity. Or man is to be a perpetual baby with a perpetual *goo, goo, goo,* padlocked in a perpetual crib, with a perpetual baby-sitter from the cradle to the grave, who will change his diapers even when he is over sixty-five. The social-democrat bids man: "For pity's sake, don't be a man, be a parasite! Receive, but never give; absorb; suck your sustenance out of the world's bloodstream. If you try to be a man, we'll have to deliver you over to the psychiatrists, for you'll be mentally ill."

But truly to be a man means only secondly to take — because first you give. A true man knows that it is more blessed to give by action than it is to receive unemployment compensation: to give joyous work, invention, artistry, skills, initiative and energy and enterprise, creative talents, genius. Man, the masterbuilder, creates plus and surplus, profits that burgeon and nourish, miracles of creation, the seedtime that brings the harvest. And in such work, man is not concerned first with utility but with the creation of great forms that incarnate noble meaning. His work is born as a child is born — out of love and passion. Man nourishes his work, as woman nourishes the child, for nine months under his heart.

John Chamberlain recently wrote: "In Britain, the so-called council houses erected by the government are horrible to behold; and if recent reports are to be believed, their deficient heating systems are responsible for an upsurge of respiratory diseases." Of course! — they were built by social-democrats.

Compare what *man* builds: The Taj Mahal, a poem in stone to a lyric love; the Parthenon, where marble was enlisted in the service of reason and the gods; the cathedrals of Chartres and Rouen, where a community of individuals aflame with faith and hope and love built upward Niagaras of stone that fortify the soul across the centuries. Or compare the buildings — great in beauty, great in use — that Howard Roark builds in *The Fountainhead*. Social-democrats can't construct a decent rest-room, or keep it clean. But man as man — humble toward God, but proud against conformity to men — builds with courage, audacity, vision, consecration, till his work endures, both beautiful and useful, in the creations of Aeschylus, Dante, Shakespeare, Handel, Bach, El Greco, Sir Christopher Wren, St.

Thomas Aquinas, Nathan Hale, George Washington Carver, Taylor Caldwell, or the good anonymous tailor who said with his dying breath, "Tell the tailors to tie a knot in their thread before they take the first stitch!" The oddballs of this world call such creators "squares" — and indeed they are four-square, and so upon them we may build the alabaster cities that shall stand and endure.

Man is a builder, when he is *man*; a creature who, this side of his Creator, becomes himself a creator.

III

AND MAN, if he is truly man, surpasses yet includes the qualities of all the living creatures — vegetable and animal — that share with him creation and the earth.

The assorted libelers of man — the existentialists, pragmatists, relativists, nihilists, social-democrats — seek to deflate man by calling him an "animal." They thus compensate themselves for their own impotence to be a man. But they know not what they do, for they know animals as dimly as they know man . . . or they would be more cautious.

Knowing neither man nor animal, the modern destroyers try to make the captive audiences of the schoolroom share their ignorance. Thus in their psychological "tests" (to be answered by our children — God save us! — with a yes or no), they write: "Man has no soul or spirit. He is just a superior animal with nothing but a physical body. Yes or no."

Man, of course, shares earth with the animals. He includes — and should include — many of the qualities and much of the nature of animals. But today's wreckers mean, by claiming man as "only an animal," that man is only blind, irrational, brutal, a-moral, lustful, violent, bestial . . . for which libels our friends the animals should bring suit. If man is an animal, he has vital instincts, noble courage, joy in living, artistry (like the beaver and the bird), a sense of property and of right and wrong, wisdom, cleanliness. One wishes that social-democrats, and better-Red-than-dead degenerates, and Beatniks, *were* animals — for then they would be better men!

Animals have a vital will-to-be that contemporary man too often has lost. Animals have courage against all odds; they will battle to the last gasp for their God-given *I am*. Mink or muskrat, woodchuck or wolf, caught in a trap, gnaws through the plastic fetter of a paw, saying in effect: "Liberty — even on three feet!" A cat grooms and washes himself to a dainty gloss of grace — proud, beautiful, clean — putting to shame the frowsy sloppiness of some students in our foremost colleges. (The hippie may be a "cool cat," but he is not a clean "cat," and so he is not a cat at all.) Animals have a sense of property and of moral right: The big dog will leave the small dog and his bone in peace . . . in the latter's yard. The killer-for-love, the weasel, is the anomaly and exception. In general, animals keep (through instinct) right reason and the golden mean; they are the good somnambulists of God.

To be a man means that we include in our rich complex being the truth of the animal — which makes us not less, but more. We, like the animals, affirm (when we are *man*) a dauntless will-to-be; we thrill with the joy of life; we trust our vital instincts; we seek to develop our innate destiny. How splendid the animals! In spite of all temptations to belong to other species, a tiger burns bright from the anvil of God; a rabbit keeps a tryst under the moon with his little cobweb tuft of tail pert and gay; the thoroughbred spends his heart to win the race; the partridge lures the fox away from her young with pretense of a broken wing; the bird fashions a sheen of plume and lilt of song, affirming the spectrum and the tonal scale. Man is more than these, much as we love them; but man cannot be less than these.

Thus man, when man, says with the animal a yes-to-life. He accepts even the pre-animal as part of his total nature — the century-scorning oak that gives food to the squirrel and shade to the violet, and stands superb against wind and lightning. Man accepts the fleet-foot bunny proud of his chic rabbity self; the joyous play of the otter enjoying his clay-slick slide; the loyalty of the dog hurling himself at the mugger to protect his master; the changeless wisdom of crow or cougar or wild goat; these, a true man knows, are something which man must not scorn but embrace. A true man does not sneer at man as "only a superior animal"; he says "I share with you, the animals, all these things. I am a man, so I must go farther than you in consciousness and character; but I will never deny you, pervert you, or betray or abjure the qualities that are yours." The trouble with social-democrats is that they are not good animals; so how can they be men?

IV

THE WISEST of books says that God has set man only a little lower than the angels. Man (especially today) may fall far lower than the demons, with Lucifer, his chosen lord; but God has set him, in the potential of his essence, only a little lower than the angels; and man, to be man, must know it.

Is it not because the social-democrats are sick and sorry, and have a deep sense of guilt and failure and sin, that they frenetically deny man any proximity to the angels? They deny the highest terms of man because they thus excuse themselves for not being men. But to be man we must reverence the height of man, as Nietzsche bade the despairing youth whom he met under the tree upon Zarathustra's hill, "By my love and hope I conjure thee: cast not away the hero in thy soul! Maintain holy thy highest hope!"

That stormy Berserker of literature, Thomas Carlyle, knew the truth: Man, he said, is *Diogenes Teufelsdröckh*, or "God-born Devil's-dung." But our modern destroyers deny the Diogenes and affirm the Teufelsdröckh.

To be man, we must aim higher than man. A man can succeed, being finite in existence but infinite in essence, only by rising to his highest possible failure. Thus man is one who lives by the tragic sense of life, finding in tragedy his triumph. Where is man more truly man than when, shaking his fist at the storm, King Lear goes mad to become sane, loses a kingdom to win his manhood, and dies at last that he may live?

Even in the world of physics we must aim the arrow, or even the high-power rifle, above a distant target if we would hit it. And in the world of metaphysics, in the realm of consciousness and character, it is equally true; we must never forget trajectory, we must aim above our target. To hit anything on this earth we must aim at Heaven. I once wrote a sonnet, "Therefore The Dream," in which I said of the arrow of our lives:

> Earth bends it from its high trajectory:
> Infinite line becomes the finite arc:
> Each arrow, curving, spends inexorably;
> And by our failure we must hit our mark.
> So in the high trajectory of the soul.
> To reach his goal man aims above his goal.

But social-democrats never aim above their goal. That is the mortal flaw and fallacy of Socialism. To social-democrats earth is all; they never aim at Heaven and so they can never hit their target on earth.

To them the good of man, the goal of man, is a one-level, immediate, utilitarian security, comfort, satisfaction of appetite and desire and "need," but never a *pursuit* of happiness, not a quest for the Holy Grail, not "immortal longings," not the magic casements, not the pearl of great price. So their blunt leaden arrows, never aimed above their target, aimed (they say) at "peace," reach only the wars they loose; aimed (they say) at "freedom," bring only the slavery they accept; aimed (they say) at "security," bring us taxes and taboos and frightened minds and shaken souls — around which psychiatrists gather like buzzards; aimed (they say) at "abundance for the world," bring us only increasingly the equality of poverty. Social-democrats aim only at earth, they forget trajectory; they reach nothing, they fail because they never aim above their goal. They ruin earth, as Franz Werfel said, because they "embezzle Heaven." And the National Council of Churches calls this "being Christian," and the Chaplain of Yale University says on television that "morality" is only concerned with "peace," with "racial equality" — that is, never with individuals, but with "society."

One of the few Liberals (maybe because he is not a "Liberal") whom I respect is the late Joseph Wood Krutch. In his *Human Nature And The Human Condition* he writes that our contemporary alienation from life is this: "It is a lack of any sense of what life is for beyond comfort and security, and it would still be so even if all these good things were conferred upon all. At best life would still remain, in Yeats' phrase, 'an immense preparation for something which never happens.' "

But to be a man we reverse all that. Man is one who seeks a "sense of what life is for." To be man, we must seek first for *meaning,* as the composer seeks for the symphony, and then all the preparation of the orchestra culminates in "something that happens." "In the beginning is the Word. . . ." And man is man only as he too, in his lesser human way, incarnates — *the Word.*

V

FOLLOWING this direction of thought even farther, to be man we must know that man is real only in his highest terms. Our contemporary destroyers say that men are "real" only in their lowest terms. Everybody is to be "equal" — but "equality" (to the social-democrat) is to be reached not by a free and noble adventure upward, but by a forced and jealous levelling downward. We humble men are not to be encouraged to rise toward the best; but all men are to be "made" equal to the worst.

But to be a man, we must see and say and seek the highest realization of man. If you would know music, go not to the Beatles but to Bach; if you would know football, don't go to Harvard, but to Jimmy Brown or John Unitas; if you'd know generalship don't go to Braddock and his bloody blunders or to Varus tossing his legions away, but to Hannibal, Caesar, Napoleon, George Washington, Robert E. Lee, Douglas MacArthur; if you'd know poetry, don't go to Carl Sandburg and his yeasty amoeba-gropings, but to Keats. If you'd know man, don't watch a human mistake doing a Bobby Baker in Washington, but cherish the good simple citizen who "does the work for which he draws the wage," who keeps the wheels turning and the wheat growing, and who carries the world on his shoulders like today's forgotten Atlas.

To be a man we need not be ourselves a champion. But we must reverence the champion in every field, and seek to follow him even afar off, and love the excellence of the champion as the standard of reality. Thus we can be good citizens even if not great citizens, and say of the champion — and gladly — "To him the laurel!" So man becomes man, rising above bitterness, jealousy, hatred, frustration. And man can do this the more happily because all real quality and attainment comes not from outward "success," but from inner being; man finds himself as man by seeking in the marble of his own intrinsic being the statue which is his own *I am.*

Man becomes man as he knows that each unique individual — and each man is unique in his own intrinsic destiny and being — is a seed cast into the dark earth of time and matter. There he must lie with the stones and the damp earthworms for neighbors, with the rain that breaks his heart so that he may grow, with the dusky mold for his bread, and with the sun as yet unseen. To be a man means for the seed to gather together all its power to fulfill the dream of its own being, to grow toward the wheat for bread or the rose for beauty. To be a man is to say: "Only as I thrust my roots into fate shall I lift my fruit into freedom."

VI

AND TO BE a man means to have contact and rapport with the reality of the living earth, with Nature as she really is.

The legend of the good giant Antaeus comes to us out of the wisdom of the ancient Greeks. Antaeus (they said) was the son of earth, and whenever he was thrown to earth and made contact with that living source of life he rose with tripled strength. But once the hero Hercules, for some good reason of his own, had to fight and overthrow Antaeus. At first Hercules lifted the giant and hurled him to the earth; but from each fall the giant arose, three times as strong. Even the great Hercules could not continue such a struggle; he saw that this was the way to defeat and ruin; so at last he lifted Antaeus and held him suspended in thin air, severed from the living earth. Then the giant, denied contact with the source of life, grew weaker and ever weaker; and at last he died. So it is with the social-democrats today. They are thin urban men, theorists and ideologues, who have lost contact with the earth, with the solid homely reality of things as they are, with Nature and God. Social-democrats, of their own volition and through no action of Hercules, hang suspended in thin air till they lose strength and die. But man, if he is *man,* lifts his head toward the sun because he keeps his feet on the earth.

And, wise in that fundamental contact, a man remains always a worker and a soldier.

A woman's life turns inward toward the child; a man's life turns outward toward his work. That is the fundamental psychological difference between the sexes, and the great spiritual difference too. Man can be man only as he knows that, and stresses that, and affirms that: Man has a destiny to fulfill, a work to accomplish, and woman must never turn him from it. His work is his child -- and no concern for the literal child should swerve him from it. To make the earth blossom like the rose; to build the house or the racing yacht, to raise the thoroughbred horse, to write the poem or compose the symphony, to turn the eye of the student toward light, to grind the wheat or tune the motor . . . these are the concerns of man. Much of the unhappiness of man, much of the flabbiness of man today, is that he has lost the sense that his child is his work and his work is his child.

And man, if really man, must be always a soldier. Much of the unhappiness of men today, and most of the unhappiness of women today, comes because man has lost his militancy, has become unmasculine in a feminized world. A world where "Mom" didn't raise her boy to be a soldier, where she puts feminine softness before virtue (in the root Latin sense of the strength-of-man), where she wishes to be the active woman amid passive men, soon becomes a soft world where a few hard men run rampant. Violence, mayhem and murder, riots in the streets, assassinations, mobs militant all around the world, wars raucous all around the world (silly wars that are never won)... these are the natural consequences of man abdicating as the soldier.

Partly this comes because the men who remain hard and tough are encouraged to be harder and tougher; partly (or largely) it comes about because man himself, when his wholesome qualities as the good soldier are suppressed and driven down into the subconscious, explodes in frustration. The noble militancy of man, softened and frustrated, erupts from the nether stew of the tortured subconscious in violence and dark splintered chaos. If you inhibit the soldier you incite the murderer.

Man, to be man, must say (as I wrote in my book *The Way Of All Spirit*): "For is not every seed a soldier; every birth an attack upon the world? The flesh desires peace; but the spirit enters the world to trouble the sleep of even the granite and to toss it, gargoyle-mouthed, in the charge of the cathedral upon the stars. The spirit enters the flesh to bring not peace but a sword. The perfect pacifist is death: and — *de mortuis, nil!* The spirit, however, is a warrior: 'He is sounding forth the trumpet that shall never call retreat.' "

The soft suicidal a-philosophies of the decadent West — existentialism, pragmatism, relativism, social-democracy — are the lapses of men who have abdicated as the soldier. Man must again cease to be Hamlet and become Laertes, saying: "My will, not all the world's." He must again say with the Hindu god, Krishna, "Arise and fight with a resolute heart. Setting no store by pleasure or pain, or gain or loss, or victory or defeat, fight with all thy might." So it is always with man the soldier. Hercules endured the seven labors and died in the grip and agony of fire; but dying he became not a corpse but a constellation.

God, in the world's greatest book, defines Himself thus: *"I am that I Am."* Man, as creature not Creator, humbly and without *hybris,* must say once more — to be truly man — "Let me become in existence what in essence I am. Let me be once more — *man."*

Feminine Woman:
The Lady Is A Conservative

To find a truly feminine woman you have to walk, today, among conservatives — for they alone are working to *conserve* the central, the essential, the vital, the real, in life and in love and in man and in woman. As the radical editors of *Look* phrased it in their issue of March 9, 1971: "What is the John Birchiest of all backlash groups? It's Fascinating Womanhood."

And since I believe that much of the unhappiness of men and women today comes because too many men are not masculine and too many women are not feminine (and do not wish to be!), I think we conservatives should be very proud of our feminine (and fascinating) women. I believe it is time to proclaim to the world how magical, how mysterious, how infinitely varied and how lovely, the truly feminine woman is. So I am going to venture to say here what I think she is like. I do so with great humility, asking as did Shakespeare in *Henry V* that you pardon "The flat unraisèd spirit that hath dared/ On this unworthy scaffold to bring forth/ So great an object."

First let me say that the finest compliment a woman can give to a man is to tell him: "You are not just a 'male' — you are also a man!" And the finest compliment a man can give a woman is to say to her: "You are not just a 'female' — you are also a woman!" But to be able to say that, a man must discover a woman who is really his deepest desire — a *feminine* woman; a woman who is utterly and supremely feminine.

What *is* a woman who is utterly and supremely feminine?

Let me first say what she is not. There are two types of woman today who come shrieking and charging to mind. One of these belongs, largely, to Middle America. She is the supposedly good and often popular "Mom."

Some years ago, I got in the habit of watching a Soap Opera called *As The World Turns*. While it disgusted me, it was so grimly incredible that I seldom missed it. Especially awful was a central character named "Nancy," the wife and mother, who was a supposedly "good" and yet thoroughly repulsive creature. Nancy is always sure she knows more than anyone else; she "loves" her husband and children, and tries to run their lives like a female drill-sergeant. She is possessive, arrogant under the mask of womanly sweetness, usually wrong; an immovable object who never realizes that there is an irresistible force called reality; and who is, in general, an ambulant pain. She is a kind of cannibal, feeding on the flesh of the souls of her husband and children, and calling it "love" to run her household like a pair of shears or pliers used as a nutcracker. Bossy, metallic, know-it-all and dominate-it-all, she forgets nothing — and learns nothing.

In the serial, this woman's poor husband, Chris, is supposed to love her, and she is supposed to love him. But it is the love of the steel-trap and the clog for a convenient (and "beloved"!) foot. She loves most her own will and way. This for the "good" of her victims — not as God loves all His creatures and pours His freedom through creation's veins, sustaining them, giving them life to fulfill *their* destinies, holding them tenderly in His hands, understanding them in terms of their own inner being.

Nancy is typically "Mom," and she defoliates all those around her, as if by chemical warfare. She seems to regard men — her sons, her husband — as erring little boys; she seems to be saying always, "Boys will be boys — more's the pity! What would they do without Mom to steer them?"

Such a woman is cock-sure — but never *hen*-sure (as alone she should be). God save the son, God save the husband, who is the prey of a "Mom"! To be married to such a woman is a catastrophe; she is a female atrocity.

The other type of which I spoke is as bad — or worse. She does not belong to Middle America, but to avant-garde America. She is "smart" — a smart-Alice to balance a smart-Alec. She is sophisticated; she knows all the chic suave answers to all the wrong questions; she talks like a computer full of Freud and Krafft-Ebing and Sartre. She is a swinger; she swings like a monkey on a liana in the jungle. She is hard, metallic, and lacks oxygen; she has the sort of face you see on the females in the pages of *Playboy* or *Cavalier,* a face like thin ice over a vacuum. It is a face that launches a thousand infidelities.

The smart-Alice has read all the latest (and fashionable) books, and knows all the clichés of the hour. If she is a hippie, she wears sweaty foul blue jeans, and hair like escaped cobwebs on a binge. If she is one of Suzy Knickerbocker's "beautiful people" she wears whatever is the chic of the moment, preferring pants especially. She "knows" everything and understands nothing, in a "smart" amoral way. She thinks she is "modern," but the ancient prophets of Israel described her fully and accurately long ago. Isaiah wrote:

> Because the daughters of Zion are haughty,
> And walk with stretched forth necks and wanton eyes,
> Walking and mincing as they go,
> And making a tinkling with their feet:
> Therefore the Lord will smite with a scab
> The crown of the head of the daughters of Zion,
> And the Lord will discover their secret parts.

My own view is that man can never really really love either the "Moms" of this world, or the avant-garde women of this world. The trouble with both is that they have lost the central charm of woman — which is to be woman as the soul of her nature and destiny would have her be.

And what is that? Consider.

Woman sometimes seems to lust for mastery; but woman can love only a master. Woman is happy only when she finds a man who is a master; him alone she can admire, obey, and love. I do not, of course, mean by "master" a bully boy with a club or a whip. I mean that the happy woman, the woman who makes man blessed with happiness, is one who sees in him his destiny and genius, his central power, his will to create. She wants him to have a will lucid with intelligence, a will richly fascinating with imagination. So seeing him, so finding him, she is happy because he says *yes* to life and to love . . . and so to her; he decides things for her, because that is what *she* desires. How could she admire a man who is neutral or neuter?

Of course, she will use her charms and her words to convince him, and to share decisions with him, but she will never really respect or love him if the court of last resort is not *his* will, *his* decision. The truly feminine woman loves essentially only the truly masculine man.

And the truly feminine woman is strong (woman is often stronger and often braver than man), and firm — as the flower is firm, as water is firm — firm to be the water or the flower and nothing else. But like the water or the flower, also, she is sensitive and pliant. She is humble, and soft, and flowing, as water is, as rose-petals are. But as the greatest of the Chinese, Lao-tse, knew, such humility and softness, as of Nature, is strongest of all and conquers all. The rose is soft, but so it wins the bee to delve for honey and to waft the pollen; the brooklet is soft, but so it wears away the stubborn clay and rifts the stern granite. Woman wins by surrender. Woman is victorious by yielding. She says, "My will is his will; in his will is my peace." And so she attains her will.

Truly feminine woman is not in a hurry to snatch pleasure; she loves, rather, to make time live by savoring all the sensuous ecstasy of time — books to read, meals to enjoy slowly with each sip and bite, "white cups and plates, clean-gleaming," dear intimate talks before the coming of good sleep by the side of the one beloved, memories of a morning of roses in the garden or of moons over the lake, the long lingering delight of caresses, the good tenderness to the (even obstinate) dog, the love of shells long ago gathered by a now distant sea.

Hers is, in D.H. Lawrence's words, "some unseen, unknown inter-play of balance, harmony, completion, like some soundless symphony which moves with a rhythm from phase to phase, so different, so very different in the various movements, and yet one symphony, made out of the soundless singing of two strange incompatible lives, a man's and a woman's . . . ." She lives, as John Cowper Powys said, "on the bread of old memories dipped in the milk of new sensa-tions." She is not fond of the haste and "novelty" of life — because life, in itself, is for her ever new, in its natural rhythm of sun and moon and seasons; and she loves to dwell on it and in it, as the lingering notes of a song nest in the heart, or as one loves to hold long a landscape before the soul's eyes.

A feminine woman (as Wordsworth wrote) is "not too bright and good/ For human nature's daily food." Life as it is, and must ever be, moves for her through a rhythm of little things that are subtly great — the smell of toast and bacon in the morning, the haunting back-ground stereo of music, the drive by the wave-striped sea, the making of beds with the sheets "that soon smooth away trouble," the shared troubles and joys that mottle every marriage, the scalloped oysters that her art fashions to culinary delight, the supreme joy when body is one with body and soul is one with soul — and, all of these, natural, innocent, simple, integral, true.

The feminine woman is Eve who rejects the apple. She refuses to be a smart-Alice. She refuses to talk like a tape-recording of a Columbia sociology professor. She refuses to be a Mrs. Bernard Shaw or a Mrs. Sydney Webb, an iron-clad Florence Nightingale in a chastity belt sitting on the *Encyclopaedia Britannica*. She refuses to be a frustrated housewife, seeing her husband as "Old Lunkhead," and lusting after a Rolling Stone. Or I should not say "refuses" — that is too conscious, too deliberate. She has no such desires, for she is too richly natural and joyous, and moves through life with the unconscious beatitude of the sun that shares the day with us and the moon that shares the night with us.

Her being is as natural and integral as the blossoming of the flower — and as joyous and as beneficent. She no more fevers and irritates herself about whether or not she is "happy" or "free" than the bird does as it rides the morning wind or sings from the blossomed bough. She does not "take thought" but thinks by living. She is a part of the conscious-unconscious rhythm of the universe, accepting the natural love of the earth (which is gravitation) as our feet do.

Hers is the natural beneficent rhythm of things, as when the wise oyster turns the grain of sand into the pearl. Her subconscious and unconscious are uninfected and sane and integral; and her consciousness keeps its rapport therewith in a pre-established harmony. She sways in the breeze of life as the blossomed rose sways in the winds of June, but always (like the rose) finds eventual equipoise on the living stem. In her presence, a man does not feel he *has* to be "intellectual," or a biped stud, or smartly avant-garde . . . so he can be simply a man. He feels wanted and one with her. Their relationship is not constantly questioned and analyzed and discussed; it is a reciprocity like wind and wave, like sun and blossom, like bird and bough, like the perfect words and the perfect tune.

Yet consider how fools work to make such splendor seem minor and "merely romantic" and unreal by comparison to the marvels of an "Electronic Age." With all due respect for the astronauts and their incredible feat, even they are not a part of the integral rhythm of life. To shoot across space like a super-arrow, to land on the eerie rocks or dust of the moon, to be temporary invaders of the realm of Artemis — this is spectacular but insignificant. But to stand on earth and look up at the full-orbed moon, to feel her attraction that stirs your inner tides like the tides of the sea, to bathe in the beauty of her wonder, to be a part of the total rhythm of things . . . that is more wonderful and more real than all the scientific monkeyshines of a fleet of astronauts.

And that is the charm of the feminine woman. One doesn't shoot rockets at her to explore her substance; one is closer to her, hundreds and thousands of miles away — because one reverences her, and feels her magic, and bathes in her beauty as God meant us to. She is eternally that satellite to which Omar beckoned in one of his happier moments, calling: "O moon of my delight!" And the feminine woman doesn't want rockets shot at her and astronauts landing on her; she seeks mystery, and magic, and distance that is the true proximity, and the natural and simple subtlety of love.

A natural man, in the presence of a feminine woman, feels always at *ease*. He feels at *home*. Her heart *is* his home. She and he talk even when they are silent. She lets him alone, yet with her he is never alone. To be with her is like being in his favorite nook of Nature; like gazing at his favorite landscape; like hearing the music that is dearest to his ear. It is an aesthetic rapport; a spiritual communion. They belong together, as the bird and the air belong together, as the flower and the sun belong together. Even when the rains come, as they will into every life and marriage, they belong to him, and they nourish his roots.

About her there is no "feminine mystique," but only the great feminine mystery (that no man will ever fully understand, God be thanked!), a mystery like that which is present in every great landscape, in every great piece of music. A feminine woman *is* a work of art, and should affect man like a work of art, and should be understood and cherished like a work of art. What *use* is she? Do you ask of a lyric of Burns', of a still-life of Cezanne's, what is its use? "The silver apples of the moon,/ The golden apples of the sun . . ." — what use are they? They (and she) are values beyond use, answers that annul all questions, the peace that passes all understanding.

The truly feminine woman is she who can understand that Love is Pilgrim of Eternity, tarrying but a night within the world; the earth is but a tent where lovers tarry till the morning breaks and the shadows flee away. Lovers merely keep, on earth, a rendezvous they made before time.

The feminine woman is made for love. Love is her life. She, therefore, seeks not her own pleasure — and so she finds her own, she has her own. She knows that it is more blessed to give than to receive; and she is royally blessed. She is not proud, harsh, clamorous, arrogant, aggressive; she is very proud of being a woman, and so she is very humble *as* a woman; she gives peace even in passion, and yet passion even in rest. She is like moonlight filling the clear night air; she is like pure water in the noontime hills, a song of sound, a melody to the thirsty lips. She is brilliant, like a dancing flame upon the hearth; but a magic flame that does not burn the arms that embrace her. That is what the heart of man really wants; that is what the heart of woman really wants. Only a truly feminine woman can give it or receive it.

A feminine woman is different from man; and the more so the better. The more different she is, the more there will be polarity — and reciprocity — and union. The more she will fascinate him, the more he will fascinate her; the more mystery and magic there is, the more joy there will be. Sometimes, just by being woman, she will bewilder and even infuriate man, but that is a part of what delights him and soothes him. Even when man cannot understand her, he wants her that way!

And when man and woman love each other, there is the great unity that comes out of the great difference, the great communion that could not be so precious were it not that physically and psychologically they are made differently. They are different — so that they may become one. That is the way the world is made; it goes back to the primal creation of God; it is something to be conserved forever. When it is not conserved, as it is not in the world as it is today, we get the brittle humbug called "sex."

You think me a Victorian? Listen then to a "modern." It was D.H. Lawrence who said, "The great disaster of our civilization is the morbid hatred of sex. What, for example, could show a more poisoned hatred of sex than Freudian psychoanalysis? — which carries with it a morbid fear of beauty, 'alive' beauty, and which causes the atrophy of our intuitive faculty and intuitive self." And he means by "the morbid hatred of sex," the hatred of the shallow sex-fanciers, "the terrible dreariness and depression of modern Bohemia, and the inward dreariness and emptiness of so many young people today." As he says: "These young people scoff at the importance of sex, take it like a cocktail, and flout their elders with it."

The conservative, on the other hand, does not wish to annul "sex," but to *conserve* it — which can be done only by reverencing it, and seeing it as something noble and great, like a rare and beautiful pearl that one wins by diving in deep and perilous seas.

The feminine woman also eschews modern "psychology" in its fashionable aspects. She does not pretend to be a secondhand Freud; she does not want to explore and expose and explain everything. She will be psycho*lyrical* — but not psycho*logical*. She knows the soul is alien to analysis and at home only with poetry. There is nothing duller, nothing more sickly and lethal, than a female Freud — unless it is a male Freud. The psyche belongs to the poet; not to the professor, not to the pedant. The feminine woman does not set mousetraps in the soul, baited with unholy cheese; rather, in the soul, she cultivates gardens. And she remembers always the great Garden that was Eden before The Fall.

The feminine woman transcends our modern time, and enters timeless life, in a way that too many women today deliberately reject: She is gentle and tender and loyal and good.

Do not suppose that I am being sentimental or unreal. I know very well that the woman who is evil can be even more terrible and cruel and savage than the man who is evil. We all know how the Knitting Women of Paris plied their stitches while the heads fell under the guillotine. We all know that in primitive times the women among the wild tribes could torture prisoners more horribly than did the men. And the woman who is good can be terrible and ruthless too — in a noble way — as was Charlotte Corday, the pure and true and brave, who drove her knife to the heart of Marat, the so-called "People's Friend" of the French Revolution. I know all that. Kipling rightly wrote that "The female of the species is more deadly than the Male."

But there is in woman, when natural and unspoiled, when not stiff with a veneer of sophistication, when not outraged, a powerful gentleness and a tenderness. When she really loves, she shows that gentleness and that tenderness, to the one man, to the lonely child. The man who has known the exquisite touch of this tenderness can never forget it; he finds it like Ariadne's golden thread, leading him out of the world's labyrinth. It is the mother in her. It is Mary the Mother of Christ, yearning to soothe His pain as she stood under the Cross. It is the gentle tenderness that draws the tired head to her breast and provides the rest that is the respite to pain.

And the feminine woman can be loyal to the end, and good as the sun is good, or the pure water, or the May breeze, or the shade of the silver birch.

Denying all this as sentimental nonsense, a magazine called *Motive*, foul with the ugly thing "moderns" blaspheme as "Christianity," has published a parody of the Sermon on the Mount; and doubtless the smart-Alices of the world applauded it as wise advice to men who would seek their favor. Consider:

Thou shalt not be crude or cave-mannish in lovemaking;
  and above all thou shalt not be guilty of chastity.
Blessed are the broadminded, for they do not disturb you
  with their Victorian scruples.
Blessed are the impure in heart, for they make
  such enjoyable companions.

If that is your taste — *that is your taste!* But if, to be "broad-minded," you must shut out Coventry Patmore and Charles Dickens and Francis Thompson and George Meredith and Robert Browning, and welcome in *only* Aubrey Beardsley and Oscar Wilde, then you are truly a smart-Alice and a fool. The "impure in heart" may play hot-cockles with you by day or night, but they are *not* "such enjoyable companions" for very long. I myself would find Emily Brontë and Emily Dickinson and Christina Rossetti much more "enjoyable." Every real man knows that dime-store "jewelry" is cheap and easy and makes few demands for what pleasure it gives, yet all prefer the diamond that is hard and pure. Fool's gold — to fools! And gold to the lover of the pure!

When you wish the best, you seek the "sainted silver" that certain Spanish monks, pure artists of perfection, fashioned so long and so lovingly, with such consecration, that it became silver purer than metal *can* be on this earth. Such is the woman I seek, such is the woman I reverence, such is the woman I find and love. She is as gracious as she is good, she is as good as she is beautiful, she is the sainted silver of my adoration. I can trust her as I trust the sunlight; I find her good like the mountain air and the tree that gives shade on the brilliant plain.

The feminine woman is good. And, wherever she is, *there* is a center of good — *not* of do-gooding, but a living center of good like the circle of the sun that purifies the water, and nourishes the wheat and the rose, and routs the ice age of the earth or of the heart. She is gentle and good, and so she soothes the frightened child, and rescues the lost kitten, and makes her home an island of order and beauty even today in a world of gray and bitter seas.

And because she is gentle and good, such a woman is inexorable to the man who would betray his country, or peddle drugs to her children, or seek to vandalize her home and pillage and rape. *Because* she is tender and gentle, she can point the gun and pull the trigger. She has no sentimental hatred and yet no pity for the man-eating tiger, the plague-carrying rat, the cobra in the house; she says, "Comrade, it is you or I! It is you — or all I love!"

But she loves all true and lovely things; she is gentle with them; she is tender to them. She will not *use* man for her own lusts; she will not use and betray and toss him aside; her word is her bond in the sense that we forget — the *bond* that is her own honor, her own integrity, her own loyalty in love. She is not the treacherous quicksand in which man sinks, but the firm earth in which he is rooted. She does not seek either to give or to receive mere "pleasure"; she gives and she receives *joy*. So she brings man sex (not "sex"!) as it was meant to be — a white flame, a lustrous pearl, a power and a glory, a consummation and a beatitude.

To such a woman "Victorian scruples" and "modern infidelities" are equally ludicrous and petty. Lady Godiva (ashamed of her own nakedness) and the modern strip-teaser (arrogant in her own nakedness) seem to her Siamese twins of folly. There is (to her) a time to be clothed, and a time to be naked; and the pure in heart know the meaning and the hour.

And such a woman is good, as sanity is good, as health is good, as integrity is good; she knows that the Puritan may build too narrow walls, but that the Impuritan breaks down *all* walls — till the cow's in the corn, and the hogs are in the roses, and no fences make bad neighbors. She knows that wisdom, and humor, and imagination, and beauty are an integral part of good. She is a center of life and of light, whence radiates love and joy and healing and creation.

The feminine woman may have no child of her own. But she never tries to escape from the mood of woman, for she knows that she is (in her own magical body) the potential cradle of life. She has a magical reciprocity with the child, born or unborn, and that gives her a unique destiny and distinction. The shadow (and beatitude) of the child is on her; the fact that she is the child-bearer of the race is with her; and this sets her apart and enriches her soul.

One of the most perverse of modern aberrations comes when a female demands abortion because it is "her" body, and should she not do with it as she wills? Life, life itself, is greater than she, and blesses her and gives her a function and unique glory by filling her with the new life of the future. It is not "her" body only, it is the body of love and of life, and the unborn child has its own body that is within her and yet that is not "Hers." I think that any woman has lost her soul when she speaks of the child conceived in true love as just a part of "her" body, a casual nuisance that she may dismiss and destroy by her own whim. Such a woman has lost unity with the source and center of life.

The great evil of the "Liberal" has been his rationalistic destruction of reality, his willingness (and even desire) to destroy things as they essentially are. The radical carries this to its grisly end. In *1984*, George Orwell reaches the heart of that horror. There O'Brien, who is Big Brother, says quietly to poor Winston Smith, "You must get rid of those nineteenth-century ideas about the laws of nature. *We make the laws of nature.*"

That is it! The "Liberal" and the radical hate the natural laws, the steadfast center of life, the essential *I Am*. They fretfully and petulantly rebel against the nature of life. They wish it to be malleable to their caprice and whim.

O'Brien goes on, "We have cut the links between child and parent, and between man and man, and between man and woman. No one dares trust a wife or a child or a friend any longer." And that, even before 1984 reaches the calendar, is the hell into which we are descending.

What has happened is that the "Liberal," by inevitable inner logic, has become the more activist and pouting *radical* (in the wrong sense, as if going " to the roots of things" meant *only pulling things up by the roots*!). The radical, who is the "Liberal" gone all out, gone hog-wild, hates the natural law, the organic and integral being of things, the universe as *cosmos* (beauty, ordered harmony).

He would "cut the links." To wrench life up by the roots, to transplant hearts with time-bombs, to stand things on their heads, to contradict and blaspheme the Word that in the beginning was (and in the end will be) — such is the lust and the obsession of the "Liberal" (in theory) and the radical (in practice). Their modern motivation is *hatred.* It is hatred of life, hatred of love, hatred of order, hatred of beauty . . . and so, naturally, hatred of man as man and woman as woman.

The "Liberal" and the radical fear life, fear love, fear reality; and so they rage against them. They hate woman as she is in herself, world without end by the fiat of God. And since woman is especially, uniquely central in the order of things, the "Liberal" and the radical lust to defeminize her, to destroy her unique being, to reduce her to something that is no longer woman. They seem today to be largely succeeding. What they do not know is that, in the end, they rage futilely and imagine a vain thing. Even if they destroy the world, it is the creation of God and is forever existent in Him. In spite of the world destroyers, the Birds of Eden shall sing again!

Meanwhile, in the mortal war of the spirit which we wage (on one side or the other) today, whenever we applaud woman as she is in the Providence of God, and encourage her to refuse to be liquidated and annulled, we conserve the meaning of the world, the destiny and the splendor of life, the freedom of the soul.

So let us who are only men uphold, and seek, and love, and reverence, and honor — *the feminine woman*!

Much of what we call the feminine woman may seem to many today to belong to the land of long ago and far away. I venture to believe that this is not so. At least I personally know that there *are*, even in the world today, *feminine women*; and the fact and truth that there are gives me faith and hope. But even if I did not know this, I would still see the feminine woman as a reality, far more "real" than "realism" can ever know. I have chosen to live not only by facts, but also by dreams beautiful on the horizon of the heart.

One summer I often passed a river; that summer, on its banks, two white herons moved, cloud-pale, stately and free; like two birds of burning snow, superb in solitude. They seemed strangers, aloof and proud and wild, who did not even know that, from my different world in the same world, I watched them and found joy in their beauty. Each time I saw them, they filled my heart with light; they were more my own than the things that were my "own." It is even so in life, it is even so in love; if we are to find the reality that transcends "realism," there must be white birds, beyond our nearer reach, free and aloof upon the horizon of the heart. There must be — the feminine woman!

The Gentleman:
A Matter Of Reverence For Quality

THE metaphysics of the late H.L. Mencken, simply, *wasn't*. It did not exist. But, this side of metaphysics, Mencken had a robust common sense that was as uncommon in his day as in our own. He had a healthy sense of inequality; a honed distrust of democracy; a raucous but refreshing scorn of Boobs and Yahoos, of "the blather of the holy clerks" today institutionalized in our National Council of Churches, of the plutocracy and the proletariat he called "two inferiorities struggling for the privilege of polluting the world," and of "the mob and its maudlin causes" which "attract only sentimentalists and scoundrels, chiefly the latter."

And, Mencken reverenced what he called "the gentleman" — by which he meant the true aristocrat of the spirit, the man of integrity, balance, poise, courtesy, courage, and honor, who has a sure taste for quality and values. Such men, he said, will always rank rightly above the false "aristocracy" of the *Insiders* of the Establishment. "Above it," he wrote, "will still stand the small group of men that constitutes the permanent aristocracy of the race — the men of imagination and high purpose, the makers of genuine progress, the brave and ardent spirits, above all petty fears and discontents and above all petty hopes and ideals no less. There were heroes before Agamemnon; there will be Bachs after Johann Sebastian."

I

I TOO would defend such a natural aristocracy as Mencken praises. But that word *aristocracy* could easily prove a troublesome one. Before proceeding we had best look to its definition. The *American College Dictionary* says of *aristocracy*: "1) a government or a state characterized by the rule of a nobility, elite, or privileged upper class." This, undoubtedly, is what the term has come to mean — but it defines a mechanical, an artificial, and a false aristocracy; a secondary "aristocracy," an aristocracy of man's contriving and not of God's creation. The definition which is listed third, however, in the same dictionary, is this: "Government by the best men in the state." And this is nearest to the essential meaning of the Greek, for the Greek word translates: "The rule of the best."

Surely Mencken did not mean, and certainly I do not mean, the rule of an "elite, or privileged upper class." That has been the artificial aristocracy that has disfigured life too often in the past — and that disfigures life today under the *Insiders* of the Establishment. Such a caricature has nothing to do with "the heroes before Agamemnon" or the "Bachs after Johann Sebastian"!

L'Ancien Régime (superior, I admit, to our present Regime) was artificial. It based its superiority on birth, on a *rigid* heredity, on *mechanical* continuity, on *closed* criteria; and its heredity and continuity were weakened by interbreeding, by perpetuation of flaws and degeneracies shielded by privileges of birth, by rigid succession irrespective of weaknesses within, or of genius and worth from without that were excluded from its boundaries. The aristocracies of the past, as they continued, became full of pride, stupidity, arrogance, artificiality. They brought about their own downfall because they did not recognize the width and wonder of God's power and man's genius; because they did not understand Napoleon's proverb: "The career open to the talents."

And the stuffy "aristocracy" of the *Insiders* and the Establishment today — that is even worse! It is founded on great established ganglia of wealth, allied with those great established conditioners of opinion, the universities, and depending on great clubs of established unity such as the Council on Foreign Relations. This "aristocracy" is one of "experts," of "planners," of "right thinkers" who are invariably wrong-thinkers. It controls, by devious means that are material and mechanical in essence, the media of communications — the "big" papers, magazines, television networks — and so it establishes a monolithic consciousness that becomes increasingly an unconscious hypnosis.

Such "aristocrats" are as far from Mencken's "men of imagination and high purpose, the makers of genuine progress, the brave and ardent spirits . . ." as it is possible to get. If such an aristocracy of an "elite, or privileged upper class," is what is meant by "aristocracy," then I abhor aristocracy. It is not. The true aristocracy that is the vital and essential being of greatness in the world lies in the *Inner* Kingdom; it is an inward and invisible grace, it is life and light, it is genius, it is life *en rapport* with Life.

That great obscure Victorian, James Thomson, in his *Essays And*

Phantasies wrote a marvelous essay on "Open Secret Societies." These are, he says, the open secret societies of the Heroes, the Saints, the Philosophers, the Poets, the Mystics. He wrote of them:

> Their members are affiliated for life and death in the instant of being born; without ceremonies of initiation, without sponsorial oaths of fidelity. Their bond of union is a natural affinity, quite mysterious in its principles and elements, precise and assured in its results as the combinations of oxygen and hydrogen in water, or oxygen and nitrogen in air . . . .

This is the *natural* aristocracy, the pattern of the best who do not outwardly rule but who inwardly are the Lords of Life. In their lifetimes they may live obscure and unknown; in their deaths they often are shunted (like Cervantes, like Blake) into an unknown, unmarked grave. But, dying, they become not a corpse but a constellation. It was they of whom Frank Harris was thinking when he wrote: "It is the dead who steer the living."

The natural aristocracy of the world! Such an aristocracy is not imposed from without, but works from within. It is the invisible light by which all things are visible; it is the oxygen in uncontaminated air that usually we ignore but without which we die. It is the confraternity of genius that lifts a people out of the little lives by which men die, into the life whereby the Athens of Pericles or the England of Shakespeare lives forever.

In what we call "time," this natural aristocracy seems to fall; in Eternity it lives beyond the teeth of time and works with the immortality of genius. The old rhyme tells us, "The lion and the unicorn/ Were fighting for the crown." They were — and they are.

The lion is the pragmatic beast, the symbol of material power, the lord of earth's gregarious ones. He dwells in London Town. He usurps the world's thrones in Moscow and Washington. The unicorn is the creature of the soul, the creature of imagination and legend, the symbol of the free spirit, the outsider who is genius. He dwells not in London, but in Camelot; he runs with ivory hoof and ivory horn under the unsubverted moon. On far hills aloof and alone, where breezes blow cool in the lilac night. He hates, and he is hated by, the commissars and the commissions, the bureaucracies, the foundations, the gelded centaurs of Academe, and albino gentle souls who elect to dwell meekly in Hell. We live today in the sorry world of the lion — grown shoddy, grown shabby, like an alley cat; but the world waits for the hour of the unicorn.

J.B. Priestley, in his excellent *Thoughts In The Wilderness*, has an essay on "The Unicorn." He writes:

> We have reached again, as we must do at regular intervals, the hour of the Unicorn. I am seeing it, of course, as the heraldic sign and the symbol of the imaginative, creative, boldly inventive, original, and individual side of the national character . . . .
>
> For if we don't back the Unicorn against the Lion, if we are not a boldly imaginative, creative, inventive people, a world that expected more of us will soon not even let us keep what we have now. The only future we can have worth living is the one we greet, bravely and triumphantly, riding on a Unicorn.

The riddle of the world is how to supersede the lion with the unicorn. So far, all attempts have failed because of the flaw that lies within fallen man. Even the American dream of the free Republic, despite the glory of the Founding Fathers and the safeguards of an explicit Constitution, is being subverted by an outward Conspiracy and by an inward Hypnosis. It is an ancient story — only an instant younger than the birth of nobility of purpose.

Even the noble conception of the Round Table and Arthur in Camelot, for example, blossomed only for a season and then fell because men could not sustain that level of excellence. But, though Arthur fell in Lyonnesse, and Excalibur was cast again into the sea, the wise resolute heart of man still believes that he lives immortal in Avilion — and will return. The symbol that keeps the heart of the world from breaking, and the star of the world alight, is such an intuition as that of Camelot and Arthur, and of their chivalry — the natural aristocracy that is.

We need today a return to the Round Table. There Arthur lives, and Merlin's magic is set free from Vivien in Broceliande; there once more the noble of the earth proclaim that honor, and right, and moral courage, and the truth that is beauty, are neither dead nor undefended. From there we shall call anew the Knights Errant, the Gentlemen who dare to ride forth to right wrongs and win glory and affirm the Lord.

Surely among the young today, and certainly among some of those who chronologically are old (but who psychically are as young as Eden), there is implicit this natural aristocracy. Surely today there are implicit the Knights Errant of essential life. I know some of them myself; I know that they live. I do not name them, because I had rather you should find them and name them yourselves — and it is safest for them to be Knights Anonymous.

But such as these *are* ready to gather again around the new Round Table. They long for honor, for nobility, for the beauty that is truth, for the everlasting right, for what Nietzsche called "the lightnings and great deeds," for a new center of essential life, under God. Youth in its soul longs for this, and even when it goes a-whoring after false gods, or confuses Camelot with San Francisco, or sees Merlin's magic as LSD, it is restless (in its heart) for the unicorn. As St. Paul knew and said long ago, the whole creation groaneth and travailleth together in earnest expectation of the sons of God.

The whole world waits for a call to arms of the Knights of the Round Table. For, the world knows that no smug trust in affluence, in "the world's highest standard of living," will save us from the *Insiders* or the Outsiders, from the Hidden Rulers or the Open Conspiracy; man is nobler than that! Man does not live by a turkey in every oven or a color TV set in every home. Man lives by faith and hope and love, by the star on the horizon, by the trumpet that will not call retreat. As Stevenson said, life is not a bed of roses but a field of battle. To live dangerously, to seek for individual freedom and national meaning, to be Knights Errant of the new Round Table — such is the way.

The world lies (or seems to lie) under the wings of Lucifer. It is riddled and raddled with the dark forces of Lucifer, it is weighted down with "the dark Satanic mills," it is dark under the psychic shadow of evil wings. It is a world dominated by outer conspiracy and inward hypnosis (the terrors inseparable), a world where the Dragon seems to have devoured St. George. Against all that, all noble men — all who seek for man as God meant him to be — must wage war to the death. Not this "social evil" or that "social injustice" is the crux or criterion of our battle; it is the *evil of the essence* that we fight, it is materialism that we oppose. (And what is more materialistic than to suppose we can set things right by pouring out money, by replacing one evil power by a new more evil power?)

We fight against those who seek to murder God, who subvert Right in the name of "rights," who commit mayhem upon Reason and call it rationality. As Knights of the Round Table, we wait the

command of the trumpet. And we crave and need a code of chivalry
for the Knight Errant in every youth, in every man whom we can call
noble.

II

WHAT IS that code of chivalry? What is the rationale of a
Camelot reborn, the concept of Arthur come again, the form of the
Round Table returned to earth?

God's will is for *nobility in man.*

Lucifer's will, which is the will of the men of the Establishment
today, is for *degeneracy in man.*

Today, in literature, in "religion" (which is not *religion!*), in art, in
music, in sociology, in "psychology," and in "science" (which is not
science!), men are conditioned to seek and to believe in the low, the
base, the mean, the vulgar, the ugly, the sick, the scabrous, the foul.
The eyes of their souls are forced to look downward; they are
conditioned to see the mud and to deny that even the mud is
stardust. They are hypnotized to deny the high and to affirm the
low.

Today the attention of man is focused and concentrated on the
pervert, the homosexual, the drug-addict, the criminal, the destroyer,
the foul-mouthed, the resentful, the ugly. That is supposed to be
"reality," whereas it is only the refuse and wreck of reality. Today it
is supposed to be "bold" and "real" to make a toilet the scene of a
play; or a creature with the soul of an amoeba, a hero. The natural
aristocrat, however, knows all this for what it is — degeneracy,
cowardice, defeatism, deliberate perversion of life's values and the
soul's qualities.

The gangsters of death today usurp the wheel and the accelerator,
and they drive mankind headlong for the pit. Only the new nobility,
the natural aristocracy, the Arthurian Knights, preserve the sanity of
the world — and renew Man as God meant him to be.

The concern of the new Knights of the Round Table will be with
the highest and the best. They *know* the evil in its stark ugliness; but
they *will* the good in its beauty "terrible as an army with banners."
Every inch and ounce and atom of their being will concentrate on
excellence, on right, on the truth that is beauty and the beauty that
is truth, on the holy and the high. Their interest will not be in
stumblebums inebriated in the flop-houses of the world, but in the
hero, the poet, the saint, the lover, afoot and lighthearted on the

open roads of the cosmos. Never denying the evil and the base with their minds (for they exist), but denying centrality to the evil and the base with their wills, they "fight on, fight on," with Cyrano.

A man becomes what he sets as a symbol and a love at the center of his soul. Love the ugly, concentrate on the ugly, set the ugly at the center of your soul — and you become ugly. But be bold and original, be discriminating and nobly selective, know that in life many may be called but few can be chosen, and you will not wallow in the ugliness that so easily besets us. Instead, by discrimination and choice, love the beautiful, concentrate on the beautiful, set the beautiful at the center of your soul — and you will become beautiful. Thus the Arthurian Knights reverse the debacle of man and make it the renaissance of man.

Their clue is what I call the Problem of Good in the world. Amid all that goes wrong, there is so much that goes right! Millions fall physically sick and mentally ill; but there *is* health. Hundreds of young men think it pertinent to turn a college building into bedlam and a latrine; but thousands of young men still desire and labor for the education that may turn the eyes of the soul toward light. The calamitous spider called Mao Tse-tung turns Mainland China into a madhouse and an abattoir; but Chiang Kai-shek makes Taiwan into a garden of life. The persistent ascent toward good endures and abides amid all the sullen precipitation toward death: Amid Lucifer's lust to destroy, there remains God's will to create. The new Knights Errant will see the clues of light and life that intersect the evils of darkness and death, and will follow them upward toward the sun.

The Gentleman is the child of the light. Therefore he is indeed the *gentle* man, even when he is inexorable and militant; he is angered by evil, but he refuses to become one of the angry young (or old) men; he is courteous even when his enemies are discourteous; he is, most of all, chivalrous. Chivalry! — O noble word! It means that you ride as the Knight rides, you fight as the Knight fights, you inexorably set your lance against evil but you (like our soldiers in Vietnam) honor the enemy with vigilance and are fair to the defeated or the surrendered. You eschew resentment and rancor, for that is the sickness of the slave; you do not let rancor fester your soul; you strike the clean blow, but you seek no revenge.

You are like Joan of Arc at the stake, saying to the English soldier who was burning her, "Step back, or you too will be burned." The finest words of praise I can find are to say of someone that she, like

Joan, is gallant — and *hearty*. To be gallant amid the frustrations, to be *hearty* amid the calamities, what is higher in virtue? And the Gentleman is hearty and gallant!

They say that once there were monks in medieval Spain who hammered silver to such gloss of purity that it seemed a *miracle* of craftsmanship — they called it "Sainted Silver." Such is the gentleman; he is "sainted silver." He has standards that endure and abide, graven in star and stone. He reverences only quality, he is not moved by quantity; he knows the *price* of things, yet he lives by and for the *value* of things. But always he is gallant and he is hearty!

And his strength lies in the fact that he knows the ground and guarantee of all values. He believes in himself because he believes in more than himself. Therefore he avoids that most terrible of sins, *hybris* or *pride*; he remains humble because he says, in the great words of the Lord's Prayer — *"Thine* is the kingdom, and the power, and the glory!" He knows that God is the measure of all things. Thus he is sceptical of man's ideologies and fabrications; knowing and reverencing the "Eternity that God hath set within man's heart," he lets his reason play like a lambent flame over the "many inventions" of man, and man's air-conditioned ant-heaps.

Because of this, the Gentleman has dignity and poise and serenity. He stands aloof from the fashions, and the trends, and the manias of the hour or the era; he lives *sub specie aeternitatis*. He is, therefore, not an existentialist — but an essentialist. He is able *"rerum cognoscere causas,"* — to know the causes of things with Virgil's beekeeping philosopher, and so can hear beneath his feet, unmoved, the "roaring of the very river of Hell." He is poised like the eagle, whose wings the wind itself sustains.

And his code of action is best spoken by that ancient and timeless proverb: *Noblesse oblige.* He knows that nobility lays upon a man a duty and a responsibility: If a man has the quality that makes him noble, he owes it to himself to shower that quality upon the world.

This is *not* to be a busybody do-gooder. Is the sun a "do-gooder" because he shines? Is the rose a "do-gooder" because she blossoms? Is granite a "do-gooder" because it gives a steadfast stance for the cathedral or the many mansions? The sun shines because he *is* a sun, because it is his generous and joyous nature to shower light upon his planets and to pursue the ever encroaching night. The rose blooms because her heart is explosive with color and fragrance, and because it is the art of her nature to be beautiful. The granite stands unshaken because that is the destiny and the essence of granite. Not to *do* good but to *be* good is the essence of the creative and the heroic.

The *noblesse oblige* of the Gentleman is the lucid flame of the sun, the lambent crimson of the rose, the stern strength of the granite. If you are a root of beauty, you pour beauty into the gardens of June; if you are a sturdy fundament of being, you bear even the skyscraper on your shoulders. The nature of your being, the destiny of your nature — *these* determine what you should do.

The Gentleman is not the rust that eats the steel, the fungus that rots the wood, the tapeworm that lives as a parasite upon a weakened host; the Gentleman is the steel of the bright blade, the living tree that grows into the centuries, the unicorn beautiful upon the plains. By being what he is, by the nature of his being, the oak gives shadow to the rabbit and food to the gray squirrel; the blade gives Cyrano his freedom amid the world's base ones; the unicorn gives the vision of supernal beauty. *Noblesse oblige!*

The Gentleman is not *heavy* even when he is grave; even when he faces the worst, he is gay. And this is because, like Cyrano (his noble examplar!) his soul is so strong it can dance even upon the darkest waters. Cyrano, dying says: "Yes all my laurels you have riven away/ And all my roses; yet in spite of you/ There is one crown I bear away with me . . . . " And this is, he says, "One thing without stain,/ Unspotted from the world, in spite of doom/ Mine own! — " Then he names it, of course. And it is *his white plume!!*

The Gentleman, like Cyrano, cherishes that inner integrity, that truth to himself, that affirmation of his own essential meaning — *his white plume*. His inviolable soul!

To The Young Who Seek Renaissance

A Father Writes To His Son Of America

I, your father, write to you, my son. But the subject on which I write makes us *both* sons of something that unites and transcends us both: We are both sons of one country, of the beloved country that gave us birth. About that land and country I wish to write to you, and also — and this should keep my words from seeming didactic — to myself. To you, and to myself, I wish to write a personal and yet open letter about what made (and makes) America great; a letter from my heart and to your heart, a letter that tries to say what patriotism means and is. I wish to write not of "the Great Society" — but of the Great America.

I know only too well the fashion of the hour among so many of those who ironically call themselves "intellectuals." They pride themselves on uprooting in themselves their instincts, the elemental loves and hates of the wise blood, the secret roots (transcending all "ideas") that thrust their being down into the subsoil of reality. They betray their intellect by severing and insulating it from living reality, from Nature, from the living God beyond and above Nature. They do not say with Whitman, "The time straying toward infidelity and confections and persiflage [*the poet*] withholds by steady faith." They seek out infidelity and confections and persiflage; and so they pervert and betray reality, and the instinct that tells us "This is my own, my native land, and I love it beyond all others."

The fashion of the hour among the false "intellectuals" who know little of intellect is to deride and mock patriotism, to reduce noble patriotism to ignoble prejudice. The final flowers of such weedy seeds are the words of some of our high-school students of recent

43

years: "To be a patriotic American is to be a blindly stupid individual" (Redding, Connecticut), or (from the Menlo-Atherton High School in California), "We must prepare for a Russian occupation of the United States by a major change in the attitude of the American people." The Menlo-Atherton High School has not changed, for an editorial in their school paper suggested just the other day that the daily recitation of the Pledge of Allegiance should be dropped. It is said that the pledge is merely routine and then it asked: "Does it have any meaning to mumble the same old syllables over and over until they either mean nothing or become a blind part of our subconscious . . . ?"

Since my blood beats in you, I cannot believe that you will ever suppose that repetition of what is profound can turn it into something superficial. I believe that there is a greatness in you that will preserve the greatness of prayer or pledge or poem or sunrise, or miracle of the body's adventure as it poises each instant over the precipice of death. So I dare to hope that you with me, and with Whitman, will "withhold the time straying toward infidelity" by the power of steady faith.

Why then, my son, should you and I be patriots? Let us try to find the answer in a study of what has made — and what makes — the essential and eternal America *great*.

I

UNDERLYING all there is the physical reality of place that is far more than space. The continental arms are around and underneath us and the continental soul is nearer than hands or feet. There is the land herself, the country, the fundamental place, with all her atmosphere and aura, that is ours . . . or are we hers? We are in harmony with the great American continent, with the country and the land, with her physique and her psyche. This continent itself, this mighty stage for majestic drama, lifted from the plangent seas by God working through terrific explosions and upheavals of the basic earth, prepared by the glacial bulldozer of the Ice Age — this continent of fiercer lightnings, of earthquake and hurricane and cyclone, of extremes of heat and cold, of bison and grizzly bear and Indian, is the *American* continent: We are her children, and she our mighty mother.

Not for you, my son who does not need it, but for the conforming cynics of the hour, let me quote a modern of the moderns, D.H.

Lawrence. The cynics cannot dismiss him as a "conservative," they accept him as a "radical," yet it was he who wrote in his *Studies In Classic American Literature*:

> Every continent has its own great spirit of place. Every people is polarized in some particular locality, which is home, the homeland. Different places on the face of the earth have different vital effluence, different chemical exhalation, different polarity with different stars: call it what you like. But the spirit of place is a great reality.

Poor Lawrence had lost his roots — but he sought those roots. And in that search he had, as he here shows, a great mystical sense of the influence of place; a great living communion with the physique and the psyche of *place*, with the body and the soul of the land.

All the great Americans have felt this. Thoreau, in his essay on "Walking, " thinking of course of the American continent, wrote:

> Here is this vast, savage, howling mother of ours, Nature, lying all around, with such beauty and affection for her children, as the leopard; and yet we are so early weaned from her breast to society, to that culture which is exclusively an interaction of man on man.

He anticipates here, of course, the socialism and the sociology that he despised and the modern distemper of collectivism that he would have loathed. And he adds:

> The Spaniards have a good term to express this wild and dusky knowledge, *Gramatica parda*, tawny grammar, a kind of mother-wit derived from that same leopard to which I have referred.

In these splendid words he speaks powerfully the very essence of the American continent.

There are, of course, some Americans whom this frightens or repels. They seek suaver ancient ties, the less savage motherland of Europe. Every decade, or every century at least, some expatriate Americans flee to London, or to Paris and the Left Bank, or to Rome. They are not Americans by nature, they do not draw the milk of human greatness from the breasts of this continent, they flee to a more civilized mother. Such were Henry James and Whistler, T.S. Eliot and Ezra Pound, Gertrude Stein and (to a large extent) Hemingway. But *William* James (a greater writer than his brother in spite of his pragmatism), Whitman and Thoreau and Emerson and Vachel Lindsay and Robert Frost, Winslow Homer and Albert Pinkham Ryder, remain rooted in the American continent and "its own great spirit of place." The expatriates, though they have great artistic skills and genuine stylistic excellencies, are yet somehow thin and brittle and lost. They are like trees whose sap is meager; like woods that are not quite lovely, dark, and deep.

How splendidly American, on the contrary, is Whitman! Starting "from fish-shaped Paumonok," he begins and ranges the land from "million-footed Manahatta" and the "scallop-edged waves" of Brooklyn ferry, to the calamus flowering in Western states, and the lilacs blooming in innumerable dooryards over the land. He loves the elemental, the essential earth of America, and draws life from the loam of the land he loves.

So you, my son, will love America — the continent, the country, the physical earth that has a soul of its own. You will love the snow-sand-dunes of northwestern Florida, the sunsets where the redhot sun falls unquenched into the Gulf; the gray rocks where the unbroken Atlantic is broken on the coasts of Maine; the strong wild unfruitful gravel and boulders of western Rhode Island; the suave corn-rustling deep loam of Indiana, where the rivers move like flowing earth and the bark-pleated sycamores rise over drawling creeks; the terrible heat of the painted deserts, and the flint or silver spears of the Sierras in California or Colorado; the rainy forests of Oregon and Washington: the multiform and multichrome landscapes of America that no Winslow Homer or Albert Ryder has painted in all their infinite variety. You will traverse it all on flying wheels or soaring wings; from it you will choose your own beloved nook and place out of the beloved orbed whole. For all the days of your years (because you are not mediocre enough to be "modern," because you are not a time-bound "intellectual" but a timeless poet), you will love your land for its physical beauty and its physical vitality. Why is America great? Never forget the "spirit of place," and what Kipling called "the Red Gods." *Not* the cheap unholy deracinated old-Europe *Marxian* "red," but the gods of Abenaki and Shoshone and Cheyenne and Oneida, the Red Gods of Thoreau's "tawny grammar," the household gods of the woods that are lovely, dark, and deep.

And what does the continent of America *mean*? It is a place of Yea-saying, the "wild and dusky" spirit of "the leopard," the place of the strong out of whom comes sweetness. In the physique and the psyche of the place called America there is no timidity, no cowardice, no compromise, no half-and-half-hesitation. It is the continent of the absolute *yes.* Stephen Vincent Benét has expressed the spirit of America splendidly in "The Ballad of William Sycamore." There is the joy of life, the delight in love (*not* just "sex"), the exhilaration in battle and the triumph even in tragedy, the individual independence that finds community in dancing the "Money Musk," the exuberance of the lusty heart and the exhilaration of the strong blood. How American the lines —

> We cleared our camp where the buffalo feed,
> Unheard of streams were our flagons;
> And I sowed my sons like the apple-seed
> On the trail of the Western wagons.

He was proud of his sons, those "right, tight boys, never sulky or slow"; he joyed in their lives — and also in their deaths, when one died at the Alamo and one fell with Custer. He and his wife took such deaths in stride, saying only, "So be it!" But they could not endure the fencing of the land, the encroachment of "progress," the bulldozing of man into mass, the communizing of individuals into sociology. So he rode an untamed colt into the fiery day, and found his youth in his death, and was "much content in [*his*] dying." That is the soul of the continent become the soul of her sons, the untamed glory of sheer American living; that is the kind of man who lived tall as the mountains and ample as the prairies. And that is what the country asks us to be, for that is what the continent itself is and says.

Ours, my son, is a mighty inheritance, a land that is our land, a great earth where our roots can grow deep. And you will never forget, as I never forget, that only as a tree thrusts its roots deep into the earth can it lift its branches high into the sun.

II

AND IN HARMONY with the tremendous and vital continent that is our country, America is great because of her sons who have conjugated and lifted into poetry her *gramatica parda.* Why is America great? Because of the heroic litany of her sons, and (as Emerson put it) their "actions that must be sung, that will sing themselves." That white soul and first American, George Washington

— surveyor of vast spaces, Indian-fighter, general who fought the seemingly hopeless battle with undying hope, patriot who despised all cabals and partisanship and treason, statesman who breathed life into the Constitutional Republic and the one nation indivisible — was such a son in his integrity and his heroism. Such was Patrick Henry, asking almighty God to forgive (if even He could) any who thought life so dear or peace so sweet as to purchase them by the chains of slavery — Nathan Hale, giving his one life to the terrible death of the noose for the sake of something greater than his life — John Paul Jones saying from the deck of his sinking ship "I have not yet begun to fight" — the words "Millions for defense but not a cent for tribute" — Admiral Farragut in Mobile Bay bidding his iron-clads steam ahead, and "Damn the torpedoes" — Douglas MacArthur declaring, in the midst of terrible loss and awful valor, "I will return" — all these are the bugle-notes of the American soul.

Never, my son, condescend to braggadocio. Do not say great words that you cannot support by great deeds. But love America because she has born sons whose words were ultimatums and battle cries, and whose deeds were swords that dared what the bugle-notes proclaimed. Remember always that you move proudly friended by those who dared to be the Yea-sayers of their country, whose words walked tall in consonance with their deeds, who said what they meant and meant what they said and marched to great music to a great goal. Remember and love the major great who were suns flaming over history; remember also the minor great, the humble men who were the quiet loam whence grow the corn and rose of freedom and sanity.

And never forget the greatness of the American *language*. H.L. Mencken wrote a major book on the American language, the language that is English and yet so much more, so much that is new. And Stephen Vincent Benét wrote a splendid poem on the American names of American places, which made him proud as they made us proud. Tanged, racy, pungent, poignant, salty with humor, sharp with insight, rich with exaggeration, sane with perception, plangent with sound and beauty — such is our language. And understand what the tepid and the cowardly of the hour are too petty to know, that a "Russian occupation of the United States" would mean the end of our language. For how can a language live and grow when the destiny of the country is negated as no longer valid and the people grow vapid with slavery?

America is great, too, because of her artists. I know most about our literature, and I say that is unique and major. There was Edgar Allan Poe, whose artistry of rhythm and meter, of assonance and alliteration, of the lips that open and shut over beautiful sound, equals or surpasses most European artists. The fastidious French, the artists of art for art's sake, the Baudelaire of finesse and those who followed him, hailed Poe as master — but never equalled him. And in spite of his artistry, he never wrote only for art's sake, but also for the spirit and the soul. In his deep purple poems there is real landscape of living objective truth — not sufficiently noticed, perhaps, because it is *Southern* landscape and too many critics are *Northern*. Great, too, the difference between Baudelaire and Poe: Baudelaire delighted in — he sought out — the dark gardens of the *Fleurs de Mal*, the Flowers of Evil; but Poe did not. Poe *suffered* from the purple shadows; he *hated* the blight of the raven; he reached anguished arms out for life and the stars. He longed for the affirmation that lies beyond all sickness of the soul. In "Israfel" he wrote:

> The ecstasies above
> With thy burning measures suit —
> Thy grief, thy joy, thy hate, thy love
> With the fervor of thy lute —
> Well may the stars be mute!

Here is no artist of the Hollow Land, but the artist of Heaven.

And there is the fine American artist, Longfellow, who is one of the great poets of the sea (as Kipling knew and said), and a poet of noble patriotism.

There is Whitman, who saw the universe as an open road for traveling souls, who affirmed himself and wished every individual man to affirm his individual soul. Superficial people suppose Whitman a "radical." But Charles W. Eldridge, who knew Whitman intimately described him thus:

> It will surprise some of Whitman's admirers to learn that as revealed by his conversation he was the most conservative of men. He believed in the old ways; had no faith in any "reforms" as such, and thought that no change could be made in the condition of mankind except by the most gradual evolution . . . . He did not believe that Woman's Suffrage would do any particular good . . . . He delighted in the company of old fashioned

women . . . . Anything like free love was utterly repugnant to his mind . . . . He was likewise very hostile to anything like anarchy, communism or socialism . . . . For the abolitionists he had no sympathy.

How greatly American Whitman's words toward the end of his life: "I bid neither for soft eulogies, big money returns, nor the approbation of existing schools and conventions . . . . unstopp'd and unwarp'd by any influence outside the soul within me, I have had my say entirely my own way, and put it unerringly on record." Is there any more American affirmation? Again and again he speaks the American soul: "The clock indicates the moment — but what does eternity indicate?" "I keep no account with lamentation." "Agonies are one of my changes of garment." "I find no sweeter fat than sticks to my own bones." "And I say to any man or woman, Let your soul stand cool and composed before a million universes." He walks the open road of immortality, he loves equally the "splendid and haughty sun" and "the huge and thoughtful night"; he sings the praise of "the fathomless universe" and "life and joy" — and also "the sure-enwinding arms of cool-enfolding death."

There are the poets and essayists of Transcendentalism (how superior to instrumentalism, relativism, positivism, existentialism!), the philosophy that says life is an involution or advolution from the Above into the Below. The great valid Thoreau, who asked no security by subsidy, who could live on ears of corn and woodchucks, or (as he said) "on ten-penny nails"; who was a "Saunterer toward Heaven," who asked nothing of "society" but to clear away its shadow, who saw the sun as only a morning star in the dawn of the soul's endless life, was a part of American greatness. And Emerson, with his brave doctrine of Self Reliance, his faith in the "infinitude of the private man," his sense of the enfolding poetry of life:

> The port, well worth the voyage, is near
> And every wave is charmed.

In poem and essay he is a fountain of sanity and freedom inexhaustible from the deep earth. Over our generation of whiners and deniers, of Nay-sayers and wallowers in defeat, he pours his beautiful disdain.

There are our novelists, too. There is James Fenimore Cooper with his epic of the essential America, the Deerslayer and Pathfinder, the celebration of the free sane elemental American and the continent of which he is worthy. There is Hawthorne, stylist of dainty rectitude, explorer of the soul, poignant and profound, who shows us how to match the outer continent with the Inner Kingdom. And there is Melville — remember Father Mapple's sermon:

> Delight is to him — a far, far upward and inward delight — who against the proud gods and commodores of this earth, ever stands forth his own inexorable self. Delight is to him, when the ship of this base treacherous world has gone down beneath him. Delight is to him, who gives no quarter in the truth, and kills, burns, and destroys all sin though he pluck it from under the robes of Senators and Judges. Delight — top-gallant delight is to him, who acknowledges no law or lord, but the Lord his God, and is only a patriot to Heaven.

You and I, my son, as patriots and genuine Americans say also that we should be "patriots to Heaven." Remember, too, the American courage of Ahab, crying as he casts his last harpoon, "Oh, now I feel my topmost greatness lies in my topmost grief." And we, like Melville, speak of life's eternal quest as: "the fiery hunt."

How greatly American, too, Mark Twain and *Huckleberry Finn*! The epic of Old Man River, the poem of America's central artery, the poem of the river and man, the essence of American speech and the American soul! Here is our love of free living Nature, of the untamed soul refusing a barren "civilization" that is a socialization, of man absorbing the winds and the sun and the stars through his naked hide as he drifts in joy down the Father of Waters. Ours the wise Huckleberry Finn who routs all ideologies and abstractions with the splendid and haughty sun of concrete reality!

You, my son, will nourish your American soul with these American classics — you will never turn your back on them, to "go a-whoring after strange gods" (as the Good Book says). And I do not need to tell you that the country which created all these is — *great.*

The continent itself, and the genuine sons of the continent, and the classics of the continent, affirm the American soul. And what is that soul essentially? It is a soul impatient of quibble and question, of debate and discussion and "dialogue," of all Hamlet-hesitancy: The American soul says *Yes* — arbitrarily, categorically. It cuts away nets of abstraction, ideology, quibble, doubt; it soars into reality on its own strong wings, like the eagle. It loves to *be*; it scorns all *not to be.* It believes in its elemental instincts, its inherent destiny, its own *I*

Am. It does not "believe in" freedom; it *is* freedom — the freedom of destiny realized. It makes the mind living and real with the wise dark blood; it is as intrinsically wise as the oak tree, the mountain lion, the canny woodchuck. Like them, it does not seek the fantastic "freedom" to be wrong, but the vital freedom to be right. This is not the assertion of the petty ego, but the affirmation of the intrinsic self: affirmation, courage, rapport with concrete reality — these are elemental in the American psyche. That psyche is as inexorable as a sword-blade, as arbitrary as the terrible swift lightnings of Heaven: It says: "I am! Such is my *will.*" It says: "There is no appeal from the T-square and the level." It says: "I am as categorical as the beat of the heart, as absolute as the pull of gravitation."

You and I, my son, love *this* America, the eternal America, the essential America, the America that forever affirms its inner destiny against its outer fate. This is the America that God meant America to be. And we say, with no Hamlet-hesitancy, with no shadow of doubt or turning, *"This America is great."*

III

BUT TODAY I KNOW, and I believe you know, that this America is being killed within herself; her soul is being stifled within her, or torn from her. Our country, our great America, is being raped by the nihilists, by the champions of death, by the Nay-sayers. A virtuous woman subjected to forcible rape is not the less virtuous, but neither is she ever the same again; that outrage may kill her, or change the balance of her nature in ways as terrible as the torture which her body may survive. Can the essential innocence and joy and affirmation of the American soul survive the ravishing to which they are being subjected?

Taylor Caldwell wrote a while ago of "Britain — no longer great." And that statement is indubitably true! Is the Britain of the "mods," of the woman-haired whining Beatles, of labor greedy for the wage and chary of the work, of the hypocrites who pass laws to keep the "coloreds" out of England and prate of the "sin" of Rhodesia, great? Of course the greatness of England, based in Eternity, can never die — Shakespeare and Blake and Browning — Clive and Kipling — Drake and Nelson and the Iron Duke — these forever are. But that greatness goes in presence, it fades in time. Shakespeare died in time but lives in Eternity; but does the nation whose soul he spoke live to the height of his greatness, in presence and in time?

If Britain remains great, it does so in a few individuals. The two magnificent Englishmen who recently *rowed* a dory all the way across the Atlantic, keep — in spite of the "mods," and the B.B.C., and C.P. Snow, and Bertrand Russell — the essential greatness of England alive.

And even so the great classic America survives, and will forever — in Eternity. But does the raped America, the ravished America, the America of dole and subsidy, survive in presence and time? What are we doing to separate our existential nonentity from our essential being? Where is the soul of the land of the free and the home of the brave, if we seek now to be secure but not free, if we seek now to be safe but not brave? If we are to "prepare for a Russian occupation of the United States by a major change in the attitude of the American people," can we survive (as a soul) that murder of Patrick Henry? Where is the America that was?

Our proud fighting men in the war-of-forbidden-victory still sustain that greatness in Vietnam. Our sons of John Birch who stand up and take "the thunder or the sunshine," with "free hearts, free foreheads," still sustain that greatness. The proud free individuals who stand even today for the integrity of the home, of private property, of the spirit untainted by the politics of surrender, of man refusing to be bulldozed into mass, sustain that greatness. The gallant young Negro who dares to walk alone from Georgia to New York bearing a placard that proclaims that he is proud to fight for the country he loves, sustains that greatness. There is, as the Good Book says, "a remnant," there are still "ten thousand who have not bowed the knee to Baal."

But too many contemporary Americans separate themselves from the essential America. They diffuse their souls in apathy. They yield to nihilism by default, because it is "sophisticated" and "smart" and "fashionable" to embrace the smartness and blight of the nihilists. They secretly loathe but outwardly acclaim plays like *A Streetcar Named Desire,* or *The Toilet,* or *The Death Of A Salesman,* or authors like James Baldwin and Norman Mailer, or novels like *Catcher In The Rye,* or "poems" that are the sawdust of death. Where are the William Sycamores, fathered by men whose "fist was a knotty hammer," who "cut [*their*] teeth upon Money Musk," who marry a girl as "straight as a hunting-knife," whose eyes are like the stars of the Dipper, and who toss the years over their shoulders like a spoor of rainbows? They are bound today by the Lilliputian cobwebs of "Liberalism," they are anemic with the smartness and blight of nihilism!

But you, my son, will be otherwise. Yours is the great heritage of the classic America. Accept it, sustain it, affirm it. Never lose "the innocence of anger and surprise"; confirm yourself to the elemental simple things like birth and the sun, like the body's death and the noble night; withhold by your steady faith the years straying toward infidelity; love water cold to the thirsty lips from the woodland spring; love the wind on the sail, the lightnings loose over the mountains; accept life from the rind to the core; say yes to truth, and beauty, and right undiluted and absolute and categorical.

Be American like an eagle staring into the very sun, like a grizzly bear splendid upon the Sierras, like Old Man River striding the continent, like the Gulf Stream bearing the heat of garnered suns in a blue river through the green banks of the Atlantic. Dare, choose, be arbitrary and affirm, hate the ugly and the love the beautiful, love, enjoy, be. Look outward with proud acclaim toward your continent; look inward with proud affirmation toward the continent of the soul within you.

And know, my son, that while one American still affirms life greatly, the greatness of America still endures and abides. And know that even if our America — betrayed by the dry rot of little men — should end in time and presence, the essential and eternal America that is great will live on in the mind and the will of God. And I know that you, since you are my son, will love with proud joy that America that God means and wills.

When Roads Diverge To Left And Right

WE live in an hour when the youths who make the publicity of TV and the headlines of *Life* and *Look* are those who fly, over the Sorbonne or over Columbia, the Red Flag of Marx or the Black Flag of Bakunin. There are fortunately, other young Americans who devote themselves to sanity and freedom; but, of them, one hears hardly a whisper in the kept Press of the Establishment. What you are about to read is addressed to all of these — to the young who seek a "brave new world" that is actually a cliched old world of slavery, and to the young who seek a renaissance of the timeless spirit of essential reality.

Perhaps it is naive to suppose that the devotees of the Black Flag and the Red Flag will read my words, or will heed me if they do. They seem, alas, to tolerate nothing but the image of their own dated perversion. Nonetheless, we do not exclude them.

As for those young Americans yet devoted to sanity and freedom, I hope that they will find in what I am about to say here something to nourish and strengthen them, though I know that, being individualists, they will (and should) differ in some things and bite each idea to test its mettle.

Most especially, I would write to uncommitted youth, to youth in search of reality, to youth who would find some coherent pattern amid the mist and hum of this lowland of modernity.

I would write to you all as one man to another, as one mind to another, as one who seeks truth by exploring what is real. And I would ignore, as I hope you will ignore, all mechanical criteria of mere youth or mere age, never assuming either that life begins at forty or that life ends at thirty. I say to you young people of America and the world: Let us forget all superficial tags of "young" or "old," let us even forget the easy labels of "Left" and "Right," and let us seek together what all men of good will and clear reason should seek: The things that *are* the truth that *abides*.

I

WE HEAR MUCH today about the "generation gap." That gap, however, is too often made a thing of mere quantity of years, not a thing of quality of being. The quantity of years a man has lived means nothing till the ancient questions are answered: "What have you done with those years? What have those years done for you?" The *quality* of our years is what matters. A teenybopper who goes into a tizzy over the Beatles or the Rolling Stones does indeed find a gap between himself and Rembrandt or Goya; but it is a gap not of quantity of years but quality of being. "Ripeness is all," as Shakespeare says. And, though Sidney Lanier and John Keats died "young," there was no "generation gap" between them and Shakespeare or Goethe who lived to the fifties or the eighties. There was no such "gap" because they all lived in the realm of timeless *quality*.

The wise and humorous "old man," who lives with every inch and ounce and atom of his being, is closer to the wise "young man," who lives with the arterial blood of body and mind, than he is to the "senior citizens" who play shuffleboard in the retirement colonies of St. Petersburg or subsist on Scotch in the saloons of suburban Darien.

The "gap," you see, is not determined by the quantity of years but by the quality of the human beings involved. There *is* a gap, irrespective of age, but it is between the fool and the wise man, between the brash and discourteous and the courteous and humble, between the human mistakes and the human achievements. In the life of a great people while its life is valid, as in classical China, the gay young blade, Li Po, who waded into the river to clasp the moon (though he could not swim) and died with the moon in his arms, could understand and be understood by the poetical oldster, Chang Chi-ho, who was known as "the old fisherman of the mists and waters" and who put no bait on his hook, "his object not being to catch fish."

Fire is fire — no matter how long it burns. The "old" fire on the tomb of the unknown soldier is closer to the "young" fire kindled for their country by American soldiers fighting and dying with honor in Vietnam than either waft of flame is to the ersatz incendiarism of, say, the President of the National Student Association. Even the "now-iest" of the Now Generation would find a trip with Socrates at fifty more interesting than a trip with a fool of fifteen . . . unless they were fools too. Any "gap" between the generations is as foolish as a "gap" between the blossom of May and the apple of September.

Actually there is a greater gap between the "sophisticate" of eighteen and the unspoiled child of five than there is between that child and a William Blake at fifty. It is as William Saroyan, in his one indubitable masterpiece, *The Human Comedy,* wrote of little Ulysses:

> He came quickly and quietly and stood beside her, then went to the hen nest to look for eggs. He found one. He looked at it a moment, picked it up, brought it to his mother and very carefully handed it to her, by which he meant what no man can guess and no child can remember to tell.

There is the very magic and lost Eden of childhood — and how far, how far, how far it is from the sophisticated artificiality of the professional "flower child"! The "sophisticate" of eighteen may have grown "knowledgeable" and smart and clever at the expense of his direct spontaneous self, and be an insufferable mental brat — but this will be as apparent to the unspoiled child as surely as to the vital old man.

Note that the teenybopper gone to college calls it a "poem" to write:

> Only knowing that within will lay what without I have not . . . and there shall be no satisfaction no depuration nor salvation — for the within continually moves further toward a distant internal . . . .*

But the child of three speaks simply in poetry from the living "within" of his being — "The noise went by so fast I couldn't see it . . . ." or "The puppy wasn't biting me at all — he was just tasting me." This is not a matter of age; it is a matter of something lost out of life — and something added of synthetic smartness and neon lights. Something has happened to youth (from the outside), something intellectualized (yet minus intellect), something artificial. The child's conscious and subconscious are integral and harmonious and one; life speaks directly to him and through him. But the teenybopper gone to college has fractured and splintered consciousness from subconsciousness (and superconsciousness) and tortured life into artificiality by draining the blood from the mind

*From *Death: kinds, two,* by Sean O'Toole, *The Campus Forum,* El Camino College, California, Issue No. 2, March 30, 1964.

and making intellect kosher. The gap is not a necessary adjunct of "age" but a loss and destruction that has fractured quality.

The trouble with life today is that this slick artificiality, begun among college teenyboppers, persists as a perpetual adolescence in people who are older. It is the great deficit of the Now Generation. It is not due to quantity (or lack of quantity) in years, but to a lack of quality in being. C.G. Jung puts it best. He asks of the psychological counselor what he can do when "he sees only too clearly why his patient is ill; when he sees that it arises from his having no love, but only sexuality; no faith, because he is afraid to grope in the dark; no hope, because he is disillusioned by the world and by life; and no understanding, because he has failed to read the meaning of his own existence." (*Modern Man In Search Of A Soul*, Pp. 225-226.) *That* is the gap that divides the Instant Generation from Timeless Man. It is not a gap in age; it is a gap vital and psychological. It is the modern distemper of splitting mind from soul.

Even D.H. Lawrence, in his genuine but darkly seen way, saw this sickness of modern man — the fracture between abstract cerebral mind and the instinctive wisdom of "the dark blood." He says, in *Studies In Classic American Literature*: "You can idealize or intellectualize. Or, on the contrary, you can let the dark soul in you see for itself." Exactly! The soul, of course, is light as well as dark; but it is surely dark in its mystery, its magic, its depth, and it should be left alone and not tortured into artificial cleverness by psychedelic lighting and a perverting electric amplifier. And today it *is* so tortured among the college teenyboppers. That is the true gap in the lives of the Now Generation.

You want integrity? So do I. But integrity means *wholeness,* and wholeness is a quality of the soul (which modern man must find if he is to survive), of the Inner Kingdom, of the fruitful union of sub-and-super-consciousness with the serene reason of the true consciousness. This has been rendered difficult for us largely by the Freudian super-ficiality that saw the "subconscious" as something rather dirty and bestial and dark (yet something to which we should give full play), as the nether stew of irrational impulses, as something nasty and base. On the contrary, the sub-and-super-consciousness, as in the instincts of the vital animal and the intuitions of the child and the genius, is a noble and fruitful thing that should and can work in harmony with the reason of the surface consciousness. The child so lives; the philos-opher (*not* the "professor of philosophy") so lives; the poet or the saint whose roots of genius go down into the depths so lives. The man who really lives find his center in his protopsyche.

But you will never find integrity when you live by rationality instead of reason; when you libel the dark side of your own moon, yet give its splinter aberrations full whim and license; when you split yourself into discord. The real gap is not between the generations but between modern man and timeless man. The "generation gap" as such is a cliché to excuse arrogance and ignorance on the one side or to excuse patronage and arrogance on the other.

"The generation gap?" Let's discard that stupid phrase, that hoary superficiality, that easy escape from thought, that pother of nonsense! Seek rather the integrity that binds the generations into the noble search for life and life ever more abundantly.

If you must stress the generation gap, you narrow and destroy your own life. *If* you are to be useless and untrustworthy once you pass thirty, you had better get a pistol in spite of Senator Dodd, to celebrate the dawn of your fourth decade not with a whimper but a bang. But this denies all richness, all depth and width and inner wealth in your life. It might even deprive you − and the world − of the glory of a Shakespeare. After all, Shakespeare had not written *King Lear* or *The Tempest* when he was thirty . . . .

II

FORGET AGE and concentrate on timeless reality. The question is − what do you truly seek? If your adventure is to fly the Red Flag or the Black Flag, you seek to wallow in clichés, in old gags, in the outmoded and the reactionary. You think I am prejudiced? Listen, then, to a darling of the Left, to Bertrand Russell, who visited Soviet Russia and summed it up in such postjudices as these:

> . . . . a closed tyrannical bureaucracy with a spy system more elaborate than the Tzar's and an aristocracy as insolent and unfeeling, composed of Americanized Jews [*sic!*]. No basis of liberty remains, in thought or speech or action . . . . Imagine yourself governed in every detail by a mixture of Sidney Webb and Rufus Isaacs, and you will have a picture of modern Russia.

And if you say: "But this is the old age of Communism, and China and Cuba are not so!" − you mistake the truth. For he so wrote when Communism in Russia was "young," just after World War I. And it is necessarily so. For ownership in common as an ideal, and dictatorship of the few in practice, are very, very old concepts. They go back to primitive tribes, to aboriginal peoples, to corruption of life into collectivism, which goes sadly back across the centuries. And as for anarchy and the Black Flag, that goes back to the origin of the perennial scourges of all history, the Catilines of history, the nihilists who live on loot as long as it lasts and prepare the way for the repressive emperors who as men on horseback liquidate the men they have driven into the gutters. The Red Flag in modern times is as old as that mid-Victorian with whiskers, Karl Marx; the Black Flag is as old as Mikhail Bakunin, Marx's contemporary and enemy (who sought the same Communist ends in a different mood and by different means). To seek either is to go back, to go backward, to retrogress to the chaos of anarchism or the ancient night of Communism.

Free men and sane men wish, rather, to transcend time and so to create eternal things within time. The men who discover fire and invent the wheel, who fashion speech into the alphabet. who with Pasteur conquer rabies, who as law-givers create a Constitution to keep men free, who freeze music into the architecture of great buildings, who create beauty on canvas or preserve wisdom on vellum, who know with Archimedes that given the proper lever and a place to stand one can move the world, who with Atlas bear the world upon their shoulders . . . these are neither "old" nor "young" nor "Left" nor "Right" — they are the integrals and the creators. But the nihilists, or the monolithic spiders of the Total State, the Bureaucrats and the Power Boys, are old, old, old — clichés ambulant, old gags who reckon themselves real, hoary cobwebs rampant. They turn their faces away from "Eternity's sunrise" (as William Blake put it), they splash the world with the blood of the Red Flag, they call in the croaking ravens of the Black Flag.

And, carrying this to its conclusion of logic, those who march under these flags of reaction are not preparing or welcoming a brave new world, but wrapping their hate in the flags of savages.

III

IT IS GOOD for youth to desire a fairer world. I am as much against the present *status quo* of the world of *man* as any rebel anywhere. I do not uphold — what civilized mind could uphold? — the *status quo* of man today — the megalopolis of Mayor John Lindsay or of Professor Harvey Cox, the smog and legislated poverty of Welfare, the crime made legal if committed by the "black" or the "poor," the alcohol and sleeping pills and LSD and "pot," the vapid

TV and stultifying commercials, the slick sophistication of the Brainy Boys among "capitalists" in *Playboy* and *Look* and *Life* and *Esquire* and *Fortune* and the *New Yorker*, the compromisers who seek coexistence with Slave States like Soviet Russia and who lust to loose troops on free Rhodesia, the lakes fouled into cesspools of death, the men turned out to pasture at sixty-five when their unique wisdom is most needed in Academe, the mass-universities where classes of a thousand are "lectured at" by invisible professors or subjected to audio-visual aids, and where "teachers" are shunted into "research," and instructors still raw from graduate schools are turned loose on students, the wars that we are forced to fight but not allowed to win, all the lies and cruelties of the Liberal Establishment . . . . *Carthago delenda est!*

But what is the climate of that Establishment that I dislike as much as you do? It is rationalism, pragmatism, existentialism — materialism and obsession with the Temporal Now uncriticized by God's Eternal Now — positivism and the worship of the Big and the Clever and the fashionable and the temporal and the secular. It is the climate of the rootless ignorance that supposes that history began with "science" and "democracy." It is the climate of forced integration of "races," willy-nilly, no matter what either race wants, but never the integration of mind and soul within the individuals of all races. It is the climate of belief that matter is a period after mind, not mind a question-mark after matter — physics but never metaphysics, biology reduced to necrology, chemistry that supposes it "explains" consciousness and is ignorant that consciousness discovers chemistry. It is the climate of the superficial fashionable Camus who declares categorically: "I continue to believe that the world has no ultimate meaning."

Yet, such is the "spiritual" climate of the *status quo*. And how can you create a fairer world of man until you find the *potentia qua* of living Nature and beyond it of the living God? You cannot criticize the Establishment if you accept the invalid "values" of the Establishment. To criticize what is wrong and to create what is right you must transcend this world and enter the Kingdom that is not of this world. Rationalism, relativism, existentialism, materialism — such are the valueless "values" that have resulted in the human "world" for which some youths blame their elders. But if these same youths still accept and carry out even more brashly these *same* "values, how can they create a different world? Philosophy, metaphysics, the spirit, or their absence — these always determine the outer world. Until and unless you find the ageless and eternal spirit of the *potentia qua,* everything that you do will only italicize all that you rightly loathe in the *status quo* of human society today.

To fashion from wreck and sediment a fairer world you must begin with light, with philosophy, with coherent thought. And so I say to you: Discriminate, discriminate, and again discriminate! Be fastidious. Choose. Select.

You see, the beginning of a true society lies not in society at all, but in the individual. We have sought for some decades to change society — and look at what we have done to society, look at the society we have — atoms, hard grains of glaze-pointed sand, fragments! As we have fractured mind from soul, so we have fractured society from community and nation. Only individuals who feel responsibility and seek not "rights" for themselves but right for their country can restore us to the "blissful seat of Eden."

We have splintered the nation into what the Founding Fathers called "factions" — into classes, fissured minorities and selfish, blind, mob-majorities, pressure groups, labor unions or manufacturers' associations, *etc., etc.* . . . Where is the one nation indivisible? Grains of sand, grains of sand . . . atoms . . . splinters . . . and the great winds blow, and we are blown with them. Only living individuals with living souls, who know the integrity of *noblesse oblige,* who seek right more than "rights," who impose *upon themselves* responsibilities, who pursue the impossible dream in themselves, and not the unattainable world of treacle that is supposed to make "society" happy, can restore the nation and create a viable "society." Ortega y Gasset in his magnificent *Revolt of the Masses* reveals the truth and the way:

> For there is no doubt that the most radical division that it is possible to make of humanity is that which splits it into two classes of creatures: those who make great demands on themselves, piling up difficulties and duties; and those who demand nothing special of themselves, but for whom to live is to be every moment what they already are, without imposing on themselves any effort toward perfection; mere buoys that float on the waves.

One need only add that these human buoys are forever calling on a perpetual coast guard to come and tow them ashore to Lollipop Land.

And you do *not* "impose on yourself any effort toward perfection" by cultivating off-beat beards, and letting your hair grow long, and drifting into a psychedelic Nirvana, and indulging in vagrancy and flagrancy, and aping the compulsive masquerades of conformity to the Now Groups. That is the *status quo* of the off-beat. It is the playboyism of Shriners standing on their heads. True individuality will not come through eccentric habits or garbs or manners. Dress as men normally dress today, because your search is for *inner* differences and so you scorn *outer* differences which only distract from what is important about you.

And do not join "groups" to "sit in" or "love in," the gang conformities of the pathetically unsure. Be alone, be *alone,* in the crowded city or the thronged college library. The way to the creative society is to shun mass, to avoid "social" groups and "reforms" and panaceas, but rather to seek within yourself the cosmos that is the healing of the chaos without you. Once a wise Indian guide, surprized by a blizzard while miles from camp, told his despairing client: "Indian not lost: wigwam lost!" As long as the Indian is not lost the wigwam can be found. Let it be so with you in your wider world yet similar predicament!

The world of "society" today is a chaos? — then be, yourself, a cosmos! And if *you* are a cosmos, you are a center of light and life and love, a sun that, like all suns everywhere, makes light of his despair and so brings light to all his planets.

"Shoulder the sky, my lad . . . "

The great benefactor to society is not the activist for "social justice," but the individual who *is* justice in all he says and does. The greatest benefactor to the life of the Negro was not Nat Turner, the revolutionist (God forgive him — I cannot), but George Washington Carver, alone in his laboratory, discovering and using the secrets of Nature; alone in the fortress of his soul and his genius. Alone, alone with Nature: alone with God; alone, alone! Only so can you be with others, creating for others; only so are you a center of light and power by which the world may live. Because he was alone, George Washington Carver could help his people, the *American* people. How much we owe him! But we would owe nothing to him, and American Negroes would owe nothing to him, if he had been another busybody, another "social" agitator, another Father Groppi in ebony. He helped society, as we too must, by finding *himself.* As Goethe said, you must *be* somebody before you can *do* anything.

If youth would have meaning for the world, it should go into the mountains and the deserts and the islands and dwell there alone until it has something to give. Not the mountains and the deserts and the islands of geography, necessarily, but those of psychography. How wise was Zarathustra! —

> When Zarathustra was thirty years old, he left his home and the lake of his home, and went into the mountains. There he enjoyed his spirit and his solitude, and for ten years did not weary of it. But at last his heart changed, — and rising one morning with the rosy dawn, he went before the sun and spake unto it:
> Thou great star! What would be thy happiness if thou hadst not those for whom thou shinest!

And so, like the sun, having generated his wealth of light and become himself a sun, he went back to the world to give what he had first created in himself, saying:

> Lo! I am weary of my wisdom, like the bee that hath gathered too much honey; I need hands outstretched to take it.
> I would fain bestow and distribute, until the wise have once more become joyous in their folly, and the poor happy in their riches.

But Zarathustra had gone first into solitude, and in his loneliness he discovered himself and so became not an ink-blot but a sun. And so must youth today. In patience, in loneliness, in solitude, in silence, youth must discover itself and learn to *be*. Only so, after apprenticeship to the years, after creation of quality, in its wisdom and its power, perhaps it may *do*. Only from the fully charged clouds fall the lightnings of great deeds; only from the garnered and deep fountains can flow the rivers that never fail.

IV

LONELINESS AND ISOLATION are a prerequisite of our eventual communion and fellowship. But that loneliness is not a tearing up of roots (the rose, the wheat, and the fruitful tree live by roots), but a thrusting of those roots even deeper into the earth.

In our deserts, our mountains, our islands (geographic or psychographic), we must draw our life from our land. The noble continent that is ours, the America that is the land we love, the mountains and the prairies and the oceans white with foam, these must be a living part of us; they nourish and support and inspire and give us a valid strength and joy. There is a mystical communion between the land where you live and the soul which you are. Your land is an *alma mater*, a cherishing mother, and it is ever with you, and about you, and in you — if you break your communion with it, you wither and die though you go on "living."

"Starting from fish-shaped Paumonok," and loving "million-footed Manahatta" and the lilacs that bloomed in à million door yards, Whitman nourished his genius. Poe filled his strange deep-purple poems with the landscapes of the South. Sidney Lanier found his way to God through the unique and mysterious marshes of Glynn. Winslow Homer nourished his genius on Caribbean waters or the surf-assaulted gray rock bastions of the coast of Maine. Thoreau found his true philosophy not in "civil disobedience" but in the Concord and Merrimac rivers and in the beloved waters of Walden.

You may differ (as I do) with the contemporary politicians who disfigure contemporary politics. But the continent and the land that transcend them, and the generations of the great dead who are part of your love of America, and the traditions and the garnered wisdom and the genius that are a part of our heritage, these remain and abide. And these are the basis of what we call *patriotism.* If you, as youth, wave the Red Flag or the Black Flag you are alienated from your land, from the genius of your land, from the great dead of your country. So you become thin and febrile and petulant and querulous and rootless; your leaf, then, withers, and you do not bring forth your fruit in its season.

To lose patriotism is to lose the very sources of your life, the very fountains of your being, the deep roots of your soul. It is a part of the fragmentation that is the curse of modernity. It is a part of the fracture between mind and soul, between the beneficent buried subconscious and the surface consciousness that must never be severed from the whole and the integrity of being.

Professor Eliseo Vivas, in his splendid *"Apologia Pro Fide Mea,"* sees the chief lack of the "liberal intellectual" — and this must include the *radical* intellectual — in his loss of piety. Piety, says Professor Vivas, in the old Roman sense, means that "a pious man is one who has gratitude and reverence and gratitude for parents, ancestors, country or people, earth, universe." The Romans, indeed, spoke reverently of, and loved, the *Lares* and *Penates,* the household gods. And all great people have known that the great dead who cannot die, the geniuses who have spoken the genius of their people, the fruitful loam and the stern rocks of their land, are a part forever of something that far transcends any "Now Generation." The eternal being, the timeless fabric of life that embraces all times and all generations, these are the love of the "pious man." And unless you have this, you are not really alive, and you are so poor in memory, so underprivileged in soul, so destitute of the wealth of life, that you are to be pitied. And thus comes, in Spengler's sense, the Decline of the West. Thence comes the end of a culture.

And then?

Then the terrible night.

I believe that you, as youth, do not want this. I believe that you want a fairer world and a truer life. And so I believe that youth, vital youth, valid youth, will not long wave the Red Flag and the Black Flag, that it will implement again the great Roman word *Pietas,* and that it will live for and by its land, and the eternal verities, and meaning, quality, and value. Then, and then only, will youth find and fulfill its destiny!

Why Revolution Wars On Renaissance

THERE is a trail that leads upward from one of the lovely valleys of Switzerland. Travelers take it to reach a broad and beautiful view, thousands of feet up, and mountain-climbers take it because it begins the ascent of the Matterhorn.

The trail is easy at first. It winds up and up, easily and leisurely, and for a long time climbers do not have to think or choose. But after about a gracious hour of such pleasant climbing, the trail suddenly forks and here the climber must pause and choose. The fork to the right seems narrow and rocky and steep, and barely trodden; the fork to the left seems easy and gradual and tempting, and it has been trodden smooth by many feet. And so the naive and unsophisticated climber chooses the easy and gradual path of the sinister fork. But, after only a few hundred yards, the path to the left bends in a sudden abrupt turn around a cliff; and just beyond the turn it comes to a precipice and a drop of a thousand feet into the valley below. And at the edge of the precipice and the end of the trail there is a sign that reads in German *Das Ende Der Welt* – The End of the World.

That image is a parable, literal and stark, of our world today. We know that those who choose the path to the left will soon stand at the edge of the precipice and precipitation into the valley a thousand feet below. Yet we know also that there are those who are not deceived by conformity to surface and illusion, but who choose the Emersonian road of self-reliance, the gay athleticism of the difficult way, and who climb the steep and narrow path toward the Matterhorn and the stars. They, and they alone, the few who are chosen among the many who are called, avoid the end of the world and may initiate the renaissance of man, the renewal of life.

The precipice that stands at the end of the world is, most of all today, the hypnosis and compulsion of those who seek what they call "revolution." Probably the most dangerous demagogue in America in recent years was the Massachusetts-Senator-by-the-grace-of-New-York, Robert Kennedy; and it was he who said that the

young revolutionists of the world "will achieve their idealistic goals
one way or another. If they have to pull governments tumbling down
over their heads, they will do it. We, in turn, are part of their
revolution."

Here, indeed, we stand at the edge of the precipice. Here is *Das
Ende Der Welt,* the End of the World! As it happened, one such
"idealistic" revolutionary pushed Senator Kennedy over the edge
before he was ready to go.

I

WHEN OUR MINDS, motivated by the obscure inner compulsion
of our grudge-sick or ambition-sick psyche, choose the sinister path
of revolution, and come to the turning to the left, and reach the
precipice at the end of the world, we need logic and reason to waken
us from our somnambulism into death. Definition, logic, philisophy
— these are the cold water of reality that may, if we are shocked into
reason, waken us in time. Therefore it may be valuable, and I am sure
it is necessary, to check our premises; to test our logic and examine
our psychic urges; and to see, by the sanity of reason and the critique
of reality, just what has led us to the impasse of the fruitless halt at
the verge of nothing or the messy death a thousand feet below. Just
what is this "revolution" that Senator Kennedy so cavalierly incited
for us and (more obscurely) for *himself?*

Let us try to define — and so to understand — "revolution."

I turn to my dictionary (*The American College Dictionary,*
Random House, edition of 1957). There I find that the secondary
meaning of revolution is "procedure or course as in a circuit, as back
to a starting point in time . . . . a turning round or rotating as on an
axis." Thus a wheel makes a "revolution" as it goes round in the
circle by which movement is possible, or the hands of a clock make a
"revolution" from the twelve of the beginning to the twelve of the
end. But this, of course, was not Senator Kennedy's meaning. He did
not mean the fruitful revolution of the wheel, reaching its starting
point in itself and so a new position in relation to the earth; or the
useful revolution of the clock that shows us that time is always a
repetition and not a novelty. He conceived — and ultimately
encountered — "revolution" in far other terms.

My dictionary defines the *primary* meaning of "revolution" as "a
complete overthrow of an established government or political
system," and that was Mr. Kennedy's meaning. Now if my dictionary

were profound and essential it would say, rather: "A complete overthrow of, and so a change in, the essential nature of something that has been *that* and is now *this*, i.e., the overthrow of and change in the light that becomes the darkness, the melon that becomes the mushroom." It is characteristic of our a-philosophical, anti-rational, existential time that a dictionary should choose the political and social, not the natural and real, and be superficial in its interpretation even of this. So it goes on to cite "the English Revolution (1688), the American Revolution (1775), the French Revolution (1789), the Chinese Revolution (1917)." It is so superficial that it does not even discriminate *between* these "revolutions" — some of which, as we shall see, are not "revolutions" at all in the sense the dictionary means.

To understand "revolution" we must transcend such superficiality and see the meaning of the word in its root meaning. To do this we need to study the term that underlies "revolution," i.e., *evolution,* and see its meaning in itself and its relation to "revolution."

What *is* evolution? By its Latin roots it means a development — literally, a "rolling out" — from the inner nature of something – of its latent and potential being or meaning. Unfortunately today it is tied up with a suggested (but unproved) explanation of the development of creation — the bumping of the amoeba up to man, the purely physical and biological progression from atom to animal, from ape to Aeschylus. If men would only use their minds, they would long ago have developed, rather, the concept of *involution* — that is, the descent, into lower levels of being, of the value and meaning that come always and only from higher levels of being. For example, we sometimes speak of the "evolution" of the automobile; but there has never been an "evolution" of the automobile. There has been, on the contrary, an involution from mind into matter, from philosophy into physics, of an idea that increasingly incarnates itself in the plastic possibilities of matter that is thus progressively invaded by value, quality, and meaning *from above.* This, of course, has been what Christianity has always said: *In the beginning was the Word, and the Word became flesh.* Incarnation, that is, *involution,* has always been the hidden dynamic and the open secret of the world.

But let us, for the understanding of our thesis, see the partial truth that does lie in the concept of "evolution." Both Aristotle and Goethe saw this in a way that Darwin never could: Aristotle, for example, saw the dynamic of life in the *entelechy* of a thing or creature — that is, in the inner destiny that is its meaning and intention. Thus the blind puppy, by its own inward intuition, "evolves" into the sagacious and efficient hunting-dog; the human embryo, by the entelechy of its implicit being, "evolves" (if it is fortunate) into Bach or Rembrandt or Thomas Jefferson; or (if it is unfortunate) into Carl Sandburg or Soapy Williams. The vital root in the dark earth, by living destiny, "evolves" into the radish for use or the rose for beauty. In this sense (the only essential sense), "evolution" means the vital rolling of the inward into the outward, of the potential into the actual, of the intention of the egg into the bird with the plumes that glow and the throat that sings. Thus "evolution," in any credible or valid sense, means the realization of latent or implicit quality; value, and meaning — that simply *becomes* in time what it always *is* in eternity.

Let us now advance to the meaning of terms that are based upon the word "evolution." Take *devolution*. Devolution means the descent of evolution in an opposite direction; it is the reversal of evolution, of the movement of child into man, of bud into blossom. By devolution, progression becomes retrogression, development becomes decay, destiny becomes fate. Devolution turns the movement toward the life more abundant into a relapse into the death more potent. Devolution means decadence.

And if there is evolution toward more abundant life, there is surely also a possible devolution toward retreat and death. If the early naive evolutionists were right, and there were evolution of man through monkeys, anthropoid apes, and missing links, we have less evidences of it extant today than we have of the devolution of man. For the quite obvious devolution of man into monkey, we have only to turn to the contemporary campus . . . .

But let us go a step further. We have seen the meaning of "evolution" and of "devolution." What, then, is the meaning of *revolution*?

II

HERE AGAIN, let us transcend the superficiality of the conformist dictionaries of the day, and see for ourselves what is the root of the word or the seed whence its meaning grows.

The Latin prefix "re" means a backward turn, as in *re*versal or *re*action. So here, in *re*volution, there is the reaction against evolution, the reversal, the backward turning, the revolt against intention and meaning. So, like "devolution," it is a relapse from or a revolt against life and being. Devolution, however, is a slip or lapse or fall; a decadence that is a passive rotting, a drifting and debacle into decay. Revolution, however, is not a mere passive drifting into decay; it is an active, deliberate, willful reaction against the intention, the life-urge or vital destiny that is the meaning of the root or the seed or the thing or the creature. "Revolution," thus, means a chosen and willed reaction against the value, quality, and meaning that lie at the heart of any valid life or creature. "Revolution" means a pulling down, or apart, of basic being, until reality comes (in the words of Senator Kennedy) "tumbling down over our heads."

In my book, *Of Perilous Seas,* I gave what I consider the essence of "revolution" in my poem, "The Titans":

> Once there was war of earth with Heaven: the Titans
>> Waged total war with Zeus;
> They tossed vast mountain on vast mountain, storming
>> Heaven's hypotenuse.
> They sought to scale Olympus in their foray,
>> Till they were backward hurled . . . .
> The Titans never breached the walls of Heaven —
>> But they laid waste the world!

"Revolution" thus means reaction; the rebellion of the Titans against the Olympians; the resentment, the sick grudge and revenge of the impotent and disgruntled of the world against quality, value, and meaning; the cancelling of evolution; the will-to-destruction, the will-to-suicide.

"Revolution" is *not* the omnipresent struggle of life against opposition and impediment. Suppose an acorn fallen upon a granite boulder: Strong with the intention of the oak, it thrusts out roots into its meager cup of loam; it splits the rock to find ampler nutriment; or it reaches out with resolute arms of being to find, around the rock, a kindlier earth. But that is not "revolution"! It is just the will-to-be; the brave determination of destiny that shatters the brute determinism of fate; the essential war that is forever the creative way of the world. Such war, Heraclitus rightly said, is "the father of all things." But if the acorn sought "revolution" it would abolish all intention of the oak within itself, or it would repudiate the nourishment of loam that alone can nourish it, and it would bring its dream and its deed "tumbling down over its head."

The seed within the earth has a war to wage with darkness, stone, mould, worm, crow, frost, drought. It does not, however, rebel against its own introstance or even against its valid circumstances, in petulant and negative "revolution"; it uses its circumstances, and it affirms its introstance, in the fruitful war that is the father of all things. It does not "tumble things down"; it builds things up.

Logic and reason require that we distinguish such creative struggle from the petulant, grudge-motivated, nihilistic reaction that Senator Kennedy called "revolution." Apply this to history. The Hungarian "revolution" against Communism, in Budapest, was not revolution at all; it was the war of the seed against the stone, the worm, the frost. Communist domination, chicanery, treachery, were not a part of true Hungarian evolution or intention; they were external negations of Hungary. The Hungarians did not revolt against, but sought to affirm, their own essential and eternal being as Hungarians, their native *I Am*. They merely warred against impediments to their own being.

(The only Hungarian "revolution" occurred when a child of Lucifer named Bela Kun tried — with no success, because the Hungarian entelechy was far otherwise — to reverse evolution and deny the Hungarian destiny by subjecting Hungary to the reversal called collectivism, the concentration camps and the firing squads, the moonless midnight and the sunless noon.)

In the same way, our so-called "American Revolution" was not revolution at all. It was, as it is correctly called, our *War for Independence*. We did not deny, we affirmed, the essential spirit of England — Magna Charta, the freedom of Milton's dream, the growth toward justice and natural law.

We rightly fought England to win our own destiny; but it was a destiny in terms of Anglo-Saxon being. This is so true that most of the Fabian "historians" I criticize in *Brainwashing In The High Schools* have to assert with angry iteration that the American Revolution was not a War for Independence, but a "Civil War," a "revolution" at home — of the "underprivileged" against the "privileged," of the "Colonial democrats" against the "Colonial aristocrats." The "poor," the "uneducated," the men without "property" (it is supposed) rose in "revolution" against the "rich," the "educated," the "privileged" — like, specifically, George Washington! — who supposedly cared only for their own pelf and power. A part of our debacle today comes because "Liberals" have implanted, by surly iteration, such lies in our national subsoil. But the War for Independence was not a "revolution" — it was the struggle of the acorn with the stone, that it might grow and lift the very sky upon its leafy shoulders.

The revolution, however, by which the Chinese Communists (with the help of our State Department) overthrew a once great nation, was indeed a "revolution" in the Kennedyan sense. Mao Tse-tung and his goons of infamy sought to reverse, deny, and destroy the entelechy of China. A people that is devoted to the family is to be denied the family and homogenized into communes; a people that reverences the gracious morality of Confucius and "the superior man," or the rhythmic metaphysics of the great Lao-tse, are to be turned into the ants of materialism, and told that truth is the most expedient wrong; the people that created the poetry of Li Po (who drowned with the moon in his arms!), and the paintings of innumerable mystics of landscape, are to be reduced to "realists" in a two-dimensional Flatland. Thus the Communist Revolution in China is indeed revolution — i.e., reaction, negation, reversal, denial. *The abolition of China!*

The Russian Revolution of 1917 was likewise, in the root sense, a revolution. It sought to erase and negate all that the Russian people by destiny and intention *are.* The Communists *use* patriotism — but hate and negate it; they *use* religion, but seek to abolish it; they *use* the classics of literature, but seek to overthrow them. They seek to uproot and overthrow the concept of Holy Russia; that is, the essence of the Slavic soul. The great Russian freedom-fighters — Tolstoi, Dostoevski, Pushkin, Andreyev, Turgenev — were the acorn warring with the rock, not the revolutionists who deny the oak, or the termites who destroy the oak from within. The Russian Revolution of 1917 was a deathwish; a gesture of Russian suicide.*

Shakespeare almost always has the final word. And so here. If you would understand "revolution," turn to *The Tempest* and study the revolution of Caliban against Prospero. Prospero is the magician, the master, the glory of imagination and the noble height of the mind — that is, all that is the intention of God for man and the aspiration of

---

*The French Revolution of 1789 was also revolution in the sense of nihilistic overthrow. It fractured the organic being of France. France has never recovered, and only when it tran- cends the "Revolution" will it become again a great nation.

man for himself. And Caliban? He is devolution of man back to brute, the lapse of mind into mud, the grudge and resentment of all that is sick and evil in the psyche. Caliban is asked what he would do if he had his will and way. Notice his answer! He would "bash in" Prospero's head while he lay sleeping; and he would *burn Prospero's books,* those instruments of magic and mastery. (The Nazis and the Communists, the Calibans of the Twentieth Century, bash in heads, too, and burn the books.) And then Caliban — O characteristic will of "revolutionists"! — discloses his heart's desire; he says, once Prospero is overthrown and "tumbled down," he will rape Miranda and "people the isle with Calibans." Shakespeare knew the nature of revolution; and he abhorred it.

"Revolution" is the parallel, in politics, of the most characteristic disease of the Twentieth Century — cancer. Cancer is the disease of the body in revolution against the body; of the reaction whereby the cells of the body revolt against the body, as a whole, as an entity and an organism; of the cells become a mob to ravage and overthrow. "Revolution," in the Twentieth Century, is our typical contemporary disease paramount and rampant, our typical disease of man as a political animal. "Revolution" is the galloping cancer of the West!

III

THE HEALTH of the world is negated by the cancer of revolution. How, then, *does* life advance, grow, evolve, and surpass itself in noble renaissance?

We may begin our realization of the advance of creative life by referring briefly to the Hebrew prophets in the Old Testament. The apostles of reaction in our "Liberalized" churches today often liken Harry F. Ward, their idol as a "revolutionist," to a Hebrew prophet. This is nonsense because Harry F. Ward is the intellectual opposite and spiritual negation of the Hebrew prophet. The Hebrew prophet, whether a seer of doom like Jeremiah or a seer of the mystical coming of Christ like the Second Isaiah, was always a conservator. He never said: "Smash the Tables of Stone and the Ten Commandments, and let us usher in the New Morality; let us become the morticians of God, embalming Him with the formaldehyde of 'God is dead'; and let us celebrate the New Gospel of Sodom and marijuana!" The Hebrew prophet said the opposite: "Establish yourself on the eternal law graven in star and stone; *renew* your little temporal existence with the great eternal and absolute being of God; seek reality where alone it is — in origin and essence and changeless rhythms; discipline your mind and heart and soul with the reality that never changes; and know that the final 'kick' of the citizens of Sodom shall be inexorable fire and brimstone from Heaven!"

The Hebrew prophet rebuked men for the novelty of their avant-garde tangents to reality, for their "whoring after strange gods." He was ever the great conservator of value and meaning; he knew that all living and fruitful changes can occur only in a world predicated on a changeless reality.

Science, likewise, contrary to the superstitions of the hour, is never revolutionary. To be sure, science advances (as well as retrogresses), expands, changes as it reads more of God's primal writing in Nature and the earth. The atoms of Democritus are dissolved into the fields of electrical energy of quantum physics. The physics of Newton expand and change with the physics of Eddington, Sir Oliver Lodge, Einstein. But science cannot remain science if, by "revolution," it overthrows all reverence for fact, or logic, or quiet weighing and measuring, or hypothesis and experiment, or integrity of mind, and if it brings all these "tumbling down around our heads." Science can change only if science remains basically changeless. Otherwise science reaches the precipice and the end of science itself.

And in the application of pure science to practical uses, "revolution" brings only failure. Man may co-operate with Nature to produce eventually a blue rose, a horse that shatters all records for strength or speed, a hybrid corn that in quantity and quality surpasses all known varieties. But man does all this only by co-operating, by reverencing being and essence and character, by enhancing inner reality and essential design in animal or vegetable. There can be no advance in thing or creature except in terms of implicit and potential quality, value, and meaning, that in destiny and nature are already implicit. Even Bernard Shaw knew that if you amputate rats' tails for generations, the wise stubborn rodent genes will still affirm the splendid appendage that we call a "tail."

Of course there are biological sports and mutations. But these are only the vital leap of genius over the slower processes of talent. No sport or mutation ever denies the essential being of the entelechy; every mutation and sport only enhances and emphasizes the potential quality, value, and meaning that are integral from the beginning. If it does not, there will be only the monstrosity, the mongoloid, the

Siamese twins, the cretin, the perversion, the headless horseman.

Even in the leaps of life that (if we were not so blind and dull) we would know are miracles — the caterpillar spinning the cocoon and emerging as the flying flower we call a butterfly — the miraculous brown cow that eats green grass and gives white milk — the seed of the quiet and relatively colorless egg that becomes the spectrum rampant and the voice brazen in the splendid parrot — there is no "revolution," but only fulfillment and realization of a psyche already given. The living process is not "revolution" — but renewal.

"Revolution," on the contrary, is always reaction toward idiocy and death. For example, if God were Picasso — which God forbid! — we would indeed have "revolution": We would have calves with thirteen legs and the heads of an octopus; our tigers would not burn bright, but writhe in darkness like cobras in a snake-pit; our eggs would not blossom into emancipated daffodils, but explode into inky tarantulas crawling away for a sit-in; our *King Lears* would fade into the grimy scraps of abstraction labelled "Guernica." If God were Staughton Lynd — which God forbid! — we would pin medals on refugees from a draft-card, and spit on good soldiers for their country, and set up wall-mottoes for Russia labelled: "God Bless Our Slavery," and see the Vietcong as men with the strength of ten because their hearts are pure. If God were Le Roi Jones — for which thought God may forgive me! — we would equate the joy of sex with the inbred perversions of sodomy, and see black and white as mutually destructive instead of the ivory and ebony keys that are both necessary on the key-board of the world, and that, in harmony, produce music for God and man. Always and everywhere, "revolution" is *not* the way of God, of Nature, or of creative man. Always "revolution" is the deathwish of the world.

How, then, does life advance? Not by "revolution" — but always by *renewal*!

Our very bodies live by renewal. Every seven years, at least, every cell in our physical bodies becomes new, so that our bodies stay young and vital by a perpetual inner renaissance of the different — and the same. This change is changeless, and so gracious and quiet that we never know it takes place, and so absolute and eternal that it is like the swing of the compass toward the North Pole.

And in the body of Nature as a whole it is even so. God does not fashion purple snow one winter and green snow the next; snow is a changeless ecstasy of white (blue in shadow of course) that is new every season yet the same every century, and within that changeless rhythm God makes every individual snowflake, in the dainty rectitude of its geometry, different. The changing rhythm of the seasons as a whole is possible only because of changeless recurrence and renewal by God's grace and power. God does not substitute avant-garde pompons of conceit and whim for the laurel or the lilac; he *renews* the eternal Spring with the renaissance of the unchanging flowers that have their roots in Eden and their blossoms in Apocalypse. God feeds the world because he renews the eternal wheat and the absolute potato and the constant fat kine, world without end, in the poetry of restoration and reaffirmation. Ever in the one mansion of the light, God renews the changeless colors of the spectrum — red is forever red, and blue is forever blue, and green is forever green, in the joyous fiat of renewal in this world and in every world. Dogs bark in joyance when Agamemnon returns from the wars at Troy, and they will bark in equal joyance when Superman returns from his foray to the stars. The purring mother cat, through all feline generations, gathers a clutch of fluffy kittens to the fountains of her breast, and renews in the Twentieth Century the catty glory of the Eleventh Century. And even in London or Manhattan, while life continues, there will be joy in the morning because a child is born, and sadness when the silver cord is broken and the mourners go about the streets. Ever the rhythm recurs — and the rhythm is renewed; such is the fabric of life, the tissue of being.

Renewal, renewal, and ever *renewal*! Reality is like the sound of a bell that is struck . . . and fades . . . and must be struck again, and again, and yet again, in eternal recurrence to the end of time and the essence of eternity. God says, "Lo, I make all things new!" — by renewing forever the *old* things made ever new from *within*. Life, like the minnow in Keats' brook, forever wrestles with its own sweet delight, and the brook never grows old and the minnow is forever young.

The way of life, while it remains life, is perpetual renewal. Thus in every age the child — unless it reaches the end of the world because it is "revolutionized" into a sophisticated brat — knows that his kitten has thorny paws, and that the way to prove the wind is there is to fly a kite, and that the Emperor has no clothes over his scrawny naked chassis. Ever the adult finds reality changeless in the novelty of renewal if, with King Lear, he wanders the world as if he were God's spy and takes upon himself the mystery of things.

Man, by becoming the "revolutionary," may by his own fatal

choice step out of renewal, and seek to wear the tentacles of the tarantula or win the carapace of the turtle. But when he does, he soon reaches the precipice where stands the sign: *Das Ende Der Welt*. Meanwhile, true men renew their youth as the eagle, and see the earth renewed with springtime and harvest, and love the grass that dares, even today, to remain *green*. If life has a coat of arms, its motto reads: *Reviresco*, I grow ever new.

What Freedom Is, And What It Is Not

A LL my life I have loved liberty with a passion and a ferocity. Always I have been ready, if necessary, to go into the wilderness and live on fish and blueberries rather than curtail an inch or an atom of my soul's freedom. Christ's words have haunted me. "What does it profit a man," He asked, "if he gain the whole world and lose his own soul?"

At the root of all that I am about to say, therefore, let it be clear that I love freedom; that I have sought freedom; that my life's joy (which is great) has dwelt in the fierce and vital climate of freedom. But just because liberty has meant so much to me, I have sought to understand it, to try to know what it is — so that I might truly hold it for my own. And especially important, in this loose and illogical day, I have sought to know what liberty is not.

But, as the "Liberals" are forever saying: Let us define our terms. My collegiate edition of Webster's *New World Dictionary* defines *freedom* as "exemption or liberation from the control of some other person or some arbitrary power . . . a being able to act, move, use, *etc.*, without hindrance or restraint . . . . " It defines *liberty* as "freedom or release from slavery, imprisonment, captivity, or any other form of arbitrary control . . . exemption from compulsion . . . ."

These are good definitions — as far as they go. The basic element seems to be *choice*, personal choice, from within and not from without; choice of what to do, where to move, what to think, what to be. And such freedom is that which I have sought; such freedom, I hope, is that which we are all seeking.

Most people today increasingly desire "exemption from compulsion" by Big Brother; compulsion which comes to us in the impertinent questions intruded into the census, confiscatory levies of an income tax that would make tax slaves of us all, reduction of private man to a social security number, or (in too many countries) an even more open and obvious boot stamping forever on a human face. In some countries, like the public Hell of North Vietnam, Mao

Tse-tung's Paradise for Bully Boys, or the imperialism of the Soviet Inferno, men are so obviously threatened by such arbitrary compulsions that any surcease, however brief or limited, seems (in itself) freedom and liberty. And, relatively speaking, it is.

But though we must struggle, abroad and at home against the ever augmented compulsions of the Total State or the Servile State, we shall never enter into the subtle and essential nature of freedom until we go further. We shall even destroy freedom in ourselves, in others, and in our society, if we confuse the freedom of anything and everything to be everything or anything, with the vital freedom to be ourselves in the context of reality and meaning. The young anarchists, for example, and even some of the sober philosophers of libertarianism, suppose that freedom means *any* choice (as long as it is *their* choice). They see it as a license to follow any whimsical desire for any capricious end as long as we make it. That is not what freedom is about at all. Not at all!

In the theology which I hold sacred, it is written that God has given us — of His own will — a will that is free. He made it possible for us to choose wrong and to refuse right. He wishes us, *of our own will and choice,* to desire and select the right; He does not, by any arbitrary outer or inner compulsion, *compel* us to be true, integral, wise, good, sound. Freedom, then, comes from within, from our own souls, from our uncompelled choice; and since it is possible to have freedom in at least many of our inner choices, liberty or freedom includes the possibility of error, mistake, sin, disaster.

But — and here is the point I wish especially to make — such freedom is temporary, for it leads into the evil necessities that co-exist with falsehood, negation, self-destruction, and (eventually if not soon) into the annulment of freedom itself. That is the risk God took when He gave us free will; and that is the responsibility we must assume when we exercise liberty of choice. Those who inhabited Dante's Hell were not forced into it; *they chose it*. It is the dead-end street they freely chose instead of the possible open road that they refused. Never forget that this free choice, for them, led to the end of all free choices.

Dante rightly saw Hell as a descending funnel, whose walls forever grow more narrow; and they finally abandon hope who enter there. You and I are faced with the responsibility of choice, the knife-edge of decision; and sooner or later this will be the inexorable question our choice poses: Does my life grow wider in possibility, freer in choices? Or do the walls close in; does the seeming freedom lead to a growing constriction; does life become a descending funnel of ever narrowing walls?

Today too many of the shouters for freedom do not realize that any release from outer compulsion means a greater necessity for inner wisdom. Freedom is *not* a freedom from responsibility, but a responsibility for choice. Freedom depends upon reality, truth, inner wisdom; it is the choice of choices, the *inner* compulsion of truth, the soul's own rule of circumstance by introstance. It is not a whoopla carnival, but the great, lonely, and noble anguish of the hero of the mind.

Freedom does not mean the liberty to do anything or everything, but the liberty to have self-responsibility. Narrow is the way and strait is the gate, and few there be who find it. Freedom is not loose, easy, indiscriminate; it is a terrible and noble thing, to be won, through blood, sweat, and tears, by the athlete of the soul. Let us examine carefully the nature of freedom.

The freedom of anything and everything is contingent on the destiny and meaning of everything and anything. It is not freedom for the mole to burst out of his tunnels into the noontide sun and dance the waltz of the light. It is not freedom for Sophocles to sprinkle his *Oedipus Rex* with the humorous gaffe of Aristophanes' *Frogs.* It is not freedom for George F. Babbitt to blackjack the pilot of a superjet and take the controls into his pudgy and inept hands. It is not freedom for a woman to grow a beard and to seek, in herself, the sex functions of the male. It is not freedom for the square to lose its corners in the circle, or the great singer to hit flat and sour notes because that is her whim, or the painter or the clothes-designer to set hostile colors in raw juxtaposition just to be avant-garde. It is not freedom for the octogenarian to diddle with hop-scotch, or the ten-year-old to slam-bang a Porsche at Sebring.

Freedom is the liberty to *become* ever more perfectly what essentially you *are*. Freedom says, "In my end is my beginning." Freedom accepts the boundaries that make it free, as the river accepts its banks; as the apple accepts the blossom and the bough, and does not demand the license to hang five feet off the boughs in air that has never blossomed. The freedom of the sword accepts the necessity of the steel. The freedom of every color accepts the vibratory rate that establishes its place in the spectrum. Red may become more fiercely and purely red, but it loses its being — and therefore its freedom — if it steps outside the boundaries of its rhythm within the total light. Only because the tonal scale is inexorable can the individual notes be free.

The great creations of the poet or the philosopher can be free — can *be* at all — only because of the laws and the necessities of language and of logic. The alphabet is given — or there can be no writing. Grammar exists and is, or there can be no firm structure to liberate the precision of meaning. Sentence structure, the integrity of the paragraph, the accuracy of punctuation, the order and pattern of the typographer — were these not here, what use would thought be, as an art of communication?

The first question anyone or anything should ask is this: *"What am I in my essential nature and being?"* Once he has found this, he has found what his freedom may be, for he will know what his life's truth is. If in his essential nature and being he is a blind appetite, an amorphous lust, a grab-bag of nothing, he can never be free. Nothing he can do will make him free, though he toss choices left and right like an antic harlequin of possibilities! He will be a Jerry Rubin, incapable of anything but license and looseness. He will be a "Burn, Baby, burn" nonentity, giving fire the wildest freedom of its nature, but he will find *in himself* no freedom to be. Being nothing, what can he be but nothing? Having no nature to become, he can have no freedom; and in his sick despairing misery, he will seek to destroy his freedom with his license and his whims and his perversions.

But if he is a true artist, of language or of life, he will seek his destiny and grow toward his meaning. He will find the truth, and the truth shall make him free.

Is he, by destiny, a poet? Then he can find freedom only by following the banks and boundaries, the substance and the essence, the responsibilities and the necessities, of the poet. The poet must be an integrity; he must descend into the roots of his own heart and ascend into the flower of his own soul; he must *feel,* without either sentimentality or cynicism, the rhythm of his own pulses and the emotions of his own being and of man's universal being. "What is the poet?" Keats asked, and he answered:

> 'Tis the man who with a man
> Is an equal, be he King,
> Or poorest of the beggar-clan,
> Or any other wondrous thing

A man may be 'twixt ape and Plato;
'Tis the man who with a bird,
Wren or Eagle, finds his way to
All its instincts; he hath heard
The Lion's roaring, and can tell
What his horny throat expresseth . . . .

That is a calling and a destiny. It demands a purity of being, a dedication, an intensity; it must not allow itself to be diluted with pleasures and dissipations and tangents. The poet has no freedom in this, that, or the other way — in any corrosion of the senses through drugs or drink — in any perversities of thought or brutalities of the spirit — in any wallowing in the obtuseness of the mind, in the corruption of the heart, in cruelties or crassness of the soul. His responsibilities to his high calling and his noble destiny give him only the freedom of the great pilot who sails dangerous seas in pursuit of Passage to India. His freedom to be a poet means that he has not the license to be a Marquis de Sade, or a pimp for call girls, or a playboy with dada and surrealism.

Milton wisely said that to write great poetry, the poet must make his *life* a great poem. Any dissipation of the great freedom with the little license is something subtracted from his meaning and his destiny. And as a poet (or a simple man) abandons his own essential destiny and meaning for aberrations, perversities, and wild licenses, he ceases to be free; he becomes a slave. The man who boasts of his "freedom" to drink and drug and whore, becomes a slave to drink and drugs and cheap sensations, and "love" becomes merchandise. He becomes a slave; he ceases to be a free man.

Charlie Chaplin has much to answer for. His stupid support of the Left, his distaste for the America that had given him freedom to fulfill his distiny, are thoroughly reprehensible. But there is another criticism, this side of all politics, *above* all politics, that I have never heard stated, and yet which is his essential sin. Chaplin had a great talent. Yet he, in mid career as it were, abandoned that talent; he ceased to be an artist of unique pictures, while he still had energy and talent to make them; and he withdrew, like a sulking Achilles, to his tent. He betrayed his own meaning. He was Browning's sinner, whose flaw was "The unlit lamp and the ungirt loin." He abandoned the freedom that God had set in his heart, for "free" ideas, "free" self-gratifications, "free" higgledy-piggledy nonsense. The "freedom" he sought destroyed the freedom implicit in his soul.

Again and again, the small fickle "free" artists destroy their freedom. I have used this instance before; I here use it again, in much greater detail, for I can find no better. In a French magazine, *La Croix,* there was a review of a book, *Libro Nero,* by Giovanni Papini, an Italian author of unquestioned integrity. There Papini cites, word for word, a personal interview he had with Pablo Picasso. I quote, from him, these words of Picasso's:

> From the moment that art ceases to be the food that feeds the best minds, the artist can use his talent to perform all the tricks of the intellectual charlatan.
>
> Most people today can no longer expect to receive consolation and exultation from art.
>
> The "refined," the "rich," the professional "do-nothings," the "distillers of quintessence" desire only the peculiar, the sensational, the eccentric, the scandalous in today's art. And I myself, since the advent of cubism, have fed these fellows what they wanted and satisfied these critics with all the ridiculous ideas that have passed through my head.
>
> The less they understood them, the more they admired me!
>
> Through amusing myself with all these farces, I became celebrated, and very rapidly.
>
> For a painter, celebrity means sales and consequent affluence.
>
> Today, as you know, I am celebrated, I am rich.
>
> But when I am alone, I do not have the effrontery to consider myself an artist at all, not in the grand old meaning of the word: Giotto, Titian, Rembrandt, Goya, were great painters.
>
> I am only a public clown, a mountebank.
>
> I have understood my time and have exploited the imbecility, the vanity, the greed of my contemporaries.
>
> It is a bitter confession, this confession of mine, more painful than it may seem, but it, at least, and at last, does have the merit of being honest.*

John Garth, in the San Francisco *Argonaut* for August 1, 1952, cites the commentary above and comments on it. He says:

> Behold the irreproachable top god of the Moderns, now fully and finally unmasked through his own testimony. At long last we have the final truth from his own lips! Now he himself has said, almost word for word, what

---

*For this, and a discussion of it, see the excellent book, *Peril On Parnassus,* by William F. Adler, Vantage Press, New York, 1954.

the editor of this page has been declaring from time to time ever since our first series of articles appeared in the San Francisco *Examiner* in 1939.

And Garth continues:

He [*Picasso*] has sold himself down the river for a mess of pottage and now, at the end of his days, he realizes that all he has seemed to have gained is nothing compared to the career in honor that might possibly have been his. The artist's mission in life is not selfishly to accumulate a lot of money by cheap trickery, but to use, in the finest manner of which he is capable, the rare gifts God has entrusted to him.

Thus Picasso today looks back upon his wasted life with a heavy sense of shame. The insane plaudits of the world's ineffectuals have turned to gall and bitterness in his mouth. Better the inner satisfaction of one fine work honestly done than all the false fame and empty, imbecilic adoration of the silly, self-hypnotized art poseurs. The fact that he now recognizes his fatal mistake and today regrets it bitterly does prove that Picasso knows the meaning of artistic integrity and feels an inner, if belated, sense of honor, self-defiled.

This is exactly what I am talking about. Freedom? Freedom, for the artist, is to be responsible to integrity, to honor, to the God-given destiny of his own soul. What does it profit a man to gain wealth, and fame, and intellectual ballyhoo, if he loses his own soul?

Picasso is acclaimed for his "freedom." It is "freedom" from reality and meaning; it is "freedom" for illusion and playboy nonsense. It is the freedom to reduce the living grain of wheat to the thin and sterile chaff and husk.

No man has the "right" to be wrong; all have the responsibility to be right!

It is not freedom if you go off on tangents into error. It is not freedom to eat a box of chocolates when you have galloping diabetes. It is not freedom to put a superjet together with putty and Elmer's glue. It is not freedom to shake hands with Leftie the Bear and bed down with him in a commune of lethal co-existence. It is not freedom to disregard the compass. It is not freedom to swallow cyanide because your whim is that it is a vitamin. It is not freedom to play kittybenders on thin ice over zero waters. It is not freedom to decide that you can confuse *a* with *x* at will, or decide that the multiplication table can multiply 6 by 5 and get 13.

George Orwell, in *1984,* wrote the wisest words I know in any contemporary secular book. There Orwell has poor Winston Smith, in what he (vainly) hoped was his private journal, write: *"Freedom is the freedom to say that two plus two make four. If that is granted, all else follows."* How sound! But, of course, contemporary revolutionists and "intellectuals" and "Liberals" and even (alas!) too many libertarians, think that the only freedom is the freedom to say that two plus two make any number your whim decides and desires.

How foolish they are. There is no freedom in telling lies!

Reality is inexorable. If you add the number of grams in a prescription, or the money in your cash register, or the quarts of oil in your car's crank case, you find no freedom in inventing the figures in your final sum. Reality will destroy such "freedom." You will sour your insides, or distort your resources, or either burn out your bearings or smother them in surplus oil. *"The basic freedom is the freedom to say that two plus two are four. If that is granted, all else follows."* And so in all politics, freedom does not mean fantastic acrobatics in the tree-tops of illusion, hanging like a monkey by the prehensile tail of your fancy, but a sober and sound (and foursquare) arithmetic of reality. It is not freedom to pretend that if you pile a debt of billions on billions, it is not a debt because "after all, we owe it to ourselves!" Only the *truth* will make you free!

And it is not saying that *two plus two make four* to say that you have freedom when you smash windows at whim, and run amok with "Burn, Baby, burn!", and loot stores at will. That is not the way the figures add up. That is not the way the compass points to the North. That is not the way the T-square shows the angle.

Anarchy destroys freedom because it distorts reality. The motivation of work, the stuff out of which even bread and circuses are fashioned, the substance of basic life, are being destroyed by it — not only in their physical being, but in their spiritual bases. For the anarchist it always proves later than he thinks, and the inexorable reckoning comes sooner than he thinks, and the gods of the copybook maxims present the bill — not to some hypothetical Paul, but to you, the quite tangible Peter.

"As a man sows so shall he reap," is the inescapable context of freedom. It is the showdown in poker, from which there is no appeal. You are not "free" to claim victory in the game when you have not earned so much as a first down and your opponents have made five touchdowns!

Even the wild votaries of the fantasy of freedom come to know this at last. In the newspapers for February 2, 1971, the Associated Press quotes a tape recording attributed to Eldridge Cleaver. This declares that Dr. Timothy Leary and his wife have been taken into "protective custody in Algeria" (*i.e.,* arrested) by the Black Panthers "because 'LSD has destroyed their ability to make judgements.' " And then the tape continues, with a sober wisdom that one would not expect from Cleaver: "If you think that by tuning in, turning on, and dropping out that you're improving society you're wrong. You're destroying your own brain and strengthening the enemy. They want robots."

Forget Cleaver's jargon about "society" and "the enemy." Think of his words in terms of your own soul. Here is Tim Leary, an idol of the freedom-set, a purveyor of the monkeyshines of "freedom." And what "freedom" does he get? Arrest even by the Black Panthers! And, far worse, the destruction of his ability to make judgments; the destruction of his own brain! That is, the freedom to exult in the wrong choices destroys the ability to make *any* choices: You start out to be the giddy freedom-fancier; you end as — a "robot"! You end as the slave to mindless oblivion.

I once thought myself a libertarian; but today I would as soon call myself a forger. I will *not* conform myself to any label; I *will* confirm myself by the compass and the T-square. I know that there is no freedom to annul the alphabet, to repeal the multiplication table, to play hot cockles with *up* and *down,* to shuffle darkness and light as an ideology, to say that poison is a proper ingredient in bread.

I may, of course, *choose* to commit suicide. But freedom means not an annulment of life — but a fulfillment of life. I may, of course, choose to blow my mind with LSD — but freedom means rather to fulfill my mind with reason and my senses with rich precision. The essence of man is to seek life and life ever more abundantly. To substitute for this the helter-skelter whims and idiosyncrasies of the gadgets of death is not freedom at all. To pickle your brains in alcohol, or to destroy the innocent Eden-glory of your senses with drugs, or to smog the splendor of love with the caricature of pornography, is not to become a free man whose feet are beautiful upon the mountains but a cripple who is a slave to a wheelchair.

The destiny of man is to find sound work to do, and to become in it a craftsman and an artist; to be honest and honorable in his relations to his fellowman; to find a woman to love with his body and soul; to love and reverence the living and fathomless universe; to seek God with your mind and your hands and your heart and your soul, and serve man's freedom. Anything that interferes with this destiny denies man's true freedom and must be fought to the death.

What is freedom in love? Today a noisy minority (or majority, who knows?), plunge into sex like lemmings into the sea, and call indiscriminate biological release and physical pleasure "freedom." These people demand and take the "liberty" to go to bed with anyone, of any sex (even their own); to be as promiscuous as death; to swap and make new playmates of sex as the wind changes. They say that this, at last, is "freedom." But if you read their all too public manifestos, you find that they soon tire of "straight" sex (for which they first clamored), and find it "boring," and have to have as many loves as flies on a poor dead rabbit, and then find "freedom" and "pleasure" only in perversions, and in the end become as blasé and bored and blowsy and miserable as addicts who begin with marijuana and end in the hells of heroin.

If this is freedom — *damn* it!

Meanwhile true lovers know the freedom of love. They know that love is a tune that means a consecration and a destiny, like that of the virtuoso who practises on the piano till the notes are right and silver-clear. They know that purity of soul means choice, and discrimination, and a joyous loyalty, because to be with *her*, to be with *him*, is a destiny and a meaning; and that to live with your one true love is like living with the sun and the moon and a sprinkle of stars in the infinite variety of the *one* love.

Modernity is full of such illusions. Thus the woman's "liberation" movement would *destroy* the freedom of woman. It seeks freedom *from* being woman, never freedom *for* being woman. It does not ask a freedom to be woman, but a freedom *not* to be woman. Its fanciers are ashamed of being woman; they do not appreciate the unique glory of woman; they are slaves to man because they envy men, and are jealous of men, and seek to be carbon copies of man. By so doing they destroy the freedom to be woman, and despoil the unique glory of being woman.

It has never been brought into the open that most of the noisy press agents for "freedom" remain old-stuff — for they remain materialists. I mean, they believe in economic determinism; in matter as a period after life, instead of life as a question mark after matter; in biology as the final necrology; in physics as final and not as a mere portico into *meta*physics. They want "freedom" in a universe that (to them) is a prison that contains only a universal death cell. Freedom is possible, really, only in a universe that is surrounded by infinity and eternity, that is permeated by poetry and magic and miracle. Only as it is our Father's House, full of many mansions, is there real freedom.

Freedom essentially is the predicate of immortality. Freedom is the grace of God streaming into the world of man. Compare, for example, the "freedom" of a Madelyn Murray O'Hair with the freedom of the great author of the Bhagavad-Gita! Compare the dry splinters or sawdust of "freedom" of a Robert Ingersoll with the living tree of the universe, Iggdrasil, in the great Norse conception!

What we really need is something truly new — and therefore truly eternal. (Eternity contains not a narrow present, but a living past and a living future made one in God's Eternal Now.) We need a real break with the materialistic establishment of modernity. We need not the "novel" but the new, not the "revolution" but the renewal. Beyond Communism — and capitalism — we need the timeless order (not system) of vitalism, the denial of matter as the reality and the affirmation of life as the essence. Thus, and thus only, shall we find the Freedom in which we may live, and move, and have our being.

Recently I heard of a tragedy that most moderns will not even understand, but which seems to me the basis and beginning of all wisdom about freedom. Let me tell you about it.

There is a certain variety of eagle (now, alas, almost extinct!), of which the last live on an island in Lake Erie. These eagles mate only in the air; and two eagles choose each other exclusively and for life. Recently some human mistake, some aberration from the human, shot at a female eagle on that island and broke her wing so that she would never fly again. Three months later, conservationists found her, crippled but still alive. Never again could she fly to mate in the air; but she was still alive, because tirelessly and faithfully her mate had fed her, and stayed near her, with a love that never failed. Never, in her need and in his lonely deprivation, did he leave her or forsake her.

That, to me, is a parable of the choice that is true freedom!

Touchstones Of Excellence

Taste And The Sane Mind

A great physician of the mind might venture the diagnosis that a major sickness of the modern soul comes from the virus of the phrase: *"Everyone has the right to his opinion."*

Everyone does not have the "right" to his opinion, but only the responsibility to see that his opinion is right. No one has the "right" to the opinion that ground glass is an excellent substitute for flour; that loaded twelve-gauge shotguns at full cock are good toys in a nursery; that fire never burns and water never drowns; that any and every passenger should have the freedom to take over the controls of a transcontinental jet; that a bat with rabies is as harmless as a dove. No one has the "right" to such opinions, because such opinions are wrong – and therefore cannot coexist with Reason. It is no arbitrary human dogma, no authoritarian human compulsion, that says this: The inexorable fiat of reality and the inexorable cogency of reason say it.

And no one has the "right" to equally false opinions in the realm of value and taste. No one has the "right" to the opinion that the stumblebums of Podunkville play the same kind of football as the Baltimore Colts; that "Vinegar Joe" Stilwell was a general of the genius of Douglas MacArthur; that Jean-Paul Sartre belongs in the same intellectual universe as Aristotle; that Edgar Lee Masters knew the Hell-of-it in Spoon River as truly as Dante did in Verona – not to speak of the Heaven-of-it; that Marx was the thirteenth disciple of Christ; that Shakespeare is the inferior of Eugene O'Neill. One has no "right" to such "opinions," if one inhabits the cosmos of reason, because such opinions are intellectual wrongs.

91

The old proverb tells us: *De gustibus non disputandum est*. And indeed, in a limited sense, there is no disputing about tastes. If Hottentots love roast grasshoppers and I love roast beef it seems a gustatory impasse. I shrug and say, "So what?" Yet even in the relatively minor field of the culinary arts, there is a hierarchy of tastes and a crudity or finesse of tasting. The man who prefers the hamburgers at Sloppy Joe's, the Truckers' Enemy, to my wife's fried chicken, may say, "There's no use disputing about tastes!" But the epicure or connoisseur knows that about food, as about all things under the sun or moon, there is discrimination, a scale of values, distinctions — that is, *taste*.

And, just so, the connoisseur of sound knows that there must be differentiation and discrimination between the mass-produced fiddle and the violin from the hand of Stradivarius . . . between the sulky child at an untuned piano, and the virtuosity of Paderewski . . . and if we pass beyond such rudimentary discriminations, there is the great adventure of delicate distinctions and ultimate appraisals among the subtleties and heights of the truly great. There taste distinguishes the lovely flutter of the butterfly music of MacDowell from the beat of Beethoven's lightning.

The intellectual adventure of life, the pursuit of excellence, the ascent from the Mazda to the star, lie implicit in every such exercise of taste. Of course, today, the relativists and egalitarians of the hour not only seek to homogenize the milk of human kindness, but also to homogenize *all* the various liquids of the world into one totality of tasteless integration. I myself use homogenized milk, though I personally miss the pure intensity called cream; but I will not accept the modern homogenizing of milk, honey, Lysol, vodka, crankcase oil, Seven Up, and swamp-water into one supposedly potable beverage. Why? Because, like the artist in tea-tasting or wine-tasting, I keep my palate pure — and so my taste is as the taste of ten. With Coleridge in "Kubla Khan," I say in paraphrase: "For I on honey-dew have fed,/ And drunk the milk of Paradise." When you have sipped such divine tipple, you can't abide Sartre-and-soda or Le Roi Jones on the rocks!

Virgil told us that the descent into Hell is easy, but hard the return. So with us. But from our contemporary cycles of the cultural Inferno — existentialism, relativism, instrumentalism, phenomenalism — we may, through discipline and pain, if only we will again use our minds and our wills, return to the sun . . . even bringing Eurydice with us. But so to return, we must regain the basic sense that we have lost – the sense of *taste*. Our contemporary descent into nihilism began with our loss of taste; our noble re-ascent into reverence for Heaven will come only through a renaissance of taste.

We need, today, to cultivate taste and the delicate and valid appraisals and evaluations that come only to those who have taste. That is why the Communist Conspiracy is one of the chief agents in the destruction of contemporary taste; for if you destroy taste, you subvert the strength of the soul and soften man for the easy kill.

Therefore let us talk of taste.

I

ONE ALMOST despairs of a common axiom or shared premise from which to begin a discussion of this subject. The modern mind is too often like Caliban as Browning saw him, who "Will sprawl, now that the heat of day is best, / Flat on his belly in the pit's much mire . . . . " And naturally Caliban wishes to "cheat" Prospero and Miranda, and "gibe" at them, and let "the rank tongue blossom into speech." Caliban so pervades and dominates modern literature and art that one sometimes forgets that there is something beyond "the pit's much mire," or the "rank tongue" that sows the weeds of speech. And since Caliban is incapable of the intuition of reality that establishes a premise, or the logic that fulfills the destiny implicit in a premise, how can you lead him to wisdom? Your best pearls are nuggets of nothing when cast before Caliban!

The difficulty of discussing taste today is that we have no taste to speak of any more. Colleges have very little. Most college courses in literature and art today are a roll in the mud with Caliban, and a tape-recording of the rank tongue that blossoms from "the pit's much mire."

Recently the head of the English Department in a Midwest university wrote a letter to a friend of mine in which he cited Langston Hughes as a great poet. I know a college in Indiana where the drama department believes that Arthur Miller's *Death Of a Salesman* is great tragedy – they don't even know that you cannot write tragedy about the writhings of an amoeba thrusting out agonized pseudopodia in a drop of acid! The amoeba is, of course, *pathetic*; but tragedy demands a protagonist who can greatly *struggle* and *grandly* suffer. I have a copy of the "literary" magazine of the University of Oregon that is crammed with "poetry" so flatulent-dull that it would put a damned soul to sleep as the demons turned him on his fiery grid, and that makes its pornography as sleep-inducing as a carton of barbiturates. The stuff that passes for "literature" in most college magazines today would incite Molière to write a new *Les Précieuses Ridicules.* In colleges, which should be islands of light in the salt seas of worldly darkness, tastelessness and the "academic freedom" to ballyhoo it, are rampant and pervasive. If such is the debacle of the ivory towers of Academe, what can you expect of the literary assembly lines of the marketplace?

Edgar Allan Poe is one of the supreme critics of American life and literature. He wrote his résumé of the end of the world in his "Colloquy Of Monos And Una":

> But now it appears that we had worked out our own destruction in the perversion of our *taste*, or rather in the blind neglect of its culture in our schools. For, in truth, it was at this crisis that taste alone — that faculty which, holding a middle position between the pure intellect and the moral sense, could never safely have been disregarded — it was now that taste alone could have led us gently back to Beauty, to Nature, and to Life.

It seems that, with exact anticipatory prevision, Poe saw "our own destruction in the perversion of our taste." Today we are full-seas-under what he saw far off as a new Flood.

Our lack of taste today is not only academic, but also vulgar. Television commercials — which represent, at least, what the manipulators *think* is popular "taste" — are the deliberate rejection of quality and value, a deliberate "Heil Hitler!" to the base, the crude and crass, the vulgar, the ugly. They remind me of a dead-beat musician, playing a saxophone afflicted with the heaves, out of a breath that is eighty percent alcohol, from lungs like a blacksmith's bellows in spite of incipient túberculosis.

Our lack of taste is rampant in popular actions. At the recent famous wedding of Jacqueline Kennedy's sister to a Rutherford, note what happened. I quote from the *Associated Press* for August 1, 1966:

> The new Mrs. Rutherford left the church in tears as she was confronted by an unruly crowd. Spectators stretched out to touch her gown and jostled her. After the wedding party left, hundreds rushed into the church, grabbing flowers from the main altar and pieces of white cloth on the aisle floor. Others ripped pieces from the canvas canopy at the entrance.

Such is popular "taste"! Its anarchy of lust for proximity to the famous is a parallel to our social anarchy in the streets — our "sit ins," and "freedom marches," and Molotov cocktails whenever we feel disgruntled.

The same tastelessness disfigures much that is called "literature." In the magazine *Oblique,* at the University of Illinois, the following appeared as a "poem":

hurry love
Fear at nighttime, but
be sure by day, by day
reply in routine
    when darkness is doing the dishes.
And when (do ba dodo, bu ba)
that evening sun goes down (goes down-wawn),
question briefly my fidelity, and
instantly, at that,
well, yes,
splendidly, I must admit
    and on an, oh, most definitely
    upward singing breath
    oooooooooooof
    Real Gusto! In a Great Light,
    dear.
and . . . where was I? Oh:
    will you love me in April
    as you may in May?

Such is "taste" in "literature" among the "avant-garde"! Contrast such inanity with the fierce simple beauty of Longfellow's great poetry of the sea:

When descends on the Atlantic
    The gigantic
Storm-wind of the equinox,
Landward in his wrath he scourges
    The toiling surges
Laden with seaweed from the rocks.

To spit out the one and to savor the other is the function of *taste*.

Recently, at "art exhibits" across the country, the art-conformists of the hour have been presenting as "art" a tableau of objects where we see the interior of a brothel with the skulls of cows set in place of human heads, and another tableau where we half-see the details of sexual congress in the back seat of an old Dodge. This is defended in terms of "artistic freedom," and even approved as "art" that realizes "life." Of course no adult mind denies that brothels exist. Of course no sane mind denies that some teenagers find fun and games in the back seats of beat-up jalopies. Nor does any wise mind deny that a great artist may treat the evil that is ugly, and yet lift it, through quality and meaning, into beauty . . . as Goya did. But taste says that in life, and so in art, there are levels — some dull and void, some rich and valid — and that the mind shows its power in knowing which is which — and that the mind must never confuse what "exists" with what essentially *is*, or evil that merely "exists" with the essence of evil as it *is*. It says, also, that the mind shows its quality by picturing evil *as it is* (as Goya did), and not by presenting it as a neutral existential "fact," neither good nor bad, but only exploitable and scabrously titillating.

Vincent van Gogh, in his terrible, magnificent "The Night Café," painted evil. But he knew that it was evil — and abhorred it. He wrote of the picture: "I have tried to express the terrible passions of humanity by means of red and green"; and he went on, "I have tried to express the idea that the café is a place where one can ruin one's self, run mad, or commit a crime. So I have tried to express as it were the powers of darkness in a low drink shop . . . and all this in an atmosphere like a devil's furnace, of pale sulphur." The modern "artists" of the brothel and the back seat, on the other hand, choose their subjects as neutral "facts" of existence, in terms of the fashionable modern prurient itch to be perverse and merely to exploit the manias of the hour. Also let us remember that van Gogh spent *most* of his paint in *most* of his painting not on areas of evil and ugliness but on areas of beauty and good. He loved and painted — and the moderns of the above oblique variety don't — the rich yet delicate beauty, the dainty yet mighty rectitude, of Nature and of man's psyche, as in "The Pink Orchard," or in his revelation of the infinite pilgrimage of the soul in "Road with Cypresses." Our contemporary lack of taste is obvious in our closed, narrowed, deliberately evil-centered art, where we concentrate on the dust of earth, never knowing that all dust is essentially *star*-dust . . . even when Lucifer treads it.

The same lack of taste occurs also in modern music. The *Boston Globe* is an extreme, intellectually unbalanced, "Liberal" paper, so no one can accuse me of "ultra-conservatism" in quoting the following from it. The critic of the paper (Michael Steinberg) wrote an article on July 27, 1966, which he entitled "New York Philharmonic Wrecks Oedipus." He wrote:

> The "visual presentation" included bleachers for the chorus with approximate human silhouettes drawn on them, and blue sky with white clouds. The orchestra, in shirtsleeves and suspenders, the latter not obligatory, sat on platforms that rose steeply toward the sides which were covered with orange paper. There were pennants on poles, various colors, with bugs prettily drawn on like comic valentines.
>
> Costumes: undershirts, sun-glasses, grey-green or red work gloves for the chorus. Oedipus, a boxer, including violet and gold bathrobe, red and white socks, sparring mask and hand bandages — no gloves, no sunglasses . . . Teiresias in clerical collar, but with tight pants unbecoming to the cloth, and sunglasses. The Messenger was a chauffeur with high peaked cap and goggles (dark) in a belted outfit. The Shepherd was Ben Casey. Jason Robards refused to wear his costume, which included a sweatshirt inscribed "O Rex," had on a business suit, but did consent to sunglasses. Lukas Foss was fully and normally dressed in white tie and tails, without sunglasses . . . .

For once, one applauds the *Globe*!

The point is this: There is no taste at all in such a presentation of a classic so great as to be sacred, and so sublimated in art as to be holy. *Oedipus The King* is one of the greatest plays of the world, that flowered from one of the greatest peoples of the world, in one of the greatest eras of the world. To any who can appreciate the peaks of man, this is a play never to be desecrated by monkey-tricks. The Greek civilization of classical Athens, moreover, regarded this play — and all tragedy — as holy and sublime. This play is the sublimation of man into Man. Its author is one of the few great artists of drama, a field where many are called but few are chosen; he is one of the supreme artist-philosophers of the world.

Here, then, is a poet and a play of which the critic must reverently say: "Take thy shoes from off thy feet, for this is holy ground." The Greeks, with their rare and splendid intuition for art, presented the play in a nobly stylized mode to enhance the realization of the grandly heroic — in poetry of the grand mode, that (as Aristotle said) was "more philosophical than history," and so tremendous that it seems the speech not of men but of demigods. Bathos, bawdy vulgarization, caricature, debasing of the great into the greasy, were, to them, outside the limits of tragedy. The good Greek knew that the tone of tragedy lies outside the key of comedy, and never the twain will meet.* To reduce pity and terror, the anguish of the heroic soul driven to such extremity that he tears out his own eyes, the billows that go over us in this world of probation and suffering, to what the *Globe* rightly calls "a fable about the public relations business," is a sin against the Holy Spirit — which, the Gospels tell us, is the "unpardonable sin." The *Globe* says of the conductors, Foss and Rivers, "The 'Oedipus' was designed to get them talked about. *'Épater le bourgeois'* was their aim . . . ." That is aesthetic blasphemy, tasteless clowning, tongue-in-cheek blah-blah. Even the *New York Times* knew this — and said so.

The worst of such lack of taste is that it destroys reality. At the last World's Fair in New York, for example, certain "religious" groups put on a play in which Christ was presented as a feeble-minded clown in a third-rate circus. Such a reduction of absolute Genius and the height of the soul to the dimensions of imbecility disqualifies the "mind" that does it from the life of the mind. It destroys the reality of Him whom Sydney Lanier rightly called: "Thou crystal Christ." When I was at Amherst under the late Alexander Micklejohn, even that crisp agnostic and mind of the Left used to read Christ's answer to the Pharisees asking him about Caesar's coin and tax, in chapel, as an example of the *height* of intellectual power. Micklejohn did not believe intellectually, yet he appreciated aesthetically; but these "religious" imbeciles pretend to believe intellectually, but aesthetically they have less taste than a mud-brained sloth in a tree by the Amazon. They have the "taste" of a "jeweler" who hands you a hunk of cheap, badly cut glass, and says: "See! — the Kohinoor diamond!" Or they are like a musical bum from tin-pan-alley beating on a sheet of discarded aluminum, while under the influence of a "fix," and saying: "Listen! — the fugues of Bach!"

Our contemporary tastelessness comes, of course, because we deliberately refuse critical standards, and fear and flee all that is high and great, all that makes demand upon us; and, in our impotence,

---

*In Gothic art like Shakespeare's, comedy can enter to enhance tragedy — but *not* in slapstick use of "suspenders" for King Lear and "sunglasses" for Juliet.

ridicule all potency, and forgive everything except honor and forget everything except shame. The result is that in the Country of the Blind, the Cockeyed Man is King; in the Country of the Tasteless, ditchwater is the Emperor's champagne.

Without taste, we narrow the many-splendored universe into a descending sphere of ever-closing walls . . . which is exactly what Dante saw as Hell. In reality, the universe is a place of many mansions, and life ever more abundant consists in appraising and evaluating each mansion — the laboratory of science, the gallery of art, the library of literature, the playing field of athletics, the cathedral of religion, the house beautiful of the home, the orchard where lovers' tongues "sound silver-sweet by night," *etc., etc.,* to infinity and eternity. Taste means that our minds and hearts and souls, in integral union, evaluate each mansion in terms of its essential being, as Hamlet said "in its habit as it is." Only reverence, humility, delicate intuition, wisdom that puts factual "knowledge" in its subordinate place, and Poe's "taste alone — that faculty which, holding a middle position between the pure intellect and the moral sense," can never "safely [*be*] disregarded" — can help us to appraise and evaluate the many mansions and see their variety and fascinating differences that are ours to discriminate. But the typical "modern" — the "realist" who destroys reality, the science-taster who destroys science, the "Liberal" who destroys liberty — prides himself on denying the many mansions. He says that the universe has only a single street, Skid Row; and only a single mansion (that is *not* a "mansion"!), the Flop House. So his "taste" is a caricature of reality, his judgments psychopathic.

The final pity of it is that he is thus incapable of the subtleties and excitements and intricacies of taste — which occur when, rising to the great argument, you use your taste not only to differentiate between the good and the bad, but to distinguish between instances and levels of the good and the great. Taste should be afoot and lighthearted upon the open roads of the great adventure: What are the differing excellencies of Poe and Whitman and Emerson, of Shakespeare and Aeschylus, of Plato and Aristotle? *There* lies the real glory and joy of the life of the mind. But amid our modern debacle, where taste has to waste itself in discriminating paste from pearl — not pearl from pearl; and punks from paladins, and not Roland from Cyrano — one cannot even *begin* the great adventure. Where the Beatles are "more popular than Jesus," one cannot begin the exploration of the many mansions! To linger in the pit's much mire means that one cannot distinguish the excellences and the overtones of the Lord's Prayer and the Sermon on the Mount. One is blind to the pearls and one is obsessed with the swine.

II

WHAT *is* taste? Perhaps a good beginning is a differentiation by Robert Frost. In Sydney Cox's excellent little volume, *A Swinger of Birches,* we read:

> In 1926 he told the boys in my writing class that the aesthetic range was from exquisite beauty, through elegant beauty, homely beauty, rough beauty, terrible beauty, to vile beauty. He had never been able to go to vile beauty, he said. He knew his limits. Shrubbery in spring with a lot of manure and straw around the roots was beautiful to him. He could go that far. That was a well-dressed garden. But in general he swung a little this way, a little the other way — as the balance of things required a shift — somewhere near the center of the scale.

That is aesthetic justice, aesthetic reality, in action.

My dictionary thus begins the definition of taste: "to try the flavor or quality of (something) by taking some into the mouth." It rises from this to the definition of what I am here discussing, thus: "the sense of what is fitting, harmonious, or beautiful; the perception and enjoyment of what constitutes excellence in the fine arts, literature, etc." One certainly should add — "the perception and enjoyment of what constitutes excellence in *character action, and life.*"

Let us consider this carefully. Taste, we see, is concrete, primary, and sensuous: That is, it does not begin with an intellectual scheme or a mental ideology, but with a sensory experience appraised by a fastidious tongue. It is sensory, immediate, aesthetic — the testing by the *taste-buds,* the synthesis of object and subject into meaning through one of the most compelling of the *senses.* This primary experience through the senses will *lead to* intellectual judgments.

Taste, in our sense, is not just tasting; it is tasting with subtlety, discrimination, evaluation. It is the perfect singer's sense of absolute pitch, over the varying range of the tonal scale; it is the colorist's sense of the dome of many-colored glass, with a subtle intuition of what colors fittingly blend and rightly cohere. On a physical level, it is the tea-taster's or wine-taster's power to discriminate; it is the great jockey's intuition of his horse and the atmosphere of the race; it is the great quarterback's intuition of the perfect play. It is what we most lack today — the concrete grasp of reality called *wisdom*. In man, as we shall see, it should be born — *and* it should be made; but in animal and insect, our elder brothers who are closer to the hand of God, it is directly and inevitably *there*. The "humble-bee" of Emerson's lovely poem *has* taste that never fails. Emerson puts it perfectly:

> Aught unsavory or unclean
> Hath my insect never seen;
> But violets and bilberry bells,
> Maple-sap, and daffodels [*sic*],
> Grass with green flag half-mast high,
> Succory to match the sky,
> Columbine with horn of honey,
> Scented fern, and agrimony,
> Clover, catch-fly, adder's tongue,
> And brier-roses, dwelt among;
> All beside was unknown waste,
> All was picture as he passed.

Such the fortunate bee, still close to Eden, still guided by the hand of God! One may be forgiven the wish that Langston Hughes had been born a humble-bee!

But man — for good or bad, for shame or glory — is different. He has a wider focus of will, a wider range of experience and *choice*; he can choose, if he will, not only the "columbine with horn of honey" — but the marijuana with mist of madness. He does not have the irrefrangible rectitude of the humble-bee's taste. "How art thou fallen from Heaven, O Lucifer, star of the morning!" Man's glory and man's peril is — *free will*; as the Stoics knew long ago, "God might have made man a chained slave, but instead He made him free." Man's free will runs the gamut of extremes — from "In His will is our peace," to "In my caprice is my excitement." As Hamlet knew, we crawl half-way between Hell and Heaven; and so we may choose the will-o'-the-wisp in the pit's much mire, or the sun that lights the prairies, and the mountains, and the oceans white with foam.

The unspoiled child — and some exist even today! — who has not yet been raddled with the smartness and blight of modern education, has natural taste like the "humble-bee" of Emerson's poem. He sees — and says — that the Emperor has no clothes by Dior (or Picasso) over his naked scrawny chassis. He says that his kitten has "thorny paws"; that the egg "blossoms" (into the daffodil that runs around on rebel roots and says *peep)*; that the smooth new car feels "like apples." That is taste — to see things as they *are.* If we could retain and maintain the innocence, the realism, the poetic power of the natural child, we should not have to discuss taste here. We would possess it. And man, becoming the adult yet never losing the child, would appraise and delight in all experiences of taste; the cool silver shock of water to the summer body; the ox-eyed daisy tawny as a jaguar by the northern roadside; the savor of sweet fern or sassafras crushed to a whiff of pungent delight; the beatitude of the dog's loving tongue; the song of the thrush and the plume of the tanager; the dew's coolth in the dawn; the splendid eagle's claw of lightning, symbol of the tragic sense of life. Such experiences, seen with taste and loved with delight, might regain, or at least lead us again toward, the blissful seat of Eden.

And this might eventuate if children, from the very cradle, were surrounded with touchstones of beauty. Their taste, perhaps already born, will be also made if they possess books like *At The Back Of The North Wind, The Arabian Nights, The Jungle Tales, Oliver Twist, The Wind In The Willows, Grimm's Fairy Tales, Mother Goose, Alice Through The Looking-Glass, Puck Of Pook's Hill,* Emerson's "Fable," Longfellow's "Paul Revere's Ride," and Alfred Noyes' "The Highwayman," and Coleridge's "The Ancient Mariner." Their taste will be enriched and intensified if they see around them fine paintings, if they see on occasions originals like "Blue Boy," and Winslow Homer's "Gulf Stream," and Ryder's "Forest of Arden," and Albrecht Dürer's marvellous sketch of the rabbit, and classic Chinese paintings of landscape. Their taste will be strengthened with genuine rapture if they often hear music like MacDowell's "To a Wild Rose," or Beethoven's "Minuet," or Irving Berlin's "God Bless America" or "Blue Skies" or "Oh, What a Beautiful Morning!", or Handel's "Dead March from Saul." The smartness and blight of cerebrality that brainwashes the child with the lie that the classics are "corny"; the splashing of the acid of false sophistication in the face and eyes of child or man: these destroy subtlety, discrimination, truth of taste. Taste comes only from integral humility, loving reverence for the excellent and the rare, a sense of the many mansions of this fathomless universe.

Children, contrary to modern superstition and conformity, should be surrounded with beauty and bathed in its great waters; they should see and hear only the best that man has said and known and done and been. They should be nurtured on Plutarch's *Lives,* the legends of Alfred and Arthur, the song of Roland and the glory of Roncesvalles, the *Nibelungenlied,* the stories of the heroes of Asgard, so their taste will set the hero above the heel. They should be nurtured close to Nature (even if they are unfortunate enough to live in our universal "Secular City"), with unsmogged skies, and broad rivers, and the surf that "cushions us soft, rocks us in billowy drowse," and pure air, blue skies, gold sun. They should grow up in the house beautiful (*it can be made so even in a "slum" if there is inner value in the parents' souls*), where they are treated with the integrity of justice and the stark validity of truth, and where cruelty and ugliness are unpardonable sins. They should be brought up as Plato, through Socrates, said: with beautiful forms leading them to beautiful meanings, beautiful meanings leading them to beautiful being, and glory lifting them onward to glory, world without end and life everlasting.

Matthew Arnold, in his masterly "The Study of Poetry," gave advice which is most creative in relation to the development of taste. He said:

> Indeed there can be no more useful help for discovering what poetry belongs to the class of the truly excellent, and can therefore do us most good, than to have always in one's mind lines and expressions of the great masters and to apply them as a touchstone to other poetry .... These few lines, if we have tact and can use them, are enough even of themselves to keep clear and sound our judgments about poetry, and to save us from fallacious estimates of it, to conduct us to a real estimate.

He gives his own touchstones — and we can add our own. *Touchstones of excellence!* Not a "discussion," not a "bull session," not acidulous cerebration, not vivisection with the scalpel of "sophistication," not the analyses that lead to statistics and death, but *touchstones of excellence,* that in themselves simply are.

The thing that the so-called modern "mind" cannot understand is that there *are* touchstones of excellence — that they are not fabricated, or determined, or fashioned by man: They simply *are*, by fiat of reality. The beauty of orchid or water lily, the splendid jaguar (so different from "the cool cat"!), the decibels of the wind's song, the pure absolutes of the tonal scale, the inexorable hierarchy of the spectrum, the magical music and images and insights of Shakespeare, the fugues of Bach, the inexorable reality of Dante, the transcendency of Rembrandt, these simply *are*. Before them the universe bows, and the mind of man should say simply: "Holy, holy, holy!"

Taste is like the light — it shines, and we see — and A is A, and B is B, and a spavined nag is different from Man-of-War. Light gives us scope for reason — the geometry and its lines, the spectrum and its colors. Light shows us a universe objective, real, inexorable, mysterious, first formless and then multiform: reality whose basis is the mind and will of God.

What Has This To Do With God?

IN his speech at Edinburgh University, wherein he explained his reason for resigning as rector (a post to which the students had elected him), Malcolm Muggeridge said:

> To see God is the highest aspiration of man and has preoccupied the rarest human spirits at all times. Seeing God means understanding, seeing into the mystery of things. It is, or should be, the essential quest of universities and their students and staff.

Such is the grave word of a sophisticated and often caustic intelligence, looking at the muddy time in which we wallow — and, beyond it, at Eternity which is the source and goal of reality and life.* He speaks the word of essential meaning; and that word is *God*.

Most of the things we take seriously today are frivolous. Our economics, our politics, our sciences and arts, our education and our amusements and our everyday concerns, are frivolous today just because we leave God out of them. They are made frivolous by the supercilious, hybritic, smart-alecky, negative men (often of Academe) who are concerned only with things verbal, derivative, and secondary — in a mood deracinated and sapless.

It is a mood that ends with a fashionable idiocy that "God is dead" — the homogenized hybris and pathos of academics who no longer seek what "should be the essential quest of universities and their students and staff." Instead, they try to vivisect God into dry bones and vestigial superstition. They are mad coroners at an autopsy, trying to prove the death of a "corpse" that isn't there. They are themselves proof that, having severed himself from God, man is obviously dying and often already dead — a corpse ambulant, a shadow that no longer even points to the sun.

"To see God is the highest aspiration of man . . . ." So let us leave

---

*That Muggeridge means this is proved later in his speech. He says that we may, on the contrary, "joyously survey the wide vistas of eternity and the bright radiance of God's universal love."

the mad autopsy in the fashionable funeral parlors, and seek our God who is beautiful upon the mountain-tops of the morning.

I

GOD, the Great Defender, needs no "defense." I do not defend Him; I do not try to prove Him; I do not argue about Him. Does the seed "argue" about the sun; do the branches "defend" the vine and the root; do the rivers seek to "prove" the clouds and the rain? I experience God, in my minor and humble way, as the Psalmist did in the days when men were nearer to the source and the essence, and so had the understanding that is wisdom:

> God is our refuge and strength,
> A very present help in time of trouble.
> Therefore will not we fear, though the earth be removed,
> And though the mountains be carried into the midst of the sea;
> Though the waters thereof roar and be troubled,
> Though the mountains shake with the swelling thereof.
> There is a river, the streams whereof shall make glad the city
>   of God,
> The holy place of the tabernacles of the most High.*

And even so:

> Thou makest the outgoings of the morning and evening to rejoice.

And, O Lord:

> Whither shall I go from Thy spirit?
> Or whither shall I flee from Thy presence?
> If I ascend up into Heaven, Thou art there;
> If I make my bed in Hell, behold, Thou art there.
> If I take the wings of the morning,
> And dwell in the uttermost parts of the sea,
> Even there shall Thy hand lead me,
> And Thy right hand shall hold me.
> If I say, "Surely the darkness shall cover me,"
> Even the night shall be light about me . . . .
> The darkness and the light are both alike to Thee.

---

*I hope the modern mind will notice that here the Psalmist is facing the destruction under the mere thought of which the modern faints — that "the earth be removed." The Psalmist could not have had a more intimate and revealing vision of the modern world, its nature and its need . . . and the answer to its need.

The thing to notice about these words is that they are — great. They are the words not of "simple," but of very subtle, men. They are not the words of naïve and superstitious men, like savages in the jungle; they are not desperate scaffolding tossed up to prop a falling sky; they are not cerebral verbalism of ideologies. They are, instead, the calm certainties of subtle and profound minds, penetrating life until they find the granite of reality and (beyond even that) the central fire that makes earth still a star. The Department of Health, Education and Welfare might question their mental health and put their authors in an Alaskan center for the mad; but anyone who knows that great style like this does not come out of illusion and delusion, would question — as many of us do — the mental health of the Department of Health, Education and Welfare.

These are, you see, words that speak a profound *experience* of the source and essence of being. No "scientific" discoveries about space and time, no weighing and measuring of matter (or the vibrations into which matter may be dissolved), no knowledge of up-to-date physics and chemistry, can corrode — or even touch — these words that speak an experience that is not *of* or *in* space and time. To try to disprove them by relativities of space and time is like trying to disprove great poetry by criteria of time and space.

Take a far-off but revealing analogy. Shakespeare wrote the great line: "Put up your bright swords or the dew will rust them." That is a truth about a world framed by time and space, that is true in every space and in all times; in the universe of Newton it is true, and even in the universe of Einstein it is true. So with all great expressions of things as they are: "And jocund day stands tiptoe on the misty mountain-tops" . . . "Beaded bubbles winking at the brim" . . . *"Sunt lacrimae rerum."*. . . These are the experience of great poets made eternal by the expressions of great poetry; they simply *are*. They are absolutes untouched by relativities. They are qualities unchanged by quantities. They express something, in time, so true that it transcends any time and pervades all times; something, in space, so real that it transcends space and is in every space.

Now I do not mean that the Psalmist was merely creating "poetry." The analogy of these lines to God is ludicrous, in that sense, and I do not make it. I mean simply that there is a way of experiencing the eternal and the absolute which is beyond all space and time, all weighing and measuring, all theories whether of Lucretian atoms or of the quantum theory. No matter how science reads ever deeper hieroglyphs graven in stone or star, all stars and stones flow from the incredible and incalculable *potentia qua* that wrote the hieroglyphs. Science can, at its purest, fashion formulae and theories of electricity — but, electricity remains and abides always *in itself* an unexplained power and an incalculable mystery that is a great *I Am*.

The words of the Psalmist are as true today as when they were written, and the apprehension of reality within us recognizes it. That apprehension may be deadened by pride-of-brains and pride-of-heart, but in the proto-psyche it cannot be destroyed. Which is why the "new breed" rages at such words and imagines a vain thing: It simply feels a truth that it dares not admit. Today we take the wings of the morning in our jets; today we make our bed in the hell of the modern city. But, even then, as always, *He is there*. Though the earth should be removed by our sick follies with the atom, *He is there*. The cloud-capped towers, the gorgeous palaces, the very globe itself, dissolve, and we end like dreams that wake; *but He is there*. Sustaining all things, forever creating all things anew in every instant by the power that transcends all instants, judging all things by the eternal Judgment Day of the Eternal Now of His being, the living God *is*. And now, as of old, He defines Himself thus: *I Am that I Am*.

II

THE PRAGMATIC effect of God's being is to create the universe not as chaos but as cosmos.

Without God — that is, without reason and will at the source and center of things — the universe would be casual, mechanistic, material only. It would be accidental, hit-or-miss, relativistic . . . a mere congeries of happen-so. Without central reason and essential will at its source, the universe would just happen, out of matter, energy, the libido, the "natural" bumping of the amoeba up to man, the blind atoms of Lucretius that roll round like witless marbles till they somehow develop eyes, the mindless basis of matter that lifts itself by its own boot-straps into mind, the mere happen-so of mere existence that somehow eventuates the miracle of Aristotle and Shakespeare.

The one value of a modern like Sartre is that, accepting such an existential universe, he sees that the best we can do if the world is like that is for each of us to fashion, in a hostile multiverse of clashing and disparate units, each his own affirmation of whatever whim he chooses for his own aim and law. The corollary of this solipsism is that a universe does not exist, a cosmos does not exist, only a chaos where we say "The other? — *that is hell!*", and where men are (as Schopenhauer said) like porcupines on a cold night, that huddle together for warmth and prick each other with proximity.

In an atheistic multiverse there is no universal reason of which all things partake, no holy will that organizes all into coherent form, but only matter and mechanism and random collision. That kind of multiverse is explicit in the characteristic art, music, and literature of the typical "moderns." It is the dogma of man-without-God. It is man denying that reason and free will are primal and central and essential in the constitution of things. It is man postulating life as a random flow of nothing out of nowhere into nothing. It is man seeing life as "just one damn thing after another." Such a conception dries up the fountains of joy in a psychic drought; hamstrings the soul that should be beautiful upon the mountains; and reduces man to the frivolous "morality" that says affluence is a misery for man and that *therefore* we should "lift" the "poor" into "affluence." It is a world of moles denying the sun and cursing the dark.

It is no wonder, with such a "philosophy," that the typical modern is like a cage full of weasels running around and gnawing his soul!

With God, on the contrary, there is a universe that can be called a cosmos. God is the living Creator; He is reason and He is will, conscious and central. And so reason and will pervade the cosmos He creates; mind and meaning, value and will, are of the essence. In the cosmos there are quality, value, and meaning, for they are rooted and founded in God; and God, beyond phenomena, makes the universe a living order full of reason and free will. A theistic universe has sense, because there is sense at the source and basis of all things.

And only a theistic universe is objective. Whatever the subjective dreams or whims of man, the objective cosmos abides — inexorable, solid, real in the mind and will of God. Because of Him, a rose is a rose is a rose; He sustains the seas that move and the stone that stands, the lion and the lightning, the redwood forests and the song of the nightingale and the music of the spheres — even where and when there is no ear to hear, no eye to see, no hand to touch. All things in Him are brave and steadfast, objective amid subjectivity, strong in line and rich in color. He sustains the slumberous reservoir where what we call "matter" sleeps, and where the strong swimmer of mind and will strikes out with joyous courage for an infinite shore beyond all that we yet know. A theistic universe, a cosmos founded in God, is predicated upon reason, free will, life, love, creation: It moves like the tiered galleys of the waterlilies, across the lake and the summer, from God *to* God.

There is, of course, an objection to the theistic universe; and it comes often to the most sensitive and the most godly and faithful of us, when we see many of the things that are done under the sun. A beautiful child only a few weeks old suddenly dies of a strange pneumonia in its little bed; cancer or rabies bring anguished death to the innocent — and the needed; normally beneficent fire leaps out in red anarchy and incinerates a family in a night; earthquakes devastate Lisbon or San Francisco; pride of power puts the pistol to the heads of thousands of the noblest sons of Poland in Katyn forest and tries to shovel them under from the knowledge of man; Keats dies abandoned by the shallow futile woman he loved, and seemingly ignored and lacerated by the men who ruled his day; right seems forever on the scaffold and wrong forever on the throne: How, then, in such a world, can there be a God both all-powerful and all-good?

Philosophers call this the Problem of Evil. The great anonymous poet of *Job* wrestled with it and sought an answer to it, and cried out, "O that I but knew where I might find Him!" And we too, often when we suffer and the world seems doomed even by the evil of the sometimes well-meaning, ask: "How can there be a Friend behind phenomena when such things occur?"

But suppose we yield to the Problem of Evil. Suppose we decide with Gloucester that:

> As flies to wanton boys are we to the gods:
> They kill us for their sport.

Suppose we find all the billows going over us, and say we are:

> But helpless pieces of the game He plays
> Upon this checkerboard of nights and days,
> Hither and thither moves and checks and slays,
> Then one by one back in the closet lays.

Suppose that we conclude that the multiverse is at best blind and random, or at worst cruel and vindictive. What then? Then we are suddenly faced with the Problem of Good!

How, in a random or a malignant universe, can there be reason and holiness and beauty and good? The love that blossomed like a flower in the lost beautiful child; the reason and the will-to-good that patiently seek the antidote to cancer or rabies; the heroism that risks death by fire to save a child, or that will not recant or crawl with the pistol at its head in Katyn forest; the Keats, who in spite of a fame he thought writ on water stood silent upon a peak in Darien or saw magic casements opening on the foam; the right that we admit is right even upon the scaffold or the cross, and the Nero whom we loathe even upon the throne . . . how, if the world is only and all random, malignant, evil, do such things blossom out of the omnipotent mud?

It is impossible to explain, if the world is essentially evil and in its central nature blind or careless, the conquests of the *Messiah* of Handel, the poetry of Shakespeare, the engravings of Blake (or, if you will, of Goya), the serene vision of Spinoza seeing life *sub specie aeternitatis* and breaking the walls of human bondage, the humble steadfast goodness in poverty and obscurity of innumerable sound men and true women, the life in us that heals the wounds of the flesh and turns the anguish of the spirit into new power, the dainty rectitude of the snow-flake and the fragrance and color of the rose (earth might have been only a lithograph!), the embracing love of Francis for his sister the water and his brother the fire, the mystery of Christ conquering by the Cross . . . .

Explain to me how? How out of the dead lion comes the honey of the swarming bees, out of blindness sight, out of chaos the cosmos of geometry and the spectrum, out of meanness holiness and out of mediocrity genius, out of random chance the architecture of order, out of nothing the supernal and the magnificent? How can this be? Grant the Problem of Evil, grant all the evil that exists under the sun, grant a universe with no reason and will in the person and presence of the Creator. But how, then, explain the miracle of miracles — *the Problem of Good?*

The typical "moderns" attempt to evade that question by denying the good. But if we deny the poets, the saints, the heroes, the good workmen; if we deny the reality of truth, of beauty, of right; if we deny the glory of man at his highest, "a free man, a proud swimmer, striking out for a new destiny," we are not realists at all, we are partialists. Or worse, we are Puritans in reverse gear, with a prohibition of good, with a censoring of good out of the universe. The good and the great exist and are, even though (in Conrad's words) they are like "The rocks, ever defeated and emergent, the sea ever victorious and repulsed." Good and evil, the nature of life, the being of God, these ever remain — as they should and must — as *mysteries*. We shall never explain life or define God — if we could, He would not be God. But mystery is not irrational. Reason exists so that we may define what can be defined, and reverence the truth of undefinable mystery at the root of reality. This we can say: Without Him at the basis of all, all is nothing. The paradox of God is that without Him nothing matters (in the wrong sense), for all is nothing; with Him nothing matters (in the right sense) — *for everything matters*.

III

IF I SHOULD seek to prove God or to argue about God you would rightly sweep up my words and deposit them in the wastebasket. And I would be disgusted at myself for such mere opening and shutting of the mouth over words, words, words; truth is nobler than that. All final and essential things are, and will remain to finite man, mysteries. You might define the snow-flake as "congealed H_2O," but you will know more about the snow-flake if you absorb its essential being into you by the words, say, of Francis Thompson:

> What heart could have thought you?
> Past our devisal
> (O filigree petal!)
> Fashioned so purely,
> Fragilely, surely,
> From what Paradisal
> Imagineless metal,
> Too costly for cost?

Here the poet has experienced the snow-flake — and proves its being by his experience of it.

And I say, very humbly *yet very firmly,* that there are men who have experienced immediately and directly the being of God. I say very humbly that I have myself. Some are mystics; some are not mystics at all. Upon the throne with Marcus Aurelius, in the slave market with Epictetus; in the modern slum or the contemporary Appalachian cabin or the Manhattan office; in any time and in every place — and so beyond time and space, it is possible to reach out and find Him — a living Presence, a sustaining Being, a source and transcendency, the Truth of truths, the Heart of hearts, the Life of lives.

Robert Frost wrote: "And there is Something sending up the sun." I say, as Christians who know the mystery and meaning of the Incarnation will always say, it is Some *One*. Toward this One the humble amoeba sends out the pseudopodia of his protoplasm, and we — also humbly — send out the antennae of our souls, to find Him in our longing and our need. And, if it is for our good, He answers us with fulfillment — and always He answers us.

So often, so often, in my own life I have experienced this — the incredible response to a question only half-articulated. There has come to me the one book or the one word that is light amid my darkness and that comes amazingly at the right moment — the sudden friend who sustains me in my lonely sadness — the one student who sees in me the person God meant me to be, and who as life goes on helps to open for me the door in what had been a wall — the one face "across a crowded room" — the mysterious guidance of which the free-thinking Euripides wrote (I paraphrase): *The way shall be opened unto you, not as you planned, not as you thought, but inexplicably* — the Everlasting Arms around your weakness, the Everlasting Presence to succor your loneliness, the Power that walks the waters and lifts you when you would drown . . . . These I have known, and these are mine forever, no matter who doubts and sneers: I know in Whom I have believed, and because of these I will trust in Him even though He slay me.

I do not possess, myself, the strange extra-sensory power that transcends the dimensions of time and space; I am not a mystic — I am too fleshly, too earthbound. Yet once I experienced, I myself, something after which life has never been the same. One Rhode Island night, many years ago, a full-orbed moon shone over deep new-fallen snow. Through that night, made by the moon and the snow more dazzling than the dawn of day, I walked alone a lonely country road for miles. Cold blaze of the moon above complemented the cold blaze of the snow beneath till I seemed to walk in a purer and more essential world.

On my second mile I seemed suddenly aware of myself as I had never been before, of myself as more than myself: I was lost, and I found myself. As if I was translated till I became a purity of light, I seemed to stand above the earth and look down at myself from a new dimension of being. A voice, my own yet more than my own, said to me: "What is life? What is death? What are 'you'?" I seemed to have died into life. It was no illusion or delusion; I had never lived so clearly, so surely, so starkly. I knew something — I do not know what — that was pure sheer experience of the essence of being. I could not long endure that transfiguration, I relapsed into the lesser experience that does not so strangely and utterly lift and enlighten. But because of it I can understand the words and the experience of the Psalmist and know that God is always there.

In that beautiful book, Kenneth Grahame's *The Wind In The Willows,* there is a chapter I can never read without becoming "so cold that no earthly fire can ever warm me." The Mole and the Water Rat are out in a little boat on the river, searching for the lost son of old Otter, little Portly, who (his father fears) has drowned in the wild water of the weir. The moon is a glory over the hills, and they row on, seeking, searching, feeling a hopelessness yet a strange hopefulness. Suddenly the moon grows dim before a greater light; dawn is on the river. But no bird sings. Then, in that strangeness of a magical dawn, Rat hears a sound or a song. He says:

> "So beautiful and strange and new! Since it was to end so soon I almost wish I had never heard it. For it has roused a longing in me that is pain, and nothing seems worth while but just to hear that sound once more and go on listening to it forever."

But he hears it once more.

> "O Mole, the beauty of it! The merry bubble and joy, the thin, clear, happy call of the distant piping! Such music I never dreamed of, and the call of it is stronger even than the music is sweet."

He bids Mole row on and the wondering little animal does, though he thinks the music is only the wind playing in reed and osier. And then Mole hears it too.

> Breathless and transfixed the Mole stopped rowing as the liquid run of that glad piping broke on him like a wave, caught him up, and possessed him utterly. He saw the tears on his comrade's cheeks, and bowed his head and understood. For a space they hung there, brushed by the purple loose-strife that fringed the bank; then the clear imperious summons that marched hand-in-hand with the intoxicating melody imposed its will on Mole, and mechanically he bent to his oars again. And the light grew steadily stronger, but no birds sang as they were wont to do at the

approach of dawn; and but for that heavenly music all was marvellously still.

They glide on through a world where the grass has a "greenness unsurpassable"; where the wild-roses were never so red before; where every fragrance of the living earth is a new experience of being. And they come to an island just above the foaming weir where they feared Portly had drowned, and make their way through the foam-feathered water, and land on the flowery margin of the island.

"This is the place of my song-dream, the place the music played to me," whispered the Rat, as if in a trance. "Here, in this holy place, here if anywhere, surely we shall find Him!"

And suddenly they felt a great Awe, an awe that bowed their heads and stopped their feet. It was a fear but not a fear, a peace that was a passion, a sense of a Presence very near. And still no birds sang.

The piping was now hushed, but its call was more imperious in the silence. So Mole lifted his head, he could not have refused though Death were waiting; "and then, in that utter clearness of the imminent dawn . . . he looked in the very eyes of the Friend and Helper; saw the backward sweep of the curved horns . . . ." He saw; yet still he lived.

"Rat!" he found breath to whisper, shaking, "Are you afraid?"

"Afraid?" murmured the Rat, his eyes shining with unutterable love. "Afraid? Of Him? O, never, never! And yet — and yet — O, Mole, I am afraid!"

Then the two animals, crouching to the earth, bowed their heads and did worship.

What, you ask, has this to do with *God* — this fantasy of imagined animals, this impossible dream? It has much to do with God, for it is true to the nature of things, to the psychology of awe and wonder and holiness and love, that we must experience if we are to see God. It is not Paganism and the mythological Pan; it is an image of the way to God. To animals that Helper and Friend and Presence would be God to them in animal guise, as He is to us the Helper and Friend and Presence in human guise. God is the God of all His creatures, or He would not be God — and His being embraces all of us, and the Angels and the Heavens. He is not made less, but more, because the Rat and the Mole see Him as they do, with little Portly lying safe from the wild water of the weir, safe at His feet. God embraces all, from the humblest to the highest; for all His creatures He makes "the outgoings of the morning and evening to rejoice."

There have been men sensitive to dimensions of reality beyond the reach of most of us, the seers, the mystics. Swedenborg; the great Spanish saints; William Blake; the greatest Quakers — George Fox and William Law; Henry Vaughan, and how many, many more, have been the Columbuses of the soul's Passage to India, eyes among the blind, voices among the dumb. They have had communion with the Being and the Presence, with the Helper and the Friend and the Burning Bush, that awe us with a noble terror and lift us with an incredible love. And any of us, if we purify our hearts, if we seek Him in humility and truth, may suddenly find Him who is always there.

IV

IN MY OWN limited way I have experienced God and know Him. I know that one speaks to Him in the silent prayer of the secret heart; I know that there is often a fulfillment, and always an answer that is a communion. In my loneliness, sometimes in my desolation, in my need and my aspiration, I have reached out; and I have found that we are not alone.

Such experience is not akin to theology. Theology is right and good when it is written by the wise and great; but that is not what I am talking about. Theology is of the mind even when its dynamic is the heart; it is a net of mind to catch the wind of the spirit; it may even be "chains of lead" around the soul's "flight of fire." But while scholars may talk learnedly of Water, those who drink it, who bathe in the surf, who rejoice with the thirsty land where the sudden rain falls, *know Water*. Even so we know God. We experience His being, as we experience water, or fire, or the deep breath where oxygen purifies our blood; as we experience a blood-transfusion — for this is a blood transfusion from the cosmos; as we experience the dawn after a night of dreams.

The experience transfigures the body; it does not annul the body, it fulfills it. It is not akin to drink or drugs, that shake the body and lessen the body; it fills you, rather, with a purity of essential being that is as natural as the light of morning or "the huge and thoughtful night." It is an experience beyond the senses, yet akin to the senses — we seem to touch God, to taste God (the very Bread of Life!), to hear Him as music, to see Him in line and color. And yet He is so beyond all that — immanent and yet transcendent, transcendent and yet immanent!

Before this experience, we had heard the great words that are too little for it, and in our inexperience we thought them only words: Nearer than hands or feet, closer than breathing . . . In Him we live and move and have our being . . . Lo, I am with you always, even unto the end of the world . . . Thou hast made us for Thyself and we are restless till we rest in Thee . . . Cleave the wood, and I am there; lift the stone and you will find me . . . Heaven and earth shall pass away, but My words shall not pass away . . . Before Abraham was, I am . . . . These seemed to us once only concepts and abstractions; but when we *experience* them from within, they become deeds.

We are in relation to God often like the late Helen Keller in relation to the rich world of sound and line and color. If only, as she did, we can reach out across our limitations and our barriers and let the unseen and unheard world speak to us! It would have been easy for her to deny the world beyond her darkness and silence, to curse that world unrealized because it teased her with the incredible and impossible; it would have been so natural for her to accept her false minor world of darkness and silence as the final positivistic and existential fact!

Even so, it is easy for the unregenerated and unawakened — for us who live in our similar world of silence and darkness and partiality — to huddle down in acquiescence. We are analogous to her, but we are too often without her insight, her patience, her courage, her aspiration, and so we continue in our world of the darkened and the dumb. But beyond the silence and the dark, where too often our eyes make us blind, our ears make us deaf, God stands. The unseen colors and the unheard melodies wait, and if we seek we shall find, and if we knock it shall be opened unto us.

That is the meaning of whatever truth there is in "evolution." There was no mindless bumping of the amoeba up to man. There was a world of color and sound that waited; there were the creatures, blind and deaf, that wanted to experience color and sound. Only so did creatures move onward and upward toward ears and toward eyes. Because creatures knew *before they knew it* that there is a world where lines speak geometry and colors speak the spectrum, such creatures moved upward and onward toward eyes. Because creatures knew *before they knew it*, that there is a world of the glories of sound and the harmonies of song, they moved onward and upward toward the wind in the leaves, the notes of the whippoorwill, the fugues of Bach. All that moved and moulded creatures then, all that moulds and moves us now toward even greater realities, lies always above us in worlds unrealized. It is the impossible dream that makes the fulfillment possible. To all creatures in the drama of life, then or now, we should say the beautiful words that Spaniards use in farewell: "Go with God!"

"Seeing God means understanding, seeing into the mystery of things." It means comprehending that there is a center of all things and a source of all things.

Suppose that man were a being surrounded by sounds (his experience of the universe), and that amid and yet over all other sounds, harmonizing all sounds into meaning and beauty, there was a symphony that he might hear and he (even he!) did hear sometimes. As he grew in wisdom and stature, he began to marvel that there was outside him a harmony of sounds to hear and within him the sensitivity by which he could hear those sounds. And one day, in awe and wonder, he began to realize that the symphony he heard was not the random chance of the wind or the casual collision of object on object; it spoke to him, and it spoke in terms of the artist who was the great Composer. That changed all things for him, deepening life into mystery and wonder, wakening him to the great quest, so that he listened to the beauty of the music as never before and longed to find in the music the meaning of Him who composed that beauty of sound.

He longed and he listened!

Thus the sounds of all things blended and deepened into the cosmos of music, and even the plangent and tragic chords became holiness and meaning and joy. And life became for a man a symphony great in itself, and greater because it led him ever toward the center and the source of the music of life: *God, the Great Composer*.

On Faith, Hope, And Charity

THE three great Christian virtues, in the words of St. Paul (*First Corinthians 13*), are these: "And now abideth faith, hope, charity, these three; but the greatest of these is charity." I retain *charity* here because I believe it will most richly make us think and see what the apostle Paul meant us to know. And, if modern usage has debased the word *charity*, even so modern vulgarity has debased the word *love*.

"Do not make war," some tell us today, "make love." But apparently they mean by "making love" only or mostly the biological release and the physical need of "sex." Of course, if you "make sex" — and sex alone — you are not "making love." At least it is not the love that St. Paul had in mind. Read the simple subtlety of all the great chapter in *First Corinthians*, and you will see that I am right. You may not agree with Paul, but you should know what he means; our whole adventure into truth, after all, must be an attempt to see what charity — or love if you will — really means. For charity is, as St. Paul says, the greatest virtue in the trinity of Christian values.

I

HOPE, faith, charity! What are they? Hope should be concomitant with youth by the nature of youth's plus of vitality; but it belongs to age also because the good marathon runners of life have won their second breath through the power of their spirit, and so find to the end the living hope that tells them that still "the best is yet to be." As Yeats' Father Hart says in *The Land Of Heart's Desire*:

> For life moves out of a red flare of dreams
> Into a common light of common hours,
> Until old age brings the red flare again.

In all the areas of life's adventure, while ever we are vital, there is the "red flare" of dreams, the sudden window opening on the horizon, the thing called "hope." Hope means the window to the

119

horizon, the unexpected road to the morning, the open mind and the soul breaking the iron curtain, the mystery and the wonder of incalculable life that has infinite variety and providential chance. Hope predicts a world that is not fixed and determined; a world of magic casements opening on the foam; a world where there may come at any time a newness nearer to the heart's desire.

"Tomorrow, by the living God," says a poem whose name and author I forget, "we'll try the game again." While ever the soul is spiritually young, while ever life is vibrant within the soul, after five years or a hundred years in this world, hope (which Emily Dickinson called "the thing with feathers") perches in the soul ready for song and flight. Hope abides! "Tomorrow, by the living God, we'll try the game again."

And faith? It is the affirmation of Columbus that he can reach the East by sailing to the West. It is the affirmation of the artist that, beyond the years, he can attain the outward form of beauty that is already the inward certainty of his soul. It is the willingness of the woman who loves to entrust her life to the man who loves her. It is the dream in the root that becomes the rose on the bough. It is the soul of the sun that affirms light in the face of the ever-encroaching darkness. Faith is the assurance of the possibility of things hoped for, the commitment to things to be, because we believe and affirm that they are real and valid, and worth seeking. Faith is the seed cast into the dark earth yet resolute to grow toward the unseen sun.

And charity? That is the subject of this essay. It is, as St. Paul said, "the greatest of these."

Let me say categorically that I am certain St. Paul is right in making these great virtues central. He knew that we genuinely live only while we affirm our faith, our hope, our charity; otherwise death — the inward death that is the true death — makes our "life" a disaster area, a coma and a paralysis — a particle of dust settling into the desert of a lifeless pessimism.

The greatest poet of classic and essential pessimism in English literature, perhaps in the world's literature, was the Victorian, James Thomson ("B.V.," as he signed himself). His was a noble pessimism in the grand manner — not the puny, sniggering, shabby, shoddy pessimism of the whimper, by the straw men and the hollow men who today "lean together." In *The City Of Dreadful Night,* a *No* to life so magnificent that it becomes a *Yes* to life. Thomson describes himself as he thought he was, and as a symbol of the eternal human pessimist. And what is a pessimist? He is simply the man who has lost hope, faith, and love. Thomson found the perfect image for this: Such a man, he says, is like a watch from which fate has removed the hands so that it no longer tells time, yet the works still tick on:

> As one whom his intense thought overpowers,
>   He answered coldly, Take a watch, erase
> The signs and figures of the circling hours,
>   Detach the hands, remove the dial face;
> The works proceed until run down; although
> Bereft of purpose, void of use, still go.

I know no image in all literature that more perfectly describes the defeat of life that comes if we lose the three great Christian virtues. And Thomson goes on to say:

> He circled this for ever tracing out
>   The series of the fraction left of Life;
> Perpetual recurrence in the scope
> Of but three terms, dead Faith, dead Love, dead Hope.

Thomson suffered because he thought that this was so for him, and he knew that for all who suffer the loss of faith, hope, and love, life is a perpetual catastrophe. And he did us all a noble service in seeing and saying that life without faith, hope, love, is not — Life! It is *death*, the intimate and inward death, the death that comes before the body dies. Thus, as Paul knew, to live we must seek and find the triune virtues — faith, hope, charity . . . .

And since the greatest of these is charity, let us try to find what charity *is*.

II

THE GREEKS had not one, but several, words for love. There was *eros*, the child of the beautiful Aphrodite of the sea-foam, a word that had to do with the sexual aspects of love. In its pristine Eden of meaning, the word was beautiful and noble and sweet and sane; it had not been degraded by sophistication into "erotic" and "erotica," till it was confused with the coldly smiling nudities of *Playboy* — as much like Aphrodite or *eros* as a zombie is like Juliet!

Eros can be a lovely thing; it would be a dreary day for man (and woman) if it ever lost its magic. But unfortunately, because of the Eros-mongers, it has already lost much of its magic, becoming a "naughty" rather than a noble word. That is why these Eros-mongers are like rats nibbling away a beautiful statue in rich ancient wood till they reduce it to a gnawed stub.

Still, as the Greeks knew, *eros* was not all of love, no matter how important its partial beauty. They balanced it with a grave sort of love, called *philea*. This *philea* was the love of the philosopher, of the man of vision and universality; the sober love that moved on the level of principle and understanding. The Stoic, for example, cared little for *eros* and much for *philea*. And *philea* was the thoughtful love, the principled love, the love not of passion but of understanding; it was the love that embraced humanity in the arms of reason.

Today *philea* has been caricatured, perhaps because of the weakness inherent in the word, perhaps because of the prissy utilitarian nature of "Liberals" and kosher "intellectuals" and collectivists, into something "philanthropic," something "humanitarian," something that has to do with a somber and constructive and dutiful "doing of good to man." Without *eros, philea* drains away into a pallid thing, an abstract virtue, a bloodless cerebration, a parlor game of philosophers in the merely academic sense. It is not the charity of which St. Paul speaks!

Life today is largely wrecked and ruined by those we are told are great (even professional) *phil*anthropists. They worship man in the abstract but hate men in the concrete. They are always trying to "do good" to their "brothers" without having love in their hearts, only a fussiness and the desire of the eternal Carrie Nation to reform and "improve." They are advocates of Prohibition (and prohibitions — of guns, privacy, danger, natural joy, *etc., etc.*), of wars to end wars, of making the world safe for democracy (and democracy unsafe for the world), of Leagues of Nations and of United Nations, of the use of force against the noble Ian Smith but not the evil Fidel Castro, of the right to Welfare instead of the right to work, *etc., etc., etc.,* . . . They are the New Cain, who does worse than murder Abel, for he is his brother's keeper in the modern sense of being the warden in his brother's prison. If this sort of thing were Paul's "charity," Christians would be of all men most miserable.

But this was never *Paul's* "charity." Paul dismisses the do-gooders in perfect words: "And though I bestow all my goods to feed the poor, and though I give my body to be burned, and have not charity, it profiteth me nothing." And it profits "the poor" nothing, and man nothing, and the world nothing. Such a philanthropic world grows institutionalized, dehydrated, fossilized; or it becomes the web spun by that paralyzing spider, the State.

But beyond *philea*, as beyond *eros*, the Christian word for love was *agape*. This was not merely the lovely but sex-limited *eros*, it was not merely the sober and sometimes heavy *philea*. It contained more than either and yet the best of both — something more and something transcendent. Something great and powerful.

Agape is a cryptogram to modern man, a code that he cannot crack; yet it is an open secret to the child, the lover, the saint and the poet, for it is as simple as the sun or the flower that opens in wonder and joy. It is a sort of initiation into the Life of lives, into the essence of being that lies in the living soul within us and the living souls without us. It is a wonder at, a reverence for, a delight in, the being of earth and life, of the living creatures (not merely man), of trees and flowers and animals and men; a delight in the substance of physical earth and in the essence of metaphysical being. The true conservationist will share it in some ways; the American Indian felt it in his sense of living Nature; Albert Schweitzer knew it partially, though he exaggerated his "reverence for life" into a somewhat rigid dogma; St. Francis knew it beautifully in his love of creature and man — and his love of fire, and water, and the great day-star of the sun.

It is this *agape* that is translated as "charity." And it is a concrete and living experience, not just an intellectual belief. It is a mood of inward wonder that finds the world an outward magic. It is much more — much, much more — than a doing of good merely to man, or finding man the measure of all. It embraces things, creatures, men, in the universe whose many mansions find *God* as their only measure; it is a mood that we lost in Eden but that we may regain in Christ. It is a charity that loves because it finds the universe magical, holy, mysterious, and reciprocal; it can love grief as well as glory, as we can love a lyric that is so sad it is fashioned out of heartbreak. It is a mystical sense of the magical essence of things, that includes the stones under our feet and the stars over our heads, the bird "multiplex of wing and eye," the fascinating animals, the prairies and the mountains and the oceans white with foam.

You see, it is not man alone that the Christian loves, for whom the Christian has charity; it is Nature too, and all the inhabitants of

Nature (we shall see the limits to this and the exceptions to this later). The Christian loves Nature *and* man, and has charity for them, because he loved God first and most, and God is the Creator of all these.

If you know St. Paul's "charity," you love the little rabbit with his fur all sunny; the roadside aster or the deepwoods gentian that blooms with beauty even though there are no eyes to see; the minnows that, in Keats' words, ever "seem to wrestle with their own sweet delight"; the dandelion-seeds like silver parachutes into the future; the chrysalis whence will break the flying flower . . . . Fascinating with mystery, dark with pathos, rich with joy, they are shining facets of the magnificent jewel of the universe. It is our function, our privilege, and our delight to experience this to the glory of God and to thank and enjoy Him forever. And in this experience we find the consummation of being, which St. Paul suggests and realizes for us in the splendid words of his poem to charity.

I cannot prove this by what Paul says, but if I understand Christianity and Christ, and what Paul means by charity, I believe that we have charity for things, and creatures, and men, not in terms of what they give us for our use or pleasure, but in terms of the being that *God gave them* — the destiny, the entelechy, that is theirs. We love the flower not because it is beautiful *for us*, but because it is *beautiful*; the cat not because it catches mice or feeds the ego when it rubs our ankle, but because the essence of feline being is a magic and a joy in itself. We love the woman we choose not because she flatters our pride or enhances our pleasure, but because she, in her beauty and her gracious worth, is noble essential *woman* in herself.

I think that is how St. Francis knew charity. It was not for any use to himself that he preached to the fishes and the birds and even the wolf; it was for their own splendid being that he wrote his canticle to the sun, and called water his little sister and fire his bold brother.

So it was, too, that Thoreau (if he did not always or often love men) saw the earth and the creatures of Nature with a pure selfless charity. And so the hunted fox (they say) would run to him, and the woodchuck would suffer his touch, and the fish would lie unfrightened in his cupped hand.

This is not, thank God, mere "altruism," it is not the surrender or denial of our self. It is, rather, the surest way to enrich our own being with the being of the stars and the forests and the gardens, with the fascinating variety and drama of the birds and the fishes and the animals, and with the idiosyncrasies of men's characters. So Dickens enriched himself and all the world with his fascinating men and women, and Dostoevski laid bare the mysteries of the human soul, and Shakespeare wrote his comedies like sunlight on the deep sea and his tragedies like lightning in the dark night. Thus charity is a joy-bringing virtue; and it is life-enhancing, as the bitter moderns who lose charity can never know. That is why so many moderns are narrow and thin and sad.

Charity means that, in receiving, you must also give. You must give awareness and concern, and the same consecration that the poet gives to his poem. Because you have charity, you cannot be callous to the destruction of great forests, to the desecration of lake and river, to the mutilation of mountains with strip-mining, to the making of Silent Spring with poison, to the slaughter of the wild pigeons and the bison. Charity knows that all these are a part of the living universe and that to be wanton and wasteful and cruel is to strike not at their lives only, but at yours also.

Charity means an ancient lost reverence; a lost ancient passion for the sources and the details of life; a sense of wonder and mystery and holiness. Charity means that we care for the earth and the sun and the moon; for the little bunny at home, clover-roofed; for the hawk at home in the wind-swept sky (feeling, ourselves, the joy of the wind on his quills); for the kitten chasing his little taper tail; for the tree "motionless in an ecstasy of rain"; for the sculptor striking marble into a glory of might; for the blinded man and all the splendors he has lost.

This, to charity, is not a moral "duty." It never says "I ought to!" — it simply feels and shares and is. Charity is most akin to the aesthetic experience of a man purged of pity and terror by the great tragedy, lifted beyond death by the "Death March" of Handel, tranced into communion with life by the "Sunflowers" of Vincent van Gogh.

Yet the result is morality. For when you see the might and beauty and wisdom of creatures and of other men, you do not "envy" (as St. Paul well says), for you rejoice that all these glories are poured into the river of life by your door, and nourish *your* roots. Charity does not become petulant that someone else runs faster, but shares the glory and joy of that speed; does not become querulous because another is wiser or more successful, but shares the success and the wisdom as a part of the commonwealth of the world.

Charity is too vivid in its own being to "vaunt itself," though it plays only the piccolo in the orchestra of life. It loves to play its own music, and it contributes the music it plays and absorbs the richer music others play, in the joy of living reciprocity. It is "not easily provoked," it does not "seek its own," for it absorbs everywhere its own; it does not "think evil" because it in itself is good; it does not rush out in resentment, crying "Burn, Baby, burn!" and so "behave itself unseemly." Charity does not fail when prophecies fail, and knowledge fails, or tongues cease. Charity is a joy forever and its loveliness increases.

As I have said, charity is *not* "altruism" nor the sacrifice of self. It does not put "others" *before* itself. It reverences and shares the being of others *as* itself, which is what Christ bade. It knows that its life, like all lives, becomes richer and more joyous as each life creates its own full being, and reverences others, wishing latitude and wealth in other lives, so receiving while it gives and giving while it receives. The gardener who has the most beautiful garden does not have it for "himself," but for the sake of beauty and for the being of tree and flower. As truth and beauty, as wisdom and integrity, grow anywhere in the world, and we have the charity to love and appreciate them, we know that the great question is not selfishness nor altruism, but the power of each man to grow in character and consciousness and to augment the productivity of the fruitful earth.

Think of music for a moment as the true symbol of life. Charity, let us say, loves music and reverences it, and delights in it, and seeks to augment and to appreciate and to experience it. It relates all things to that central beauty and meaning. The earth itself is the ample hall where the music is played, and the sky is the roof. Therefore it is charity, for those whose function it is, to be the janitors who serve the hall; and it behooves us all to preserve that hall and to keep the air within it clean and sweet.

And those of us who play in the orchestra should not quarrel about the instruments — one plays the flute, one a percussion, one the first violin; we have charity when we reverence music first and most, and play our own instrument as it should be in the orchestra of the world. To play the score, to follow the baton of the Great Conductor, to love the music not because it is ours but because it is beautiful . . . such is charity. And only so, as St. Paul knew, shall we know even as we have been known, and hear not as though felt dimly. Then, instead of discords and cacophonies, we may hear again the music of the spheres and the song that the Morning Stars sang together.

III

WE HAVE seen and said that charity reverences life. But that means essential life — pure life, life in its value and quality and meaning. It does not mean to reverence death in the body merely because it exists. No one loves dogs more than I do, but that does not mean that I call it "charity" to allow a pack of dogs gone wild and wrong to tear a child to pieces or wantonly to kill a flock of sheep.

The weasel is a creature gone wrong, murder ambulant, cruelty for the sake of blood-letting; it will wantonly, and not for the sake of its necessary food, invade a hen-house and sever the throats of thirty hens in a night: Shall I call it charity to let the weasel run amok? Shall I condone tetanus; the tiger corrupted from his own natural hunting of wild animals to be a man-eater; the tsetse fly that blankets an area with death for man and beast; the rats allowed to devour in India as much food in a year as America can send, because the people "reverence life"; the pestilence that wipes out the chestnut and wastes the elm; the skunk or wolf run rabid, because I have "charity"? Charity does not mean this!

Charity, just because it *is* charity, knows that if it is moral to say *yes* to life and life ever more abundantly, it is also moral to say *no* to death and death ever more abundantly. I loathe those who kill wantonly the narrow fellow in the grass known as a snake; but when copperhead or cobra or mamba strikes with deadly venom, I do what I can to kill, saying, "Comrade, it is you or I!" Once I was walking in Rhode Island woods when a weasel, whether rabid or just cantankerous I do not know, ran at me with bared teeth. Having a .22, I shot him dead. And I regard that as in perfect harmony with charity. If someone stocked my pond with the terrible pirhana of the Amazon, the terrible little fish that eat the flesh from the bones of beast or man before they can swim ashore, I would at once poison the water and save life from piscatorial death.

And so it is in human affairs. The man who proclaims on his tattooed flesh, "Born to raise Hell," and who shoots and stabs and strangles a bevy of young women, should not be an object of charity.

The victims dare not be passive; they should use their group strength to defend themselves — it is better so to die, if die you must, than to die passively delivering yourself to evil.

The Vietcong as Dr. Thomas Dooley knew them, thrusting chopsticks into the ears of children lest they hear the Lord's Prayer, tearing out tongues with pliers lest men should have the freedom to speak against their evil, are not to be allowed to perpetrate their horrors in the name of "charity." Snipers shooting firemen who try to save a city (and its innocent inhabitants) from death by fire — madmen of flame who toss bottles of gasoline on black and white — creatures that once were men who cry "Burn, Baby, burn!" — are not to be given license, by "charity," to destroy. If they were themselves fellow human beings in a fire, or victims of earthquake or flood, I would succor them as I would myself. But if I were doing what they do to mutilate and hurt and kill, the only self in *me* which would have value and worth would say, "Prevent me even if it means that you must kill me." That is what my true human self would wish to have done to my fallen human self; and I would do unto them what should be done to me.

Of course, to preserve the charity that is the symphony of life, we ourselves should not hate, we must not let ourselves become cruel, we cannot seek "revenge." If you hate, if you are cruel, if you seek revenge, you yourself become the thing you rightly loathe; you yourself become a soul metallic and poisoned, a destroyer, a man perverted from charity. And by hatred, lust for revenge, cruelty, even by anger, you are blinded to objective reality and even to efficient action. Dante saw the angry in Purgatory so blinded by a sudden red mist in eyes and brain that they could not see their way. And against the evil of the world we *need* to see our way.

Always in judging creatures or men, charity must see things as they are, with objectivity. Even St. Francis, when he converted the wolf, surely did not expect him to eat broccoli — or hay. And the carnivores, while they act and eat with the natural rhythm of their entelechy, unperverted, must be fairly seen and fairly judged by charity.

Gerald Heard, in his excellent book *Is God Evident?*, makes one mistake; he says that the great carnivores are like cancer, a malignity, a disease. But cancer is a perversion of nature, a running wild of cells in exaggeration and destruction of the body that is their own. It is unnatural, degenerative, malign. The carnivores, on the contrary, are a part of the benign and vital rhythm of Nature. If you wipe out the cougar and the wolf, the deer multiply without check or balance, they destroy their own food supply, they gnaw brush and sapling to the root, till they become stunted caricatures of themselves and die of the slow misery of starvation. The tensions of the world are a part of *God's* charity. There is a proverb of the Eskimo (I do not quote it exactly) that says: "The wolf is the health of the herd." Charity must see life steadily and whole, and be just to the tiger as to the lamb.

But! – if the lion falls into the ways of the man-eater (a perversion for lions as well as a disaster for men), if the rogue elephant becomes a morose and psychopathic death for beast as well as man, charity sees things as they are and judges as it must. Charity must have insulin in its blood, or it falls into the spiritual diabetes which we call sentimentality.

Here, as St. Paul knew, we all see as through a glass darkly. But we must try to see face to face – and, if we do not, we shall not know charity – which is like sunlight ... and, like sunlight, casts a shadow.

IV

FAITH, hope, charity! Faith is the integrity of mind and heart that knows in what it has believed, and follows it steadfastly though the skies fall. Faith is the determination in the heart of Odysseus that keeps him journeying over the wine-dark seas to reach Ithaca – and Penelope. Hope is the resilience and the generosity of the soul that keeps the door open to the future, and expects the unexpected, and awaits, beyond desolate seas, the Happy Isles. And charity?

Charity is life come at last to life. It is the glow, and the color, and the music of life. It is the heart of light; it is the seed of love that blossoms in the inner Spring; it is reverence and wonder transfiguring life because it brings a second birth and an Eden regained. It begins at home. *All* great things begin at home, for you can do nothing for yourself or for others unless it comes from within. It is you, you yourself, your own inward being, kindled by God's grace into rapport with outward things, that relates your own state of being to the true being of outward things. You waken them, they waken you; you find the reciprocity and the mutuality that alone brings life and joy. Of such is the Kingdom of Heaven – which the child may know by innocence, which the man may regain by experience if he knows humility and wonder and rebirth. In one of his letters Vincent van Gogh wrote:

> But I always think that the best way to know God is to love many things. Love a friend, a wife, something — whatever you like — you will be on your way to knowing more about Him; that is what I say to myself. But one must love with a lofty and serious intimate sympathy, with strength, with intelligence; and one must try to know deeper, better, and more. That leads to God . . . .

Such is the way to Charity.

How do you reach it? Not by activism, not by deeds, not by taking thought, not by the fury of forty infuriated beavers in flood time; nor yet by stiffening life into institutions. Do you catch the wind in a net, the sunlight in a lobster-pot?

Let charity grow *within* you as the bloom of the rose grows within the root, and let it do its outward work through its inward being. Plant the tree by the rivers of water because *you* cherish it; cultivate your garden because *you* love the cabbage or the rose; care for your two dogs and three cats because they are dear to *you*; be just to him who works for you because *you* and he are both men; reverence and love the mystery of individuality as Kipling did; share all the grief and glory of the human soul with Euripedes and Shakespeare.

Thus reverencing and cherishing the things that are true, the things that are right, the things that are beautiful, you may *become*, yourself, charity and an instrument of God's joy. They say that a Stradivarius, played over the centuries by the masters of music, becomes itself ever more able to play beautiful music because its very being has become a storehouse of beautiful sound. So let it be with us!

"For now we see through a glass, darkly; but then face to face: now I know in part; but then shall I know even as also I am known. And now abideth faith, hope, charity, these three; but the greatest of these is charity."

A Matter Of First And Last Things

FIRST and last things.... The phrase is from H.G. Wells.

Yes, I know that Wells was a "Liberal," a relativist, a Fabian (though he quarrelled with the Fabian Society). But I also know that a talented man of error, by the Providence of God, may sometimes also say that which is both good and true. I know that Wells wrote that sound and brilliant book of individualism, *Mr. Polly*; and that he wrote that great short-story, "The Country Of The Blind," in which by splendid image he contradicted everything he had elsewhere said as "Liberal" and modernist. And I know that just before his death he wrote his desperate *Mind At The End Of Its Tether,* in which he confessed that modernism and relativism and "Liberalism" lead only to negation and horror and despair.

It should be a matter worthy of our eternal thanksgiving that we who seek the origin and the goal are not also buncoed by the con-men of secularism into supposing that our essential lives begin and end in material "security," subsidies, "reform," revolution, biology and physics and Freud, or the spangles and bangles of "Great Societies" and "Men like Gods" and Secular Cities. For we know that we live and move and have our being in cities not made with hands, in the many mansions of God's living universe – in, as Wells discovered at the end, first and last things.

We know that our lives are real only as they retain continuity with their origin and attain fulfillment in their end. The things that happen between the origin and the end – the material interludes that "Liberals" suppose causative and compulsive and cumulative – are *only* interludes in which all abiding satisfactions and all enduring meanings come only as they serve the soul.

Long ago Matthew Arnold wrote:

> Ah, love, let us be true
> To one another! for the world which seems
> To lie before us like a land of dreams,

So various, so beautiful, so new,
Hath really neither joy, nor love, nor light,
Nor certitude, nor peace, nor help for pain;
And we are here as on a darkling plain
Swept with confused alarms of struggle and flight,
Where ignorant armies clash by night.

Those poignant lines describe accurately the world in which "Liberals" and collectivists put their trust. From Marx to Harvey Cox, collectivists and "Liberals" are like spoiled children crying for lollipops, ice-cream cones of dribbled subsidies, colored balloons that escape the grasp, and soap-bubbles that break in the air. A mordant but wise modern like Malcolm Muggeridge, in his magnificent rebuke to the drug-seeking, birth-pill-pushing, psychedelic students of Edinburgh University, reminded us recently:

> I increasingly see us in our human condition as manacled and in a dark cell. The chains are our mortal hopes and desires; the dark cell our ego, in whose obscurity and tiny dimensions we are confined. Christ tells us how to escape, striking off the chains and putting a window in the dark cell through which we may joyously survey the wide vistas of eternity and the bright radiance of God's universal love.

But "Liberals" want to make the chains heavier with the "security" of things, and to add fluorescent lights so that we can see more clearly the finite limits of our cell!

The indefatigable little fairies who never grow up — the "Liberals" — keep saying that if we only had "Civil Rights" and "urban renewal" and billions poured out as carelessly as dishwater — we would all be as happy as kings. But when were kings ever happy? When was man meant to be wholly "happy" in the interlude of this world? When did "billions" ever make anybody happy or valid — or even safe? When has man ever found joy except in the Inner Kingdom, in the soul, in the true security of a character that is firm and a consciousness that is wise? We conservatives know this; and so we seek first and last things.

What are first things? They are the living source whence we come. They are the origin that transcends matter and the atom and the crass ignorance of materialists become "intellectuals.

The greatest book in all the world begins with the greatest phrase in all genetics: "In the beginning God." Beyond all the proximate and intermediary actions and adventures of the seed cast into the dark earth and growing toward the sun, lies the power of the spiritual within it and the destiny of God's will above it. The mystery and the wonder, the infinite and the transcendental, the power of the Divine, lie in our *origin*. "My Kingdom," said Christ, "is not of this world." And our origin is not of this world. It lies in the first things on which all the intermediate depend. The mystery and the wonder, the Creator who alone makes land and sea, the Nth power and the dimension that contains all dimensions, the incalculable and the unconditioned, alone create and sustain the land and sea, the calculable and the conditioned, the proximate and the material, and our three present dimensions. *That* is our origin!

The random and rootless who are the petulant rebels of the hour see origin as merely physical "birth." And oddly they are fearful even of physical birth — they clamor for "the pill" and for unlimited license for "abortion." Listen again to Malcolm Muggeridge:

> No doubt long after I am gone someone will be saying on the indestructible "Any Questions" program that a touch more abortion, another year at school and birth pills given away with the free morning milk, and all will be well.

But origin is more than physical birth, though as Wordsworth and Plato knew, birth is close to incalculable sources of being that bestow intimations of immortality. We conservatives *reverence* birth because it is a wonder and a mystery, because even in our physical origin there is the miracle of human love and the miracle of God's power. In birth, a wonder that transcends the world enters the world. Therefore we distrust the whimsical addiction to birth pills and the frantic escape from responsibility that comes from all licensed abortion. Birth is too wonderful and too sacred for that! We are amazed at the irony of generations that "worship youth" (as such) and say that anyone over thirty is not to be trusted, *and yet that so hate youth that they would cut it off in the womb*. It hardly makes sense.

These fantastic generations of the illogical and the contradictory say they wish to "find their identity." They say they wish to be "original" — they mean *different,* they mean *novel.* But "original," by inescapable derivation means *having to do with origin.* And indeed *all* originality, all new creation, comes only when we enter into our origin, *i.e.*, into the living transcendental sources of genius that enter this world yet are beyond this world. To return to wonder, to the incalculable power of the seed and the sources of the seed, alone will make us original. We must ascend into ourselves by descending into the transcendent power of the fountains of life. Through the generations, through traditions, through living continuity of being, through history inwardly felt and relived, we find the origin and become original.

The trouble with most "adults" today is that they have lost tradition, living history, the classics, continuity, the abiding reality of race and nation and religion and genius. And the "young" will fail even more by denying the traditions that their elders have long lost — the reality of race, of nation, of religion, of God. In origin lies metaphysical reality, the *élan vital*, the power not ourselves by which alone we can become ourselves. Most people today ignore this and are unconscious of this. Our young rebels think that it is concern with "tradition" and "origin" that makes adults brittle and charred — and so their tragic error carries them deliberately and consciously farther from the originality they seek. They forget that one is born out of, as well as into. They think that one can create from nothing — they do not understand origin.

If we maintain our rapport with our origin we do not lose, we *discover,* the wonder and the beauty of intermediate material things. For in that Eden-mood, our lands and houses, our gardens, our politics and our work and our country, and earth and Nature, remain forever young and wondrous, forever mysterious and sacred. There shines over them a supernal light, the light that never was on land or sea. Such as these are infinite and eternal; they cease to be existential *facts* and they become living *truths* that *are.* If we transcend them we can possess them safely. They then bring us the joy of meaning, whereas if we think them central and *all* there is (like "Liberals" and collectivists), they are like snowflakes that petulant children grasp greedily in hot little hands.

And in our origin, also, lies our end. Origin contains (study Aristotle!) our destiny. Destiny means destination — a self-chosen, a God-based, destination. In the origin of the seed lies the destiny of the seed — the tassel-whispering leaves, the full ear in its sheath. In the origin of the blind, squirming tiny cub lies the destiny of Blake's "tiger, tiger burning bright." In the infant Bach lay the patterns of all the fugues that glorify the Eternity of God. For what are "last things"? They are *not* "final" things, like an end in time; but destined things, like a *goal* in time that leads into eternity.

An end in the true sense is not a cancellation but a fulfillment. The end of Dante's life is not an ending in time — like his death — but a fulfillment in eternity that is the essence of his life outside and beyond time. The end of Dante's life was the creation of *The Divine Comedy*, as the end of the life of the lilac's bloom is the creation of its Japanese lanterns of pale lavender. The end of the Founding Fathers was a goal (end) at which they aimed — the great Republic. Such are "last things" — ends, goals, fulfillments . . . . And, as such, they are closely bound up with "first things" in a spiritual continuity that can never be broken if life is to maintain its integrity. The meaning of life, the immortal joy of life, lie in such ends that are goals. They come only as we find and feel the destiny that is in our origin.

Too many people today are ignorant of such things. They try to find happiness in proximate, intermediary things — the things that come between, the temporal things. So their lives are time-ruled and not eternity-based. And they suffer because time-ruled things fade and fail and die, and these shadow-people have nothing beyond and nothing real. Real life comes only when we live in and for and by first and last things.

There is nothing more unsatisfactory than pie here and now — *if that is all.* Only Heaven can satisfy our immortal appetites. Unless Heaven is our destination, earth is only a dead-end street.

Recently I found a new intensity in all this. I was very ill and even faced what seemed — as I suppose it always must — a too imminent death.

What remained real?

All the material things I love: house, lands, possessions, "security," Nature, the earth, *etc.,* grew thin and pale and shadowy. But the *real* things — character, consciousness, integrity, faith and hope and love, grew more real. The existential things were seen as they are — mere lendings, mere gifts of God for a little while. The things that *are*, the immortal longings, the unseen things, the principles and meanings that lie in our origins and our ends, grew more tangible and valid.

Miguel de Unamuno said, rightly, that only peoples and individuals who are death-conscious are life-conscious. "Liberals" and modernists always pretend that death doesn't exist in their playboy world of all-important secular gimmicks and gadgets. But death is always with us to make life real. The thin "Liberal" world of balloons and soap-bubbles is an ephemeral — and so a false and unhappy — world. But always, beyond the next moment, there lies the world of first and last things, where our mortal unhappiness ends and our unmortal joy begins.

And when we thus see life in terms of first and last things, "time" ceases to be "time" and becomes *real* time. Think of life in terms of music. A true life is a musical composition, and as such it lives not in the progression of sounds on the keys of the piano, but in the composition as a whole that creates and makes possible the performance of the progression of notes. The tune *is*; the progression of the notes only *exists*. The composition (which is in eternity, and so can be played over and over and over again) unites the source and the goal, the first notes and the central notes and the final notes, in one living reality that binds the never-ending past and the already living future, and the intermediate present into one complete harmony and meaning. The whole composition simply *is* in God's Eternal Now. Past, present, and future move *through* the pauseless procession of the notes, but transcend the progression of the notes.

Life is a music that *is* outside of time, and uses time only as a field for its expression, and comprehends first things and last things in unity, so that all things may live. Life is music! Live in the composition as a whole, and do not be deceived by the passing notes; life is music — uniting first things and last things, and being real only when it follows the conception of the great Composer and obeys the baton of the great Conductor.

Soldiers Of God

Cast Not Away The Hero In Thy Soul

THIS is the Age of the Anti-Hero. And the worst of it is that the age boasts of being exactly that, and trumpets this infirmity as a virtue. It is an age when the ugly and damned sneer at the lion and praise the jackal; when the sick and the lost and the weak proclaim that it is good to be weak and lost and sick.

So a Jean Genet invents a new morality whereby "dishonesty is better than honesty; cowardice is better than bravery; betrayal is better than loyalty; homosexuality is better than heterosexuality, and so on." So an Edward Albee, in his hideous *Who's Afraid Of Virginia Woolf?*, shows us a fashionable world so worthless as to make us forget that beyond the Great Dismal Swamp there is stern granite and fruitful loam. It is the age of the Madison Avenue sales pitch for cowards and spiritual cripples: It is the Age of the Anti-Hero!

Naturally, as a consequence or cause of this, it is also the age of the Decline of the West. Long ago Oswald Spengler, that wisest of modern historians, observed:

> You [*the Western World*] are dying. I see in you all the characteristic stigma of decay. I can prove that your great wealth and your great poverty, your capitalism and your socialism, your wars and your revolutions, your atheism and your pessimism and your cynicism, your immorality, your broken-down marriages, your birth-control, that is bleeding you from the bottom and killing you off at the top in the brains — I can prove to you that these were characteristic marks of the dying ages of ancient states — Alexandria and Greece and neurotic Rome.

Even so! Spengler understood that only as an age upholds the hero in the soul, the true and integral and brave in man, is it great; only so does it live, and prove its greatness through the life it creates. Nietzche saw the psychology of all this and wrote of it in *Thus Spake Zarathustra.* There he wrote:

> Ah! I have known noble ones who lost their highest hope. And then they disparaged all high hopes. Then lived they shamelessly in temporary pleasures, and beyond the day had hardly an aim . . . . By my love and hope I conjure thee: cast not away the hero in thy soul! Maintain holy thy highest hope!

Yet in most of our literature today, in much of our life today, we have cast away the hero in our soul, we have trampled on and defiled man's highest hope. Today the mad ones who pretend to be the heroes of youth are Anti-Heroes, frenzied with trampling and defiling. As Weatherman leader Bernardine Dohrn recently assured us, such Mad Mods glory in the murder of even a helpless pregnant woman, and the thrusting of a fork into her stomach.

Ours is an age in which those who stand in calm integrity for something noble and brave and great, like the young soldier, Daniel Fernandez, who in Vietnam threw himself on a bursting grenade, and died that his comrades might live, are sneered at as fools. It is an age in which a General MacArthur is, like a man in a pit of cobras, attacked with all the icy venom of the cold-blooded snake-creatures of the earth, even as he plans and executes the great Inchon landing. We *do* have heroes — God knows! — and they are as great as the hero ever was; but all the bias and conformity of the age war against them.

Meanwhile, men like Jean-Paul Sartre and Jean Genet and Albert Camus stand life on its head, and proclaim that the resulting intellectual tizzy and spiritual coma are a damnation preordained by the nature of things — in a world that, in their favorite cliché, is "absurd."

To answer this, America must look to her heroes. What youth — especially American youth — most needs today is to know the example of heroism. Only the "hero in the soul," only the "highest hope," can give quality and value to life, and so joy and meaning to life, today as in *any* day. I feel disgust, but I also feel a poignant pity, for the anti-heroic conformists of the hour — the cobras that should have been men! America must look away, and pass by. She must look to her heroes.

But what *is* a hero? He (or she) is a character and a consciousness touched by something far beyond the self, and therefore able to find and create the great self. The hero is he who seeks not the unformed marble of mere existence, but who senses and seeks always within the yet unshaped marble the potential statue. He ignores quantity, because he seeks quality; he does not demand a price, because he seeks to give a value; he does not worship matter, for he knows that it is only space and weight unless or until it expresses a meaning.

The hero finds and creates a self because he yields his finite self to his infinite destiny; he knows that, in himself, he is weak as water, but that in God he may take on the strength of the river or the tide. The hero says: "What is man that Thou art mindful of him? But if man is mindful of Thee, what may he not become — only a little lower than the Angels, clothed in glory and honor!"

That faith, or rather that vision, gives man the courage to be a Man. To be a hero. He knows that narrow is the way and strait the gate; that the reward of genius may be the white flame of St. Joan or the cup of hemlock. He is no citizen of Fun City, as he is no roisterer at Vanity Fair. Joy comes to him on the wings of the lightning. He takes with a frolic welcome the sunshine — or the thunder. And for him there is *always* thunder! Well did Emerson write:

> The hero is not fed on sweets,
> Daily his own heart he eats;
> Chambers of the great are jails,
> And head-winds right for royal sails.

And yet he does not break. Neither does he bend. As the great Victorian poet and essayist, James Thomson, wrote in "Open Secret Societies":

> The mystery which he [*the hero*] understands so thoroughly and feels so triumphantly is simply this: That in the whole range of the universe, from highest heaven to deepest hell, there is no thing or circumstance, creature or being, dreadful to man; that out of himself there is nothing which a man need fear; that no nature can be born into a realm unconquerable by that nature; and, moreover, that the most dazzling lightning of ecstasy leaps from the blackest storm of danger.

That is the philosophy of the hero, played to him by the noble march-music of his own heart's rhythm. And he is confirmed in that faith because he has mystical roots that draw life from beyond the world; because he has mystical hands that reach for life beyond the farthest stars. In that climate of the soul the hero lives.

But *who* is the hero? He is George Washington in New York, when the American militia broke and ran, charging alone upon the muskets and bayonets of the British landing . . . he is Nathan Hale, giving up a brilliant career for his country, and dying in the noose of a spy . . . he is Pickett and his men in gray, charging hopeless into the Union guns at Gettysburg . . . . He is Keats writing his great Odes under the smog of stupid critics, with death in his lungs, and Fanny Brawne turning away from him, and his fame (he thought) "writ on water" . . . he is Henry David Thoreau, dying too early, and saying quietly to a friend who asked him if he had made his peace with God, "Why, you see I never quarreled with Him" . . . . she is Emily Dickinson, dying unpublished and unknown, but writing to the end the great poetry "too intrinsic for renown" . . . .

These are the heroes who justify man in the eyes of God. And the best of it is, as Kipling knew and said, that the hero includes the quiet humble men and women who do the world's work and bear the world's weight, like an unsung Atlas, on their shoulders:

> Not the great nor well-bespoke,
> But the mere uncounted folk
> Of whose life and death is none
> Report or lamentation.

Such humble and nameless heroes are the honest men who pay their just debts; who do the world's work for which they draw the wage; who know that bravery is better than cowardice, that loyalty is better than betrayal, that love is greater than lust, that the lilies and the languors of vice (to reverse Swinburne!) are tepid as compared to the roses and rapture of virtue. They are the salt of the earth that has not lost its savor, these people, the light that shines in the darkness. They are the heroes, by whom alone the world lives, and beauty and truth and right endure — even if hidden or scorned — and, yes, even today.

The essence of heroism that unites them all, whether they fight on the battlefield, or create in the workshop, or live brilliantly in the depths of the soul, is that they have the courage to serve the great and the high — the courage that does not bow to Fate but serves Destiny; the courage that sets the impossible dream above the too possible expediency; the courage by which one lives to do what is right even when to do so means that, alone and lonely, one must die for it. Courage is lonely business, and almost always the hero stands alone. It was in *Self-Reliance* that Emerson wrote:

> It is only as a man puts off all foreign support, and stands alone, that I see him to be strong and to prevail. He is weaker by every recruit to his banner. Is not a man better than a town? Ask nothing of men, and, in the endless mutation, thou only firm column must presently appear the upholder of all that surrounds thee. He who knows that power is inborn, that he is weak because he has looked for good out of him and elsewhere, and, so perceiving, throws himself unhesitatingly on his thought, instantly rights himself, stands in the erect position, commands his limbs, works miracles; just as a man who stands upon his feet is stronger than a man who stands upon his head.

So the hero! Though he be alone he is integral, and therefore great — as the T-square, or the compass, or the sun, is great, because they are what they are, and endure and abide in their own rectitude and power; because theirs is an objective integrity transcending subjective whim. The unheroic of the earth, the weather-vanes who turn with the wind, have their place; but they are saved and preserved only by the integrity of others.

The fashionable spokesmen of this day and hour are either fools or liars. They are fools to make a hero of the anti-hero, to make a virtue of cowardice and betrayal and cheating, or they deliberately lie because they know themselves and are ashamed. What sort of fool tries to escape his shame by honoring it? Yet that is *exactly* what they do. And, as a result, a whole generation of Americans is coming to adulthood believing that heroism and honor and personal courage are both foolish and dishonest. Good and truth and beauty are said to be no longer real, but mere "value judgments." And every hero, every genius, every artist is pared down to inferiority to serve the egos of our cheapjack Associate Professors of Nihilism. Thus is America's youth robbed of its heritage. Thus is it betrayed.

The hero, in all great ages, among all great peoples, has been the champion of good against evil, of truth against falsehood, of beauty against ugliness. Hercules, enduring the seven labors, and becoming not a corpse but a constellation . . . Aeneas, tossed on the surf of seas and the waves of wars, that he might found the city of Rome . . . Israel Putnam, crawling into the dark bowels of the hills, to shoot (by the light reflected from her own eyes) the she-wolf that had wantonly murdered some twenty of *his* sheep . . . Sir Walter Raleigh, telling the dreadful headsman with the lethal axe, "So the heart be right, it is no matter which way the head lies" . . . . Patrick Henry asking if peace be so sweet or life so dear as to be purchased at the price of slavery . . . Robert Browning, facing death with the words: "I was ever a fighter, so one fight more,/ The best and the last" . . . such are the stars by which youth may navigate to maturity without ever growing old.

But youth must learn that it is impossible to be great unless you stand for great things. It must see the hero as champion and paladin and preserver, not as liar and cheat and revolutionary. Heroism, wrote Emerson, "is the state of the soul at war, and its ultimate objects are the last defiance of falsehood and wrong, and the power to bear all that can be inflicted by evil agents. It speaks the truth and it is just, generous, hospitable, temperate, scornful of petty calculations and scornful of being scorned." Mere courage is not enough. An Attila had courage — but it was the courage of the scourge and the vandal; St. Augustine, writing his great *City Of God* even while the barbarian thundered at the gates of Hippo, was the true hero. The courage of the weasel, wantonly slitting the throats of a score of hens, is not heroic; the courage of the beaver in the trap, gnawing off his foot to win freedom, *that* is heroic.

Heroism is the consecration to noble things, to the gracious and the true, to integrity. The hero protects the innocent and the helpless — the threatened forest, the kitten cold and hungry and lost, the great poet torn by the jackals of contemporary criticism. The hero stands firm, like the Guatemalan Colonel who saved his country from Communism only to be assassinated by a murderer planted among his bodyguards; like General Mikhailovitch who fought for the West only to be betrayed and shot. Long, long ago the Heroes of Asgard showed the Northmen courage, and kindness. The very gods are said to have fought against darkness, and frost giants, and the traitor Loki, and all that debased the life and nobility of men. St. George and Kings Alfred and Arthur were, equally, the paladins of good — whether seen as warring against the dragon, or the vandalizing Dane, or the anarchy of a dark land and a divided life. The whole history of our culture affirms that the hero is the soldier of God.

Around us today, as in the Alexandrine decay of great cultures into mere civilizations, there are many clever men, many "sophisticated" men, some of them brilliant; they bulk large in the world's eyes, and have reputation; they represent the fashionable opinions and conformities. Always they would tempt the hero to join them, offering him the kingdoms of this world. The true hero knows the danger of their kindness; the pseudo-hero accepts it. And the true hero, who is not of this age but of all ages, who is the seer of invisible realities, who is the champion of unfashionable faith, stands in perpetual opposition to the cleverest and the most knowledgeable and the most brilliant of them. He knows that the soldier of God is born not for peace but a sword; that he, who will not yield under the lightning, dare not rust under the rain.

Since he is what he is, the hero expects no fame or fortune in this world — he suspects from the beginning that his can be only the laurel of Heaven, the crown of the stars. He will likely find in the end, as Sebastian Juan Arbo wrote beautifully of the great Cervantes, that "they were all too busy to remember either Cervantes or his grave. They did not even find time — or the means — to erect a gravestone with a simple inscription. There is nothing to mark the spot where he is buried." But what does it matter? Is not Cervantes, after 350 years, yet one of the dead who steer the living? The cosmos is his tomb, and the stars his inscription. And when they buried him, they rightly set in his hands "a cross shaped like a sword."

It is well that there are such heroes even in our own day. Always, as is natural and right, they stand tall under the thunder. The Reverend Richard Wurmbrand, of the underground church in Romania, stamped down beneath the iron heel of the Communists, writes in *Today's Martyred Church* of such men:

> The following scene happened more times than I can remember: A brother was preaching to the other prisoners when the guard suddenly burst in, surprising him half way through a phrase. They hauled him down the corridor to the "beating room." After what seemed an endless beating, they brought him back and threw him — bloody and beaten — onto the prison floor. Slowly, he picked his battered body up, painfully straightened his clothing and said, "Now, brethren, where did I leave off when I was interrupted?"

The Reverend Wurmbrand tells of a pastor named Florescu who was tortured with knives . . . with iron pokers heated till they were red hot . . . who was beaten . . . who was shut in a cell into which starving rats were driven. The Communists demanded that he betray his brethren, but he steadfastly refused. Then they brought his only son, a boy of fourteen, into his cell; they began to brutalize the child before his eyes. At last, he felt he could no longer endure the sight of his tortured boy, and he cried out: "Alexander, I must say what they want! I can't bear any more your beating!" And the son – a teenager, a mere child – answered him, "Father, don't do me the iniustice to have a traitor as a parent. Withstand! If they kill me, I will die with the words 'Jesus and my fatherland.' " And then "the Communists, enraged, fell upon the child and beat him to death, with blood spattered over the walls of the cell. He died praising God." There is integrity. There is courage. There, by God, is the hero!

And in our own country, there are heroes too. The late Senator Joseph McCarthy stood almost alone – hated by the President and the chieftains of his own political Party, betrayed and abandoned by fellow Senators, unsung by the countrymen whom he had served, reviled and libeled in the Press, allowed to die under the most suspicious of circumstances in Bethesda Naval Hospital . . . yet he never faltered. Not even in the face of betrayal and death. John J. Shaughnessy ("Mr. Mark American") was similarly abandoned and dismissed, because he wished the generosity of his country known abroad; yet he never faltered. Otto Otepka, dismissed and thrown to the wolves because he fought to safeguard the security of America . . . . took the worst that America's enemies could hand out, yet he never failed or faltered. General George Smith Patton Jr., who won victory and glory for America, refused to stifle his vision and his faith, refused to placate the Communists, and so was deprived of the army he had led to victory and degraded by an Eisenhower who was afraid of his integrity. But Patton did not falter. Neither did General Douglas MacArthur, who refused to gag his convictions for the sake of political expediency at the hands of a mediocrity like Harry Truman, and took the thunder as he had taken the sunshine, a hero to the end.

We have had heroes! We have them yet. The question is whether the American people recognize them . . . whether America is worthy of them.

The greatest battlefield, of course, is not where the guns roar and the tanks roll; it lies in the mind and the soul. And *there* is where the hero is born. The crux of heroism may lie in a man's stillest hour, in the thought and the will that enhance the consciousness and the character of the soul. The greatest deed is to see and affirm the values and the qualities, the absolute essence and the eternal meaning. The greatest hero, always, is the Columbus of the soul, seeking Passage to India in the Inner Kingdom.

The distinguishing mark of the hero is that he does not dwell on the surface of things. He is not moved by "ideas" and "opinions" that belong to the hour. He descends and ascends into the real essence, the heart's blood, the uncompromising *potentia qua,* the way, the truth, the life. That is the difference between the journalist and the eternalist. The journalist is of the day and the hour; he flourishes in his own time (like the Quarterly Reviewers who laughed at Keats), and then − if he is remembered at all − it is only because he was the enemy of the hero, and is now held up to obloquy and scorn. The eternalist lives in the great daylight of Eternity, and so the owl-eyed night-creatures cannot see him as he is. But he will not die nor go away; he belongs to the great Life that knows no season.

Yet, as a man finds the great meaning which he must serve, and as he consecrates himself to its service, he does not talk about being a hero. Often he does not even know that he is one. "Who am I?" he asks. But he is one who has found the essence of life, the heart of the cosmos, and that is enough. Thus he can never be "bored" − he can never find time hard to kill, for he is busy making time live − he knows the perpetual dawn of life's sunrise and morning hour. And he pities the mariners of the Dead Sea, who churn the waters of bitter salt with futile oars, and spread vain sails that get them nowhere because (to them) there is nowhere to go, and who sing the dull sailors' chantey: *"The world's absurd, absurd, absurd!"*

In the hero's heart the birds of Eden sing, the sun is a golden lion, and love − because he loves and is loved − is eternal joy. Absurd? Not while a single flower opens its heart in beauty; while a single chipmunk, climbing atop the wall, flirts its tail for a furry roof; while the one woman for the one man gives herself, and takes him to herself, and lives in the bliss of union and loyalty; while the poet sees the glory of joy which is at its greatest in noble tragedy; while good bread and pure water delight the hungry mouth and the thirsty lips; while, as Mahomet saw, Paradise lies under the shadow of swords. Not while there are heroes who know that life is a great *I Am.*

As always, the current of such truths returns us to the Great

Truth. The greatest of heroes, of course, is God Himself. He, the Word that was in the beginning, became flesh and descended in that involution which is known as the incarnation.

Yet, as such, even He is still misinterpreted, under attack in the Age of the Anti-Hero. He is supposed to be merely "meek and mild" — He who said that the corrupters of children had better have a millstone tied about their necks and be drowned in the deepest sea . . . He who said He came to bring not peace but a sword . . . He who walked the waters and stilled the storm.

Yet, we are told by the cultists of the Anti-Hero that this God of ours, this Ultimate Hero to be debunked into a timid and bloodless prophet of weakness, faltered under His cross on the way to Calvary, so that it had to be borne by Simon of Cyrene. How they smirk at the very thought! And how little they know the God who fashions the oaks and sustains them even in the hurricane, who tosses the lightnings over the world, who spreads the stormy ocean . . . . and stills it. Falter under the cross? He who bears the redwoods in His hand? Rather, Christ the Ultimate Hero bore His cross like a standard, like a flag, like a banner, so proudly and so mightily that men gasped and feared and even the Roman legionaries were afraid. And so they took from Him the cross that was His banner; and said that He was too weak to bear it; and gave it to Simon the strong, who bent beneath its weight.

And even on the cross itself, under the lightning-anguish and the worst tortures of death, He spoke to His Mother and gave her a second son, and said to the Thief who repented: "This night shalt thou be with Me in Paradise," and roared unto the heavens, "Father, into Thy hands!"

Was there ever hero like to this — in courage, in integrity, in faith, in greatness? This gladiator of God, this Soldier who *is* God? No wonder that still, by His power, even the people of tortured Russia are won over and die for Him! No wonder that He still walks the waters; that still He says "Can ye drink of the cup that I drink of?"; that still He not only lives that the world may be, He dies that the world may live, and is resurrected again and again.

Here is the inspiration of heroes; here *is* The Hero. Here, with us in our agony and our joy, here in us, and yet beyond us and above us, is The Hero who was, and is, and ever shall be; the living Christ who speaks the eternal *I Am that I Am!*

This is the great strength that inspires us and comforts us and sustains us. God Himself descended into the world to bear the worst that we can bear, to affirm the faith that in our lesser and minor way we would affirm, to show us by example that even we may dare to seek to be the hero. And the mystery and wonder of it, the comfort of it, is this: Though He was God, He took upon Himself the flesh and the limitations of man, so that He could truly suffer as we suffer, and experience pain and death as we experience them, and never insulate Himself in divinity. He bore what He bids us bear. Would you understand the hero? *Sursum corda!* — let your heart look upward!

C.S. Lewis:

A Gladiator Of God

CAESAR used to throw Christians to the lions; today he throws them to the "Liberals." But even in our day there arose a gladiator of God, superb with the armor of reason, magnificent with the sword of style, a soldier of the Lord who made lightnings in the sun and routed "Liberals" . . . or lions . . . like a rabble of shadows. He was the Christian whose name was Clive Staples Lewis.

C.S. Lewis, physically, is dead: But as Frank Harris said, "We are immortal only when we die. It is the dead who steer the living." Never was Lewis more alive; never was he more potent; never was he more surely the helmsman of the future. For he is a timeless spokesman of that which is beyond time; a champion of sanity and freedom. The Bertrand Russells and the Jean-Paul Sartres *were*; C.S. Lewis *is*. He was and is the paladin of the great *I Am*.

It was C.S. Lewis who spoke the powerful phrase that essentially reveals and delineates the predicament of contemporary man, that essentially defines the catastrophe of modernity. He called it "The Abolition of Man," and chose it as the title for one of his major books. In that volume, he says, thinking of "Liberalism," of "rationalism," of collectivism — and of their modes and tones and ends —

> But you cannot go on "explaining away" for ever: you will find that you have explained explanation itself away. You cannot go on "seeing through" things for ever. The whole point of seeing through something is to see something through it. It is good that the window be transparent, because the street or garden beyond it is opaque. How if you saw through the garden too? It is no use trying to "see through" first principles. If you see through everything, then everything is transparent. But a wholly transparent world is an invisible world. To "see through" all things is the same as not to see.

And that is the abolition of man . . . that is the abolition of the world . . . and that is where the thin albino nihilism of the modern mind is bringing us. May we, with C.S. Lewis, cease to "see through" – *and begin to see*! Only thus will we initiate the renaissance (not the abolition!) of man.

Meanwhile, as Lewis says in this same splendid book:

> The process which, if not checked, will abolish man, goes on apace among Communists and Democrats no less than among Fascists . . . . many a mild-eyed scientist in pince-nez, many a popular dramatist, many an amateur philosopher in our midst, means in the long run just the same as the Nazi rulers of Germany. Traditional values are to be "debunked" and mankind to be cut out into some fresh shape . . . . *

Thus are "ideologies" to be invented at pleasure, and all men to be treated as "specimens," and so Man will be "abolished" as man.

But C.S. Lewis is not abolished; he remains. Of what are such men made?

Lewis's great spiritual autobiography – *Surprised By Joy*† – is his Pilgrim's Progress, his safari in search of Heaven, through disappointments and losses and detours, till at last he found what he had sought as a subjective mood, now become an objective reality. There he writes:

> Inexorably Joy proclaimed, "You want – I myself am your want of – something other, outside, not you nor any state of you." I did not ask, Who is the desired? only, What is it? But this brought me already into the region of awe, for I thus understood that in deepest solitude there is a road right out of the self, a commerce with something which, by refusing to identify itself with any object of the senses, or anything whereof we have biological or social need, or anything imagined, or any state of our own minds, proclaims itself sheerly objective. Far more objective than bodies, for it is not, like them, clothed in our senses; the naked Other, imageless (though our imagination salutes it with a hundred images), unknown, undefined, desired.

Brilliantly Lewis goes on, "it matters more that Heaven should exist than that we should ever get there." *For if it does not exist, no one can ever get there . . . and the world that hungers for joy is (then) a vanity of vanities.*

Thus does Lewis describe the experience that came, as Lewis says,

---

*The Abolition Of Man, C.S. Lewis, The Macmillan Company, New York, 1947.
†Surprised By Joy, C.S. Lewis, Harcourt, Brace, and World, New York, 1956.

"before God closed in on me." He had been an atheist — or at least an agnostic — desiring the mood of joy without the substance of joy; the freedom of thought without the ground of freedom; the subjective mood without the objective mode. Surprised at last by the Joy that he had always sought (only to lose), C.S. Lewis now found it. And how?

> Really, a young Atheist cannot guard his faith too carefully. Dangers lie in wait for him on every side. You must not do, you must not try to do, the will of our Father unless you are prepared to "know of the doctrine." All my acts, desires, and thoughts were to be brought into harmony with universal Spirit. For the first time I examined myself with a seriously practical purpose. And there I found what appalled me; a zoo of lusts, a bedlam of ambitions, a nursery of fears, a harem of fondled hatred. My name was legion.

That is, he did what is the beginning of victory — but which the typical "modern" never does: he applied realism to *himself*, and saw there the original sin which is the heritage of Man from Adam. And that meant that only as man reached up and touched more than man could he find the salvation of joy. In Lewis's magnificent phrase, "if Shakespeare and Hamlét could ever meet, it must be Shakespeare's doing." And in the desolation of what Lewis saw himself to be, he heard the substance of Reality say: "I am the Lord"; "I Am that I Am"; "I Am." Shakespeare entered his own play and spoke face to face with Hamlet!

And so C.S. Lewis became a Christian.

And, once he found the firm ground of reality objective beneath his feet, the power and the glory of God flowed through him in great books. Already a brilliant scholar, already a great teacher, he became more — a philosopher and artist. In such a book as *Miracles*,* he became like the drowning Peter who suddenly could walk upon the dark waters of "modernity." There he sees that there is a door into the Subnatural . . . and a door into the Supernatural.

In *Miracles* Lewis sees and says that *if* all is matter, and chaos, and what we may call *irrationality*, then there can be no reason and no knowledge. "The whole disruptive power of Marxism and Freudian-ism against traditional beliefs has lain in their claim to expose irra-tional causes for them." But if you expose *all* as irrational — if there

---

*Miracles, C.S. Lewis, The Macmillan Company, New York, 1947.

is *nothing* in roots but tentacles of matter — then you expose yourself and your own "thinking" as irrational, as unfounded except in nonsense and absurdity; and whatever you say is "sound and fury, signifying nothing." Unless there is the granite of earth, and the core of living fire beneath even that — unless there is an absolute world of value, quality, and meaning — unless there is a world of mind that transcends matter and a world of Reason and Right that transcends flux and whim — all we can have is not philosophy but random whim and subjective whimsy. A transcendent absolute is the basis for all thought.

With the substratum and objectivity of the Supernatural as the necessary ground of all thought, Lewis is ready to discuss miracles. As he says: "Nature can only raid Reason to kill; but Reason can raid Nature to take prisoners and even to colonize."

> Every object you see before you at this moment — the walls, ceiling, and furniture, the book, your own washed hands and cut finger-nails, bears witness to the colonisation of Nature by Reason: for none of this matter would have been in these states if Nature had had her way.

And if this is so — and Nature bears witness to it, for the Mayan City, or the White Horse carved on English cliffs, or the science built up through patient centuries, perish and pass once Reason fails and ceases, and Nature and matter relapse into primal formlessness — then our salvation, *no, even our very existence,* depends upon the door that opens from *beyond* Nature, the door into Supernature. This world can *exist* only by a world beyond this world!

Since this is so, why wonder at miracles? Miracles do not "break" the patterns that we call "laws" — they *fulfill* them in a way not "caused" by what lies antecedent, but initiated by the direct intervention of the Supernature (that *usually* works in slower rhythms). Thus: "In calling them miracles we do not mean that they are contradictions or outrages; we mean that, left to her own resources, she [*Nature*] could never produce them." How truthfully Lewis says, "only Supernaturalists really see Nature. You must go a little away from her, and then turn around, and look back. Then at last true landscape will become visible."

Miracles are supernatural — and therefore natural. (Once you see the universe as it is, with many mansions, and levels that transcend and yet intersect, and the *potentia qua* of God.) They are the events that compress and telescope the processes of time into the action of Eternity.

The way to see them is the way Lewis sees them. "In science we have been reading only the notes to a poem; in Christianity we find the poem itself." And so:

> I contend that in all these miracles alike the incarnate God [*Christ*] does suddenly and locally something that God has done or will do in general. Each miracle does for us in small letters something that God has already written, or will write, in letters almost too large to be noticed, across the whole canvas of Nature.

And to illustrate:

> Every year, as part of the natural order, God makes wine. He does so by creating a vegetable organism that can turn water, soil and sunshine into a juice which will, under proper conditions, become wine. Thus, in a certain sense, He constantly turns water into wine, for wine, like all drinks, is but water modified. Once, and in one year only, God, now incarnate, short circuits the process: makes wine in a moment: uses earthenware jars instead of vegetable fibres to hold the water. But uses them to do what He is always doing. The Miracle consists in the short cut; but the event to which it leads is the unual one.

Once you see this, *you know that it is so*; you know that it is reasonable; it leaps at you from that buried (but now remembered) truth that, as Plato says, you have always known.

Such are "the Miracles of the Old Creation." Thus God *always* multiplies the wheat or the fishes to feed the many millions, working in and through Nature. But *once,* God incarnate worked directly from Supernature, and performed the Miracle of the Loaves and Fishes, for the five thousand. God stills every storm; but once, God incarnate stilled by His word the one storm. God is behind all healing, as every great doctor knows; but once, God incarnate did in an instant what He does always through time. "The Power that always was behind all healings puts on a face and hands." Thus seen, miracles become God doing by sudden command what God is always doing by the gracious patterns that take time.

But there are also "the Miracles of the New Creation." Here God incarnate, "the ultimate Fact, the fountain of all other facthood, the burning and undimensioned depth of the Divine life," is creating out of the old Nature a new Super-Nature, a new Adam, a new Man, and a new world . . . . Granted the Super-natural, without which there is no basis for Reason or Right, and that is possible; and (according to the Gospels) actual.

And Lo! — Nature that today has been debased into "realism" by those who worship "matter" and "mechanism," suddenly becomes alive and joyous . . . a music, a poem, a dance, a splendid charger for paladins to ride beyond time (as we know it) and space (as we misconceive it). By Miracle and the Supernatural, we *regain* law and pattern and Nature. Our name is Lazarus — and we live!

Miracles, indeed, is a book so fundamental and so great that until we have read and absorbed it we are prisoners of modernity, chained in the Siberia of the contemporary world; blind men who boast of sight, deaf men who scoff at the fugues of Bach.

The Screwtape Letters are perhaps Lewis's most popular book, and they are very good. Here he imagines the mentality of Hell, in the mind of a clever Devil who writes to another sub-Devil named Wormwood. Lewis beautifully says, in his Preface, "My symbol for Hell is something like the bureaucracy of a police state or a thoroughly nasty business office." Out of such a Hell, Screwtape speaks — clever, "Intellectual," "Liberal," modern.

How clever a Devil — and how reminiscent of so much today, including my friends of the Friends' Service Committee, is this: "The great thing is to direct the malice to his immediate neighbors whom he meets every day and to thrust his benevolence out to the remote circumference, to people he does not know." Of course! Hate Americans — and love the Vietcong! Hate "Whitey" — and love Castro or Mao Tse-tung!

And how modern is Screwtape. He wishes to destroy Christ by the modern trick of making Him seem "a 'great man' in the modern sense of the word — one standing at the terminus of some centrifugal and unbalanced line of thought — a crank vending a panacea." And he brilliantly sees the poison of the "Social Gospel" — "The thing to do is to get a man at first to value social justice as a thing which the Enemy [*Christ*] demands, and then work him on to the stage at which he values Christianity because it may produce social justice. For the Enemy will not be used as a convenience. Men or nations who think they can revive the Faith in order to make a good society might just as well think they can use the stairs of Heaven as a short cut to the nearest chemist's shop."

And how patently he sees into the perversion of modernity! — The Christian, Screwtape says, "so far as I can see, wants men to ask very simple questions: 'Is it righteous? Is it prudent? Is it possible?' Now, if we [*the Devil*] can keep men asking: 'Is it in accordance with the general movement of our time? Is it progressive or reactionary? Is this the way that History is going?' they will neglect the relevant questions." Screwtape speaks the essence of the modern debacle thus: He wants to spread the cumulative heresies that "edge the man away from the Light and out into the Nothing."

It is a book of delicious wisdom, of sly and profound insights into the modes of the *Insiders,* of a lambent humor playing over the dull gravity that is the distinguishing characteristic of every Commissar — and Devil. Read the book! And, for yourself, thrust in your thumb . . . the plums are many, and they are delicious.

To C.S. Lewis, "Liberal" Christianity is "Christianity and water." He says: "Liberal Christianity can only supply an ineffectual echo to the massive chorus of agreed and admitted unbelief." And "education" ("Liberal" education, "modern" education) cuts man's roots that should feed from the rich soil of history, and "every generation off from all others," lest the "characteristic errors of one may be corrected by the characteristic truths of another," and starves the mind and soul "for solitude, silence, and privacy . . . "and (therefore) "for meditation and friendship." To him, modern education — and materialistic "science" — resembles the fare of voyagers in the old days. It is all dry biscuits and salt beef, with never a lime or an orange; and naturally the result is *intellectual scurvy*.

To Lewis, government, the news media, and society, are modes used by the Dark Powers for the abolition of man. And he adds (how prophetically!), "And those who resist conformity increasingly tend to become prigs and cranks who have a sinister pride in being a deviationist, an attitude equally fatal to finding God." For collectivism of all sorts — Communism, Fascism, "Liberal" democracy — he has a distaste that is total abhorrence. Through the ravages and perversions of "Liberal" Christianity, "modern" education, the State in league with "science," collectivism, rationalism, and all their allies, man is today a random and rootless creature, a cut flower withering in a vase of fluoridated water . . . . This is the most just and true appraisal of the world today that we have in modern literature.

It is beautifully summed up by Ransom in Lewis's *Perelandra*:

The poison was brewed in these West lands but it has spat itself everywhere by now. However far you went you would find the machines, the crowded cities, the empty thrones, the false writings, the barren beds; men maddened with false promises and soured with true miseries, worshipping the iron works of their own hands, cut off from Earth their mother and the Father in Heaven . . . . The shadow of one dark wing is over all Tellus.

As this great passage suggests, C.S. Lewis sees earth and man as the prey of a Great Conspiracy. But it is a Conspiracy greater and deeper than many or most of us imagine! It is not a conspiracy *only* of the political *Insiders,* of such as the modern Illuminists or members of the Council on Foreign Relations, of the spider-men of economics and politics; all these exist as agents, but their instigators and masters are far more sinister, far greater and deeper. The *Insiders* are moved and "inspired" by the Dark Powers, by Lucifer and his Children, who would spite God by perverting earth and man: Spiritual Forces and Powers of Evil that conspire to ruin and wreck, to negate and destroy. Our battle is vaster than we know. It is as deep as Hell and as high as Heaven.

Ours, then, is a Holy War against an Unholy Evil, whose field of war is earth, and all the stars, and the heart of darkness that is in man, and life and death. And the hope of man, and the possible victory of man, lie in the immortal Heart of Light, and the "something sending up the sun" that opposes eternally the "shadow of one dark wing." To Lewis, collectivism and modernity are manifestations of the vast Powers of the Shadow — that conspire to blot out the suns.

Such a book as his *That Hideous Strength* reveals and realizes this spiritual conspiracy in a way that is one of the clearest and the fullest that I have ever known. The Conspiracy is insidious; it is sinister and ruthless; it works by indirection and nuances toward the victory of darkness and the lie. All champions of God who work for the salvation of man should read it, to understand how in education, in religion, in life, the Dark Powers work. Not so great a work of art as *Out Of The Silent Planet* or the incomparable *Perelandra,* it is splendidly valuable in its revelation of the methodology of Evil.

In *Out Of The Silent Planet* Lewis anticipates the space ship. But it is a ship spawned by the Dark Powers in union with a Professor Weston (the "Liberal" intellectual and scientist). The object of the space voyage is to explore another planet, ravage its inhabitants (the fascinating *hrossa* and the wise *sorns*), and find a way of keeping "humanity" and the race of man materially "alive." The invaded planet (with the ancient name of Malacandra) is Mars. There the space ship of Professor Weston and the evil exploiter, Devine, lands to explore and destroy. With them they bear Ransom, the champion of God, kidnapped from Thulcandra (Earth). And on that planet a war between Good and Evil rages, until Weston is finally defeated and returned to Thulcandra by the Oyarsa, or planetary spirit, of Malacandra.

It is a beautiful and haunting book. It is full of vistas of insight, realizations of possible planetary life as yet unspoiled by the creeping anemia of The Fall, and inhabited by creatures so fascinating that one longs to live among them. Yet always it is *real*, because it speaks the essentials of life and death, absolute and eternal.

Yet, to me, the greatest of Lewis's space tales is *Perelandra*.* In this book, Ransom (notice the symbolism of the name) is chosen to go to Perelandra (the planet Venus), that is still in the unspoiled state of Eden. It has been invaded by Professor Weston, the agent of Lucifer, who seeks to tempt its Queen and Lady-Mother, *i.e.*, its Eve, as the Serpent once tempted our Eve. Here is the greatest of spiritual dramas: — Will Perelandra choose His will and joy, or will it follow earth into corruption and The Fall? Ransom versus Weston! — one the servant of God, one the agent of the Bent Will, the Un-Man. For, beyond Weston, there *is* the terrible Un-Man, the incarnation of sheer essential absolute evil . . . .

Ransom has argued with Weston in the presence of the Eve of this new world, and the issue hangs in doubt. Suddenly Ransom knows that, for him, *words are not enough.* There is a battle to *fight,* an enemy to *kill.* (Lewis in all his work, as in his life, made it very clear that he was not a pacifist, that ideas have consequences, that ideas made flesh must be met on the plane of flesh.) This, to Ransom, is an agony and a struggle. Should he kill; can he kill? He is not a trained fighter and the Un-Man is terrible with metaphysical power. Ransom loathes descending to the plane of physical battle. What should he do? What can he do? And then the Voice out of the silence speaks to him — and reminds him that his name is *Ransom* . . . and that he has been chosen to decide for time and eternity the fate of a planet. Thus he closes in deadly *physical* battle with the Un-Man . . . .

Perelandra, C.S. Lewis, Macmillan Paperbacks Edition, Macmillan Co., New York, 1965. All three of the Lewis space tales are available in this edition.

Ransom comes upon the Un-Man tearing a beautiful bird to tatters, and bids him stop. Then:

> "But this is very foolish," said the Un-Man. "Do you know who I am?"
> "I know what you are," said Ransom. "Which of them doesn't matter."
> "And you think, little one, that you can fight with me? You think He will help you, perhaps? Many thought that. I've known Him longer than you, little one. They all think He's going to help them — till they come to their senses screaming recantations too late in the middle of the fire, mouldering in concentration camps, writhing under saws, jibbering in mad-houses, or nailed on to crosses. Could He help Himself?" — and the creature suddenly threw back its head and cried in a voice so loud it seemed the golden sky-roof must break, *"Eloi, Eloi, lama sabachthani."*

And yet Ransom, knowing that the fate of a planet depends upon him, closes with the Adversary:

> The energy of hating, never before felt without some guilt, without some dim knowledge that he was failing fully to distinguish the sinner from the sin, rose into his arms and legs till he felt that they were pillars of burning blood. What was before him appeared no longer a creature of corrupted will. It was corruption itself to which will was attached only as an instrument. Ages ago it had been a Person: but the ruins of personality now survived in it only as weapons at the disposal of a furious self-exiled negation. It is perhaps difficult to understand why this filled Ransom not with horror but with a kind of joy. The joy came from finding at last what hatred was made for. As a boy with an axe rejoices on finding a tree, or a boy with a box of coloured chalks rejoices on finding a pile of perfectly white paper, so he rejoiced in the perfect congruity between his emotions and its object. Bleeding and trembling with weariness as he was, he felt that nothing was beyond his power, and when he flung himself upon the living Death, the eternal Surd in the universal mathematics, he was astonished, and yet (on a deeper level) not astonished at all, at his own strength. His arms seemed to move quicker than his thoughts. His hands taught him terrible things. He felt its ribs break, he heard its jawbone crack. The whole creature seemed to be crackling and splitting under his blows. His own pain, where it tore him, somehow failed to matter. He felt that he could so fight, so hate with a perfect hatred, for a whole year.

And at last — O miracle! — the Un-man fled, torn, bleeding, defeated. He pursues it, casts it into the great void . . . and, when Weston too dies, the new planet is saved from corruption and The Fall.

And afterwards, Ransom meets the Lady Queen and the King, whom by word and deed he had saved from The Fall. He meets, too, the strange and magical planetary spirits of other worlds, gathered to celebrate his victory. He listens to their voices that turn speech into the beauty of wisdom. They speak of the Great Dance, of the Eternal Music, of the Poem of Creation that is in Him, and for the joy of all worlds and creatures. You must read it; it is too long to quote. And yet a little here, a little there:

> And another said, "It is loaded with justice as a tree bows down with fruit. All is righteousness and there is no equality. Not as when stones lie side by side, but as when stones support and are supported in an arch, such is His order; rule and obedience, begetting and bearing, heat glancing down, life growing up. Blessed be He!"
>
> *   *   *
>
> "All that is made seems planless to the darkened mind, because there are more plans than it looked for. In the seas there are islands where the hairs of the turf are so fine and so closely woven together that unless a man looked long at them he would see neither hairs nor weaving at all, but only the same and the flat. So with the great Great Dance. Set your eyes on one movement and it will lead you through all patterns and it will seem to you the master movement. But the seeming will be true. Let no mouth open to gainsay it. There seems no plan because it is all plan: there seems no centre because it is all centre. Blessed be He!"

This verbal music played for what is called "the Great Dance" is superlative in rhythm and supreme in meaning: It is one of the most beautiful things in modern literature.

This is a book which, if it were used in courses of literature in colleges, might help to end the abolition of man and begin the renaissance of man. But it will not, at present, in the English courses we now have, so be used. And therefore we have the students who blindly revolt because they blindly long for the wisdom from which they are separated.

Such is *Perelandra,* the epic of a planet's salvation, and of the Great Dance of all worlds and creatures and souls who obey the Will that is our joy!

We must not think that C.S. Lewis found life easy or faith cheap. Marrying late in life (and most happily), he had to watch his wife die of cancer. He himself, at the height of his powers, with new fields of work opening radiantly before him, had slowly to die because of the mistake of a doctor. He had to renounce invitations to speak and write, he saw noble doors of earthly hope closed to him, he faced too early the death that takes at last our mortal flesh . . . . He knew the Gethsemane of the soul, the question: "My God, my God, why hast thou forsaken me?"

But in the face of death, as in the glory of life, C.S. Lewis remained steadfast to the end, saying (as a Christian must) "Thy will be done, on earth as it is in Heaven." One can trust Lewis all the more just because he was so tested, and because he stood steadfast like the oaktree in the storm. The Gladiator of God, he said "Hosanna to Life, Hosanna to Death! Blessed be the name of the Lord!"

G.K. Chesterton:
Fighting To The Hilt Of The Sword

UNLIKE such sons of the wind and chaff of the early 1900s as Bernard Shaw and H.G. Wells, Rudyard Kipling and Gilbert Keith Chesterton stand ever taller and ever greater. Kipling and Chesterton were different in their subjects and their art, in their emphases, in their philosophy; they often were opposed (as about Kipling's supposed "imperialism"); but they both stood with the God of things as they are — for the qualities and values that endure and abide, and for the meaning of a world that is not meaningless. In this respect they were both conservatives — that is, they fought to preserve and conserve the things that are excellent, the realities that have endured, the bases that, beyond time, are eternal.

I wrote in AMERICAN OPINION for January of 1969 about Kipling. I write now of G.K. Chesterton — to try to discover and disclose the things that make him, for those of us who face the Seventies, a champion of the power and the glory of conservatism. And perhaps a verse from what I believe the greatest poem of our time, his *The Ballad Of The White Horse,* may suggest something of why:

> But some see God like Guthrum
> Crowned, with a great beard curled,
> But I see God like a good giant,
> That, laboring, lifts the world.

Much as I admire Chesterton, I could not for a moment see him as a usurper of the place of God. Not that! But I do see him as a good giant (and he was, physically, a giant) laboring to create and to sustain a living world of sanity and freedom. He was a magnificent artist and philosopher; and, as such, he was a good giant who supported the world amid the stars.

I

THE FIRST thing to say about Chesterton is what he says himself

160

in that early and brilliant book, *Heretics*. There he points out that an "enormous and silent evil of modern society" — and how super-true this is today! — is its gross pride in being "heretical," its crass pride in not being "orthodox." Rebels, he says, against ancient emperors or kings, against the Babylons of this world, against the Insiders of the world's Establishments, did not call themselves "heretics." No, *they* were the *orthodox*! For orthodoxy simply means "straight thought"; it means that one does not conform, but *confirms* — by the stars in their courses, the reality of two plus two that are four, the laws and rules set in Nature by God, the absolutes and eternals, of reality. Chesterton stated and restated the fundamental truth that, first of all, we must have *light*; that we cannot think except from right premises; that his philosophy is the most important thing about any man. First — *light*! First a philosophy that is orthodox; *i.e.*, that is straight and true. That is basic in Chesterton, and that is the basis of conservatism.

In *Heretics* he makes this beautifully clear. One finds there a passage that should be the creed of all colleges:

> Suppose that a great commotion arises in the street about something, let us say a lamp-post, which many influential persons desire to pull down. A grey-clad monk, who is the spirit of the Middle Ages, is approached upon the matter, and begins to say, in the arid manner of the Schoolmen, "Let us first of all, my brethren, consider the value of Light. If Light be in itself good — " At this point he is somewhat excusably knocked down. All the people make a rush for the lamp-post, the lamp-post is down in ten minutes, and they go about congratulating each other on their unmediaeval practicality. But as things go on they do not work out so easily. Some people have pulled the lamp-post down because they wanted the electric light; some because they wanted darkness, because their deeds were evil. Some thought it not enough of a lamp-post, some too much; some acted because they wanted to smash municipal machinery; some because they wanted to smash something. And there is war in the night, no man knowing whom he strikes.

How perfect a criticism of the mindless rage of the New Left, of the insistent, arrogant, established heresies (which are conformities) of the "Liberals'" and *Insiders*, of the ignorant armies that clash in the night of our day! We can begin the slow, terrible, seemingly impossible, but essentially fundamental renaissance of sanity *here*. Consider essentials; seek the primal *light*: find a philosophy that is parallel with the straight lines of the universe — find *orthodoxy*.

That is a primary emphasis in Chesterton, and it underlies all his work. By it he criticized the heresies of his day. Yet, we too may hope to find that living orthodoxy — by its light, patiently and rationally, to criticize the heresies of *our* day.

II

ANOTHER of Chesterton's beautifully fascinating books is his *Tremendous Trifles*. The title suggests the philosophy. To Chesterton, as to the true conservative always, the rich "trifles" of life — the sunrise and the sunset, the skies and the chalk cliffs, the everyday adventures of seeing flowers and meeting people, the wonders of the world — are indeed "tremendous." The sons of power — the *Insiders* of the Establishment — do not know this, or want to know it. They want money, they want power, they want crafty ways of establishing themselves; but the simple, and natural, and beautiful, and vital things that are "tremendous" for life, to them are "trifles."

Chesterton at the beginning of this book imagines two boys in a garden, Peter and Paul, to whom a good fairy comes and offers to each a single wish. Paul wishes to be a physical *giant*; and he becomes a giant. So he goes blundering over the world, seeking for power and dominion and the thrills thereof; but he is so huge that the Himalayas seem molehills to him, and Niagara "no bigger than the tap turned on in the bathroom." The world seems to him small, it bores him; he worships power and size, which destroy the values of the world. And at last the giant Paul lies down on seven prairies, and has his head chopped off because he is "out of proportion to the universe."

That is the parable — let us hope — of the giant Establishments!

But Peter is wiser. He wishes to be — a pygmy. That is, he wishes humility, and wonder, and a world made ever larger and richer, and not the worship of his own size and power. And to him the very grass becomes forests of adventure, and a rock garden Himalayas to climb, and flowers like trees with hearts like suns. The world is a perpetual wonder, for there is wonder and humility and romance in his heart, and everywhere he finds quality and value not in material riches or political power — but in the world enriched by his own heart. And the only way out of the evil world of the *Insiders* and the raucous world of the New Left, is the way of Chesterton — to find the world a wonder full of Tremendous Trifles.

I try to read *Tremendous Trifles* every spring. I marvel with Chesterton at what he "found in his pocket"; at his discovery (when on an outing and needing chalk to draw pictures) that he was on one of the chalk cliffs of England; that somehow financiers in banks, and postmen who serve the State, don't *sing* . . . but men *ought* to sing at their work; that the wise forgotten man in England (seeing convicts on a special car of a train) is neither a "Liberal" humanitarian nor a brutal "flog-the-brutes" fellow; at the two voices — one that sings England's doom, and (the other) England's glory . . . . It is a beautiful book, that *should* be read every year. It enriches the world, it revitalizes the life within us that makes the world without us great with quality, value, and meaning. It touches earth with the magic of Heaven, and so makes earth more real.

As Chesterton says: "Earth will never fail for lack of wonders, but only for lack of wonder."

Many of the best of Chesterton's books are full of short essays in literary criticism, like *Varied Types*. I know no better insight than his, there, into the crotchety iconoclasms of Tolstoi. And how great he is about Rostand, St. Francis, and Savonarola! How marvelous for our shallow, brash rebels, these words: "To let no bird fly past unnoticed, to spell patiently the stones and weeds, to have the mind a storehouse of sunset, requires a discipline in pleasure and an education in gratitude." The whole essay is a masterly diagnosis of the sickness of the modern world.

A central and noble book is Chesterton's *Orthodoxy*. In this he says: "The thing I propose to take as a common ground between myself and every average reader, is the desirability of an active and imaginative life, picturesque and full of a poetical curiosity, a life such as western man at any rate always seems to have desired . . . . We need so to view the world as to combine an idea of wonder and an idea of welcome."

Chesterton seeks, in *Orthodoxy*, a key that fits and opens the lock of reason, so that, when the door opens, the complexities and paradoxes of the world fall into a pattern of order. Materialism and mechanism never give such a world. But a world of life, where God is both immanent and transcendent, does. This is a world of "wonder and welcome," a world where paradoxes add up to reason, a world where complexities become a pattern like the picture by a great artist. This is orthodoxy.

As an example, take our attitude toward the world. We should love the world, we should be patriots to earth. But if we blindly accept the world and its ways, if we in blind and literal subservience accept the world as it is, we soon find ourselves accepting evils, tyrants, monstrosities, things gone crooked with man's original sin, mad Establishments, and "social" orders that cannot be called noble or high. *But* if we realize that beyond the world there is the Creator, and a transcendent order that gives life to, and yet is greater than, "the world" of here and now, we can be both patriots to earth and life and yet critics of and rebels against "the world" – *i.e.*, the Establishments, the *Insiders*, the Heresies into which the original sin in men's hearts lead us and others. The paradox is clear. The complexity is resolved into a harmony.

Even so the militancy and the gentleness of the Christian is made a harmony, in a way that neither a Nietzsche nor a Tolstoi can ever resolve it. For example, think of Joan of Arc. She fought, while Nietzsche *talked* of fighting; but was anyone ever gentler than she? She was a peasant, and knew poverty and the burdens of the earth, as Tolstoi never really could; but she did not make the mere peasant an ideal. So orthodoxy embraces complexities and resolves paradoxes, and gives us "an active and imaginative life, picturesque and full of poetical curiosity." It is the philosophy Chesterton speaks of in *Heretics*; it is the philosophy he exemplifies in *Tremendous Trifles*.

For Chesterton's view of history and the place of religion and of Christ therein, one must read *The Everlasting Man*, a book too rich with truth and meaning, a book too formidable with power, to allow even narrow treatment here. You must *read* it!

III

ONE of the delightful things about Chesterton is his variety. He writes, for example, *detective* stories – a favorite form of literature with me – that are classics. There is Poe, of course, with his Dupin – and his almost mathematical precision of psychology and of analytical logic. There is Conan Doyle, with his forever memorable Sherlock Holmes. But even with these Chesterton can hold his own. The Father Brown stories, especially the early ones of the "innocence" and the "wisdom" of Father Brown, are classics.

Chesterton's little Catholic priest, round like a dumpling, seemingly quiet and nondescript, is a modest fountain of insight and wisdom. Because he deals intimately with the sins of man, he knows the secrets of the heart of man. Here is detection that is not merely logical or brilliantly clever, here is insight into evil and into good, into the soul, and a motivation and a revelation that go to the roots of the heart of man and so of the world. Here are stories where, it seems, the Hound of Heaven is on the track of the soul, and there is the beauty of vision and meaning.

These are stories where the mystery yields insight into the moral or spiritual nature of the world and the soul. Yet they are so rich in style, so free in vision, so touched with humor (a great virtue in Chesterton), so brilliant in narrative, that you absorb philosophy as you absorb sunlight on a clear day, with innocence and joy and aesthetic delight.

And of course there is his poetry. Chesterton, in a poem or two, is the supreme poet of our time. *The Ballad Of The White Horse!* "Lepanto"! These are *tours de force* of genius, sudden smiting masterpieces. Color, imagery, clangor of music, romance bringing reality to life, originality that never was before or since by land or sea, depth of insight into history and life, all these are the sun-stuff and the moon-stuff of these great poems. The splendid rush (as of galloping horses, as of eagles outstripping the wind) in "Lepanto" is an experience no man can forget. Take the lines where Mahomet speaks:

> "But a noise is in the mountains, in the mountains, and I know
> The voice that shook our palaces four hundred years ago;
> It is he that saith not 'Kismet'; it is he that knows not Fate;
> It is Richard, it is Raymond, it is Godfrey at the gate!
> It is he whose loss is laughter when he counts the wager worth,
> Put down your feet upon him, that our peace be on the earth."
> For he heard drums groaning and he heard guns jar,
> (Don John of Austria is riding to the war.)
> Sudden and still — hurrah!
> Bolt from Iberia!
> Don John of Austria
> Is gone by Alcalar.

One can read "Lepanto" a hundred times, and every time it will be a greater experience. A richer joy.

But Chesterton's supreme poetical triumph is *The Ballad Of the White Horse.* The two English historical figures who rise into epic and myth are Arthur and Alfred. Here Chesterton chooses Alfred. He makes Alfred the statesman, philosopher, and Christian; and he projects him against the Old Left of violence, of nihilism, of destruction — the Danes. It is for us, as we read, a sort of parable of our own situation today. We, like Alfred, stand for a world where grain might be golden in the fields and apples crimson upon the trees, where men might write wise books on vellum, where man might live in the wonder of humility and the wisdom that is joy. But the wild Danes break in — nihilists, destroyers, the bearers of violence and power — to lay waste. And even the songs that they sing have a snake of venom in the very music.

Beaten, hunted, seemingly hopeless, Alfred (and this is the historical Alfred) fights on, fights on . . . as we do; he finds the word to rouse and unite the great creative peoples of Britain — Mark, the Roman; and Eldred, the Saxon; and Colan, the Celt. He wins them spiritually with the great word that the Mother of God gives him, the word that must always be the word of the great who timelessly fight the evil of nihilism and the world's nihilists:

> "I tell you nought for your comfort,
> Yea, nought for your desire,
> Save that the sky grows darker yet
> And the sea rises higher."

Free men, brave men, then and now, know the terror of the struggle, and yet stand and press on, because they know "The joy of giants, the joy without a cause." They know, that is, the very roots of the spiritual mountains whence cometh their strength . . . the spiritual world, the power of God.

So through magical episodes — the marshalling of Roman, Saxon, Celt; the burning of the old farm woman's cake; the songs the Danes sing, and that Alfred, disguised among them, also sings . . . we revel in poetry unequalled in our time. And so we come at last to the epic battle, the battle of Ethandune. I will not spoil it by trying to tell it. Read it!

And in the temporary peace that follows victory, Alfred foresees (through Chesterton) the New Danes of a later day (our day) — the nihilists of mind and spirit, the destroyers that raged in his day and that rage so much more terribly today. He warns of them; he describes them; he foresees the enemies of man and God. It is a great revelation of the danger of the spiritual destroyers.

And one thing that is fundamental to conservatism emerges. There is the great White Horse that from time immemorial men have made by plucking out the grass and leaving the great, bare, chalk hill clear and distinct in the shape of a great and beautiful horse. Of this Alfred says that, when he was young and inexperienced, he thought that evil could, like the encroaching grass, be defeated *once and for all*; but now he knows that it is not so. Unless again and again, patiently and every hour and day and year, men are on guard — unless again and again men pluck out the weeds and grass — unless they constantly restore and renew beauty and truth and right (the White Horse), evil will return to ruin the earth or the soul:

> And I go riding against the raid,
>   And yet know not where I am;
> But ye shall know in a day or year,
> When one green star of grass grows here;
> Chaos has charged you, charger and spear,
>   Battle-axe and battering-ram.
>
> And though skies alter and empires melt,
>   This word shall still be true:
> If ye would have the horse of old,
>   Scour ye the horse anew.
>
> One time I followed a dancing star
>   That seemed to sing and nod,
> And ring upon earth all evil's knell;
> But now I wot if ye scour not well,
> Red rust shall grow on God's great bell,
>   And grass in the streets of God.

So says Alfred. And so is the world. Is this not the soul of conservatism? The "Liberal," the collectivist, the Utopian, suppose that some one act (always hasty, often foolish) will abolish evil forever; but the conservative knows that only patient, unending, creative and preventive *work* — day by day and year by year — will keep the White Horse forever beautiful and young.

IV

It is hardly necessary to say that Chesterton was the enemy of Communism and of socialism. He was such because he believed in the freedom and worth of *individual man*. The collectivity, the arrogant "experts," the commissars, the State usurping the choices of man and the sovereignty of God, seemed to him an evil to be fought to the death. He saw Communism or socialism as a bulldozer driven by stiff-minded and groove-minded madmen to obliterate not the grass but the White Horse itself. He regarded both as a sort of arteriosclerosis of the soul, stiffening man toward an existential death. He abhorred both.

It is interesting and heartening, also, to know that Chesterton distrusted and opposed the *Insiders* of finance-capitalism. He saw the wealthy of the world assuming the *mask* of socialism to destroy both socialism and the freedom of individual enterprise. Like his great friend, Hilaire Belloc, he foresaw the *Servile State* — i.e., the Welfare State — where the *Insiders* use the superficial easy panaceas of socialism (applied to most men but escaped by themselves) to seduce men into servitude at the price of freedom. He and Belloc both saw, as the alternative, what they called "distributism" — *not* a distribution of wealth such as the Establishment pretends and upholds today, but a capitalism in which many, indeed more and most *individuals*, own capital property — land, businesses, resources — so that free enterprise may indeed be both enterprise and free.

This may not be the way, this may not be possible in our day, but Chesterton saw no other way . . . . And neither do I. G.K. Chesteron was a champion of free individual man, of man mastering his own fate and standing as the captain of his own soul.

V

CHESTERTON was so generous, so courteous, that sometimes he seemed *too* generous and *too* courteous to those he opposed. Hilaire Belloc saw this and said: "Now without wounding and killing, there is no battle; and thus, in this life, no victory; but also no peril to the soul through hatred." Chesterton hated wrong ideas; but he seemed incapable of hating the men who held them. A noble virtue — and yet sometimes, it seems, a weakness! At least let us remember that he *could* strike a mortal blow, as in his "Elegy in a Country Churchyard":

> The men that worked for England
> They have their graves at home:
> And bees and birds of England
> About the cross can roam.

> But they that fought for England,
> Following a falling star,
> Alas, alas for England,
> They have their graves afar.
>
> And they that rule in England,
> In stately conclave met,
> Alas, alas for England,
> They have no graves as yet.

And is not that the trouble with England — and places nearer home?

Yes, Chesterton was a fighter to the hilt of the sword. Gallant, generous, courteous, gay, yet he saw the mortal evil and he sought the immortal goal. He used what Belloc called *parallelism*: "he made [*us*] *know*. He was an architect of certitude . . . . " He revelled in a richness of verbal splendor, "innumerable of stains and splendid dyes"; he touched style with the end of the rainbow, and beneath the beauty was the gold of truth; he wrote with a zest and joy. He loved not only wit — which may be merely intellectual — but humor (which is of the whole man); so he said, "It is another thing to discover that the rhinoceros does exist *and then take pleasure in the fact that he looks as if he didn't.*"

Chesterton was, in his greatest books, so splendidly the artist that we absorb his philosophy as we absorb sunlight or the full moon, with sheer innocence of joy. And then we find that that joy of artistry has changed or reinforced our philosophy and the quality of our souls.

Take, for example, a passage from *Tremendous Trifles* ("The Orthodox Barber") that says the final word on all the "New" people who are going finally to do away with shaving, or the Constitution, or God, or whatever doesn't suit them:

> In the first and darkest of its books it is fiercely written that a man shall not eat his cake and have it; and though all men talked till the stars were old it would still be true that a man who shaved had lost his beard, and that a man who had lost his razor could not shave with it. But every now and then men jump up with the new something or other and say that everything can be had without sacrifice, and that bad is good if you are only enlightened, and that there is no real difference between being shaved and not being shaved. The difference, they say, is only a difference of

degree; everything is evolutionary and relative. Shavedness is immanent in man. Every ten-penny nail is a Potential Razor. The superstitious people of the past (they say) believed that a lot of black bristles standing out at right angles to one's face was a positive affair. But the higher criticism teaches us better. Bristles are merely negative. They are a Shadow where Shaving should be.

But Chesterton points out that any baby (who is still close to the Kingdom of Heaven), if you try to kiss him, will know at once whether or not you have shaved!

What perfect — and what pertinent — conservatism about the "New" this or that . . . including the "New" sex, the "New" society, or the "New" thing-um-a-jig!

Somehow when I think of Chesterton I think of a Mediaeval troubadour, a *jongleur de Dieu.* Or sometimes I think of him as his own Don John of Austria, or his own King Alfred. He speaks of Alfred, as of the Christian hero, as "The child whom time can never tire"; and so was he, himself, to the end. A great romanticist, he was therefore (in the right sense) a great realist, seeking "the combination of something that is strange with something that is secure." That combination, which is romance, is what his other contemporaries (save Kipling) lacked; and that is what keeps him forever young and forever true. So let us salute and let us cherish Gilbert Keith Chesterton — valiant soldier for the freedom of individual man, and for the glory of the living God.

Mr. Belloc:

At War Against The Servile State

HE was born Joseph Peter René Hilaire Belloc, but he sharpened his name to the melodious yet arrow-trim Hilaire. As man and writer he has grown in reputation for insight with the decades, and he still stands, as poet and philosopher, in the forefront of the modern battle for sanity.

Belloc and G.K. Chesterton were complementary artists and philosophers, friends and fellow workers, greatly different in style and temperaments but one in their belief that never could "any increase of comfort or security [be] a sufficient good to be bought at the price of liberty." That is, they were both enemies of Socialism and of Communism; and, of course, enemies of the Servile State that is the device of the ruling *Insiders* — a crafty device which would reduce the many mansions of God's universe to a stockyard feeding the greed of hidden men, and bring on "One World" where the riches of the fugue of individual man are muted to a monotone.

Shaw called these two "the Chesterbelloc" — and he and Wells regarded them, on the whole, as a sort of mythological and erratic monster that, like Lewis Carroll's Jabberwock, "Came whiffling through the tulgey wood/ And burbled as it came." Actually, the Chesterbelloc was the "beamish boy" whose "vorpal sword" flashed out against the Jabberwocks of positivism, of collectivism, of the modern distemper.

G.K. Chesterton and Hilaire Belloc, temperamentally and as artists, were greatly different. Chesterton was fluidly alive, flashing and flowing like a river that makes glad the City of God — humorous, imaginative, audacious, gay and playful, and rich with life in varied gusto. Belloc, on the other hand, was more like craggy mountain country, strong with rock ridges, less fluid and rich, more stoney and restrained, less given to gorgeous rhetoric and headlong paradox, less exuberant with life. Belloc wrote a purer and more essential prose that, at its best, is as much a model of bare power as Swift's, and in its essence a strength forever.

And it seems right that it was the unadorned and fiercely strong

Belloc who wrote of the positivists and collectivists the noble words of dismissal. They seemed (and seem) victorious; they seem to occupy, triumphant, the battlefield of the world today. But Belloc knew long ago that they had already failed in time because they fail in Eternity; and so he wrote: "Do not, I beg you, be oppressed by forces already dissolved. You have mistaken the hour of the night. It is already morning."

Why did Belloc oppose Socialism as a sort of boll-weevil in the fields of the world? Robert Speaight, in his fine *Life Of Hilaire Belloc*, wrote that to Belloc:

> The Socialist State was a state in which all the means of production — transport, land and machines — would be owned by the politicians. The politicians might be democratically elected, or they might not; that was irrelevant to the Socialist thesis. They might enforce their distribution of wealth equally, or at least equitably; or they might not. The point was that the moral responsibility of ownership would be exercised not by the people but by the politicians.

Belloc had been in politics. He had been a member of Parliament. He had seen the politicians in action. So he knew what a State in the hands of the politicians would be like, and he did not want to live in it; and he knew that no happy and creative people could live under it.

Hilaire Belloc (says Speaight) wished "a form of society where personal honor and personal freedom would be safeguarded; the only form of society natural to western man." He knew that the baseness of so much of the modern world made men desire quick, immediate salvation by the cheapest and easiest means. He knew that, in their longing become panic and haste, men might turn to *man* for salvation — and find themselves betrayed. As he wrote in *Survivals And New Arrivals*:

> The expectation of better things — the confident expectation of their advent — affects the vileness and folly of our time everywhere. Let one individual appear with the capacity or chance to crystallize these hopes and the enemy will have arrived. For then Anti-Christ will be man.

Always Belloc knew that the problems of economics and politics, while they needed solution, left a void that no economics or politics could fill. Suppose by some miracle that they were solved:

But after that? Will there not remain the chief problem of the soul? Shall we not smell what Chesterton so admirably calls "the unmistakable smell of the pit," shall we not need salvation with a need greater than the need for water upon a parched day?

This is even more evident today, with crime, rebellion, drugs, obscenity, and anarchy drowning us. That insight into the primary need of a faith, a philosophy, a religion that transcends Man and the devices of Man, is one of the things that makes Belloc central and sound. He saw, always, the great danger of the proud arrogance of Lucifer, returning to complete the abolition of Man in the name of Man. He saw and knew that we live under the shadow of peril; that the enemies of God plan the subjugation of Man; and that the bugle blows always for battle.

Belloc knew, long before Whittaker Chambers, what the latter came at last to know: Communism "is the vision of man's mind displacing God as the creative intelligence of the world." And (again before Chambers knew and said it): "Economics is not the central problem of this century . . . . Faith is the central problem of this age. The Western world does not know it, but it already possesses the answer to this problem — but only provided that its faith in God and the freedom He enjoins is as great as Communism's faith in Man."

Belloc knew and said this; it was his central strength.

I

HILAIRE Belloc's *The Servile State* was an analysis of a situation and a preview of things to come. It foresaw our present Welfare State, that "planner's Paradise," where the means of the Socialists are used to serve the ends of the *Insiders*.

A superficial mind might easily be misled by his terms. Belloc was a mortal enemy of Socialism and of Communism; but he was also a drastic critic of a *kind* of "Capitalism" — the "Capitalism" where capital was not diffused among many; where enterprise was no longer free, but stifled by giant corporations, foundations, bureaucracies, cartels; where canny *Insiders used* capitalism as a pretense, and Socialism as a means.

Belloc saw the world coming under the control of a very few (largely hidden) manipulators, with the power of the banks and financiers depriving more and more of us of money and, even more, of capital and the means of production. He really was *for* a true capitalism, but he saw around him a world where "Capitalism" was becoming confiscatory of the capital of the forgotten man. More and more men were becoming wage earners rather than free workmen on their own land, with their own businesses, by their own capital. Belloc knew that liberty however — *freedom* however — came only to those who had their own capital. Increasingly, as men lost their sense of property — their own property — they became less and less free . . . . less and less concerned with freedom . . . . What they sought, then, as a desperate *need,* was security. And the *Insiders,* the finance-capitalists, the spiders spinning their calamitous webs in the shadows, realized that they must concede security as they took away liberty. Belloc believed that the planner-Socialists — the Ramsay MacDonalds, the Sidney Webbs, the Bernard Shaws, "were confiscating income . . . they did not even propose to confiscate capital" from the *Insiders.* Speaight saw it this way:

> *The Servile State* did, indeed, fulfill the minimum condition of prophecy, in so far as it saw through a glass darkly. It saw that men in modern industrial societies would willingly give up their freedom to secure sufficiency and security. It doubted — and with good reason — whether the instinct of property was sufficiently vigorous in these societies to enforce that distribution of productive wealth (not of income) which Belloc believed to be the only social doctrine consonant with a Christian philosophy. The moment, he feared, had passed.

Yet, like him, we fight on, fight on, knowing that the only life worth living by free men is a life where every form of collective control is broken by men secure because of the free possession of *their own property productive of wealth.*

This explains many things that otherwise would seem incredible and inexplicable. Why do so many "Capitalists," why do so many "men of wealth," make a truce with Socialism, and use Socialist means like the income tax, and all the "social" panaceas, and all the coercions of Big Government? Because, by so doing, and by so giving "social security," they seduce men into docility, they lure men into servility, they establish their own hidden control under the pretense of "social justice." The Servile State — which is the state in which we now live — is a strategy of the spider-men. It is, on their part, a conspiracy and a crime. But it is also due to the blindness of the many men whose true life would be one of freedom; men blinded that they might sell their free Republic for mere security.

Belloc saw the State as becoming a "more or less benevolent slave-owner." He believed that "the rich would organize the poor with the poor's consent." How true today — with the white and the black recipients of "Welfare" allowing themselves to be *organized* by revolutionaries financed by the Establishment foundations. The riffraff of men allowing their freedom to be taken away for a pretence (how fragile!) of "security." Speaight did not fully understand all of this, as I think Belloc did, and he did not recognize that the "State" was only a front for the *Insiders*. To Belloc, this was the drift of the modern world — only to be arrested in a renaissance of freedom by the will of men who see the truth and use it to make the world free.

The answer as Belloc saw it, if it was still possible, lay in what he called *distributism*. This was not the distributing of income; it was the accumulation of more and more property among more and more men. The owner of land, of a printing press (or presses), of a store or a medical practice, of a shop and an industry or art, was on the way toward a true freedom. He was an emigrant from the Servile State to the Free Republic. He was an individual man and not a mass man.

Could this still be done? Belloc believed, as Chesterton believed even more hopefully, that the answer lay in the soul of man.

The Servile State, in style, is somewhat bleak and formidable. It is neither pleasant reading nor fine art; it is like the naked bones of thought. Nor can we say that it is the final work, nor the most perfect thought or statement that we shall have; but it is a book so enlightening, so revealing, so prophetic, that no one who would understand our dilemma and our predicament can afford not to know it. The book was written in 1912. We today have passed through the hypocrisies of a Woodrow Wilson, of an F.D.R., of their shoddy successors, and have been increasingly entrapped in the Servile State Belloc foresaw. Today Americans are beginning to see this — the correlation between Communism on the outside and the Conspiracy on the inside. And as we see it, and as we say so in terms that ordinary men can understand, we prepare for a possible renaissance of man. To know the truth is the only way to make salvation possible.

The basic thesis of *The Servile State* — that too many men will relinquish liberty for security — that the crafty few will use this to establish their own power and control — that capital in the hands of individual men will be the only answer and salvation — is essentially sound today even more than in 1912, when the condition was only incipient. Clearly *The Servile State* is a classic. It foresaw, more than half a century ago, what too horribly we see all around us today.

II

IN a more literary and delightful book, a book of travel, *The Path To Rome,* Hilaire Belloc makes his thesis more artistic. There he says:

> And I have a number of friends who agree with me in thinking this, that art should not be competitive or industrial, but most of them go on to the very strange conclusion that one should not own one's own garden, nor one's bee-hive, nor one's great noble house, nor one's pigsty, nor one's railway shares, nor the very boots on one's feet. I say, out upon such nonsense. Then they say to me, what about the concentration of the means of production? And I say to them, what about the distribution of the ownership of the concentrated means of production? And they shake their heads sadly, and say it would never endure; and I say, try it first and see. Then they fly into a rage.

There you have it! Property in the real and vital sense is the issue. A lot of our unsophisticated youth who object to "property," to "private property," have never done primer-class thinking about the matter. But Belloc, in this passage, might begin their education: Property is the basis of freedom and of the fruitful life.

And Belloc, in the same book, makes the matter not only clear but beautiful:

> But I said that we live as parts of a nation, and that there was no fate so wretched as to be without a country of one's own — what else was exile which so many noble men have thought worse than death, and which all have feared? I also told him that armies fighting in a just cause were the happiest of places for living, and that a good battle for justice was the beginning of all great songs; and that as for property, a man on his own land was the nearest to God.

This is the spiritual subsoil which must be firm and *there* if man is to build upon it the city of God. The Greeks fabled realistically that as Orpheus played upon his lyre, Thebes the city rose, wall and building, strong and beautiful. So with all of man's cities! Philosophy and poetry are the lasting basis of all material things.

And in a book like this, Belloc opens the secrets of things — and we see and live. Thus, speaking about "windows," he writes: ". . . in winter windows are drums for the splendid music of storms that makes us feel so masterly around our fires . . . . But for windows we should have to go out-of-doors to see daylight. After the sun, which they serve, I know of nothing so beneficent as windows." There is something here that transcends all economics, all social orders, and lets us see through the windows of the world the truth and beauty of God's universe.

And the depth and probity of Belloc lie in his wonderful sense of *life* — life magical, life eternal, life founded on God. He writes, laughing at the rationalists, the pedants, the positivists:

> What! here we are with the jolly world of God all around us, able to sing, to draw, to paint, to hammer, to build, to sail, to ride horses, to run, to leap; having for our splendid inheritance love in youth and memory in old age, and we are to take one miserable little faculty [*intellectuality*], or one-legged, knock-kneed, gimcrack, purblind, rough-skinned, underfed, and perpetually irritated and grumpy intellect, or analytical curiosity rather (a diseased appetite), and let it swell till it eats up every other function? Away with such foolery.

What headlong zest, what audacious wisdom! What humor!

Hilaire Belloc knew that the root of false modernity lay in a lack of integrity, or wholeness; in a human pride in the arrogance of the intellect divorced from the soul. He put the matter beautifully before us in *The Path To Rome*. The dry-as-dust men of positivism, he wrote, may "go back to their rationalism and consort with microbes and make their meals off logarithms, washed down with an exact distillation of the root of minus one; and the peace of fools, that is the deepest and most balmy of all, be theirs for ever and ever."

Yet all humor aside, Belloc knew that the situation in the modern world was perilous and critical. The anti-Christ was incarnate in the *Insiders,* in the men who thought that man (in himself) was all. Christendom as it once had been was under attack; the enemy was inside the gates; the disintegrators were blatant and brash in their assurance of triumph. It was a mortal struggle — not only economic, not chiefly economic — but spiritual.

It was a battle between the Faith — and the Fashions of the hour. Belloc was a soldier who confronted the enemy with his sword naked in his hand, and who never cried "compromise." He knew that to be "Red" *is* to be dead!

III

HILAIRE Belloc was also a poet. He was a poet of meticulous art, into whose art at its greatest a natural lyricism flowed like the juices that flood the blossoming tree in spring till the petals open and shine. Music, condensation, and meaning were his strength. Take a stanza from his "The Prophet Lost In The Hills At Evening," where he sums up himself as he saw himself:

> I challenged and I kept the Faith,
> The bleeding path alone I trod:
> It darkens. Stand about my wraith,
> And harbour me, almighty God.

The flowing grace of his lovelier lyrics is well realized in these lines "On A Sleeping Friend":

> Lady, when your lovely head
> Droops to sink among the Dead,
> And the quiet places keep
> You that so divinely sleep;
> Then the dead shall blessed be
> With a new solemnity,
> For such beauty, so descending,
> Pledges them that Death is ending.
> Sleep your fill — but when you wake
> Dawn shall over Lethe break.

One is reminded of the lovely classical stanzas of A.E. Housman in *A Shropshire Lad*. But there is a depth and width in Belloc's vision; a freedom from Housman's despair; an emphasis on *life*. And his classicism, while not as scholarly as Professor Housman's, had a natural recitude that was close to the tone of the Greek or Latin lyric.

His poetry, like graving on marble, perfected the epigram. Thus "The Statue":

> When we are dead, some Hunting-boy will pass
> And find a stone half-hidden in tall grass
> And grey with age: but having seen that stone
> (Which was your image), ride more slowly on.

In his verse, also, he had a marvellous wit and humor, as in his rhymes on animals — for children, and with reference to man — *The Bad Child's Book Of Beasts* and *More Beasts For Worse Children*. Such was his "The Frog":

> Be kind and tender to the Frog,
>   And do not call him names,
> As "Slimy-skin" or "Polly-wog,"
>   Or likewise "Uncle James,"
> Or "Gape-a-grin," or "Toad-gone-wrong,"
>   Or "Billy-Bandy-Knees";
> The frog is justly sensitive
>   To epithets like these.
>
> No animal will more repay
>   A treatment kind and fair;
> At least so lonely people say
> Who keep a frog (and by the way,
>   They are extremely rare).

In his poetry more than in his prose, Belloc's fluent wit, his dancing humor, broke through the solemnity of the Establishment like a flood of sunlight. He was not as great a poet as Walter de la Mare, or the incomparable Chesterton at his greatest, but he was a true poet; and this increases the width of his work.

IV

HILAIRE Belloc believed that life was a consecration to God. He wrote:

> That great word which every man
> Gave God before his life began:
> It was a sacred word, he said,
> Which comforted the pathless dead,
> And made God smile when it was shown
> Unforfeited before the Throne.

He was by nature (unlike Chesterton) naturally a skeptic; he had, by nature, no sense of mystical communion with the Transcendent and the Supernatural; he did not find or feel the presence of that world invisible of which another Catholic, Francis Thompson, wrote. He accepted the Faith as a premise of thought, which could never be *proved* by mere reason (though it was reasonable), but which commanded our allegiance by its majestic architecture of harmony and rectitude.

Here was a sad man who could yet be jovial in the presence of the compelling grandeur of the Faith and the joy of beauty and love; but he was a man who lacked the exuberant river of romance which made Chesterton great. Yet he held the Faith! He saw it as the great antidote to the degradation of life into collectivism, relativism, obscenity, social compulsions, destruction of the great and the rare. We need his like today.

Belloc's sense of history gave him what most men now lack. He had a sense of the tangible reality of *Christendom*, of a Europe united in creed and purpose, of a Western World that had been an entity in creed and culture. Because of this he had a feeling for discipline, for order (a living organic order), for life integral and harmonious. Today when youths without any living sense of the past, or any conception of tradition that is the soul of living order, shout for they know not what in terms of the hasty, the extempore, the random, we most need the fundamental sense of an Hillaire Belloc. We need his intuition of the soul of history.

In his sense of historic continuity, and of a central meaning in the Western World, Belloc possessed and expressed the most important element in history. Today men are too often inorganic, rootless, minus any sense of destiny or purpose. We forget that all *living* things have, and must have, that inner sense of meaning. In the oak tree, every drop of sap is *oaken*, willing the strong fiber of the wood, the shape of leaf and acorn, the strength that endures the winds and the lightnings and builds for the centuries. In the caterpillar there is the will to become the butterfly, that flower with wings. In all that lives there is this inner meaning that becomes the outward form. How much more in great peoples, in nations, in the life of man! – or so it should be.

When the continuity, the central will, the meaning of a people or nation weakens and becomes fissured and diffused or denied, degeneracy sets in. A people, a nation, is no longer great. Belloc never lost this sense of continuity, of a central meaning, and to him it was the very soul of the Western World. He knew it was being – that it *had* been – weakened and diffused and was under attack; but he also knew that without it the Western World was lost.

On the day that Hilaire Belloc died, in July of 1953, one may imagine a scene that is far removed from temporal time and the limitations of earth. There he who on earth had been born a Frenchman, and who had become a great Englishman, stood at the beautiful and terrible gate. And there Saint Peter, who holds the keys, said to him: "And who are you?"

Doubtless Belloc answered, "I am a soldier from earth, who fought with the sword and the pen for the Faith. But I often failed and I always fell short of the glory of God."

And then Saint Peter said, "I know of you, and Heaven knows of you. Strong in a time of apostasy and betrayal, you stood for the great and the high and the integral. Your sword and your pen never faltered, though every pen and every sword sometimes fails. Heaven sees you — and Heaven's sight is always clear — as a promontory of rock standing unshaken among the surf of a wild and angry sea. And on that promontory is a shrine and a cross where, unharmed by the sea, men may still worship and be free. And there Heaven's sun shines.

"We know you well, Hilaire Belloc, and we welcome you to the Great Company: Good and faithful soldier, enter into the joy of Heaven!"

Preserve Thy Integrity

Integrity: What To Tell Your Son

FOR you who are parents, today is a difficult time. The men who seek to rule us, and who wreck us, have fractured the harmony of the family into ideological discord. Theoretically they uphold "one world," a new global unity, a fusing of all men into "the family of man," a world of integrated races and homogenized classes; in practice they divide men in order to conquer man, and separate us as individuals in order to solidify themselves as our collective masters. By their "philosophy" they fracture the "one nation, under God, indivisible" into a chaos without God, where "class" wars with "class" and "race" with "race." In relation to the family, they incite and accentuate a conflict between "youth" and "age," between child and parent. By such discords, they incite division among individuals in order to establish their iron-curtain rule over man collectivized.

In areas where life is natural and right, there is wholesome tension but no unwholesome conflict between child and parent. The partridge chick trusts and obeys the mother; the baby rabbit learns from his parents when to hide and where to run, to drum signals with his hind paws, to follow the guiding star of a powder-puff tail. So it should be with man. There should be reciprocity between the rookie and the veteran quarterback; a Namath — to become a master — will learn from Tobin Rote or Otto Graham. The young painter will watch Michelangelo fashion his frescoes, and absorb all he can, instead of playing the cool cat and calling his elders "Daddy-O." Only in our unrealistic, unnatural age of "realism" and "naturalism" is the "conflict" between age and youth exacerbated, or the family splintered by the deliberate wedge of false philosophy.

Youth and age are complementary. Age is younger than youth suspects; youth is older than age admits. The soul is a timeless pilgrim traversing the space that we see as "time"; youth is one aspect, age is one aspect, of that journey; there is no irreconcilable conflict between travelers just because they stand at different places on the map. What we need is a transcendence of chronology, a vital sharing of experiences more fascinating and more fruitful because dissimilar. Youth and age should cease to "war" with each other, since both are fellow pilgrims in the noble adventure that is life.

In Kipling's great *Jungle Tales*, Kaa, the rock python, wise with long experience, is a sort of parent – a guide, philosopher, and friend – to young Mowgli, the wolf-boy. And thus he speaks to the boy he loves: "The python dropped his head lightly for a minute on Mowgli's shoulder. 'A brave heart and a courteous tongue,' said he. 'They shall carry thee far through the jungle, Manling.' " So we should speak to those who are young today. So, I hope, I shall speak.

I

WHAT shall I, as a father, tell you as a son? I am a father – therefore a man; you are a son – therefore a man. I write to you man to man, mind to mind; I write with no presumption because I am older, with no condescension because you are younger. I ask the same courtesy from you. I write, and I ask you to read, as a human being, whose worth and wisdom as a man are more important than the more or fewer days of your years. I cannot be as young as you, but I have been young; you are not as old as I, but (God willing) you *will* be, as your youth fulfills itself in age. So let us share a fruitful discussion of the life that we both wish to live as wisely as we can.

What then, from my experience as a man, shall I tell you who hunger for experience as a plant hungers for the sun? First I tell you what is too obvious to say, yet too essential not to say: You are a *man*.

What does that mean? As I have observed you, as I remember my own youth and study the youth of others, I think it means to find *personal integrity*. You sometimes feel that your elders do not have the integrity you desire; you sometimes wonder how you can attain and preserve your own integrity in a world like this. I agree with you that personal integrity is the essential thing that any man should have – and hold; so I propose to tell you what I think integrity is, and how we may attain it.

The simple criteria of Kipling's Kaa are a good beginning: *A brave heart and a courteous tongue.* If man is to be man, he must have courage in a world so splendidly dangerous – where it is unsafe to be born, since a birth-certificate is a death-sentence. I do not – I think you do not – admire a man who has not a brave heart; I do not – I think you do not – admire a man who has not a courteous tongue.

But these are fruits that grow from deep roots. They come from personal integrity, and we must find what that integrity is and how it may be cultivated. We shall not find it in circumstances (*i.e.*, the things that lie around us), but in introstance (*i.e.*, the quality that lies within us). Society cannot give you integrity; integrity is a quality of the private man.

Integrity is not easy in the world in which we live. This present, established, orthodox world of "Liberalism" does not cherish the true masculine (or, for that matter, the true feminine) virtue; it does seek, however, to reduce the true masculine virtue to a false feminine nature. Ours is not a "paternalistic" world – it is a maternalistic world. "Liberals" seek to soften and wash away the man in you, and to seduce you to the false feminine abominations of the possessive, fussy, sentimental "Mom" whose unhappy and unholy wish is to keep you forever in her womb, never to be born as a free man. Socialism, national or international, means – a womb-society.

The world around us – in so far as it is the world of man's contriving, the social world – is one where activism (by irony and paradox) seeks to enthrone passivism. The "revolutions" of the hour, with all their blatant activism, are not revolutions at all; they are reactionary retrogressions of man afraid of freedom and individuality, yearning to be again the happy foetus carefree in the womb. Not to do – but to be done for (in several senses!); not to give – but to receive; not to become free – but to be freed . . . such is the ideal of the hour. Slaves were sometimes made "freedmen" – they were manumitted – someone else struck the fetters off their hands. That is the nature of "social revolution" today; it is not the American Revolution where free men freed themselves; it is *manumission.* "Society," "government," "the state" is to manumit men. We are not to be free men – but freedmen. All the noise in Africa and Asia and the United States – like the quieter established socialism in Scandinavia and England – is activism in the service of passivism. The world today is not a world of revolution but of socialist reaction, where submen never care or dare to be free through their own worth, their own work, but clamor to be *freed*men. "We have rights," the submen say, "to freedom from want, from fear, from poverty, from all the troubles of our proud and angry dust." And they always add, "See our shackled hands? *Come manumit us!*"

You think this view old-fashioned? It is as "old-fashioned" as the pull of gravitation, as the multiplication table, as the circulation of the blood, as the rainbow after the rain. My statement is as "old-fashioned" as logic and truth: The *freedman* is not the *free* man; only *you* can deserve, only *you* can win, freedom. Freedom cannot be given from without but must always be won from within. Integrity alone gives freedom — or rather wins freedom; and integrity means self-reliance, the hero in the soul, a clarity of consciousness and a rectitude of character.

Life gives you a bit of canvas, a chunk of unshaped marble. It may be that "society" or "government" can daub a pleasant picture on that canvas, or hack a reasonable facsimile of a statue out of the marble. But if you call that a life, if you accept that as a work of art, you have no integrity — for you have no soul. Integrity means that, in the agony and joy of birth, through the travail of your own being, you fashion a picture on your own canvas, you carve out a statue from your own marble. It may be small, it may be crude, it probably will be imperfect; but it is *yours* because it is *you.* It is the word within you that becomes the work outside you.

Or take a different approach. One of the great symbols of the world's literature is the story of Jonah. Jonah was afraid of the still small voice within him, afraid of his own destiny, afraid to be the artist of his own canvas. So he fled to the uttermost parts of the sea, and took ship (he hoped) not even God knew where . . . . He fled his own soul, his own identity, his own integrity; he fled. So man today, the new Jonah, flees his integrity — not only to the far places of the earth, but to the farther places of space beyond the earth . . . in rockets and moon-shots and as spacemen on Mars . . . anywhere, anywhere out of himself. Or into the limbo-dreams of surrealism, and Picasso's nightmares full of spoiled liver. Especially he takes passage in the *Leftward Ho* of socialism, and sails desperately away from himself. But the great storms come, the ship is shaken, he is cast overboard into foaming seas. There he is swallowed by Leviathan, the State, that great beast. Such is man today, fleeing himself, fleeing integrity.

But now Jonah, as in the great ancient timeless story, must be cast out of the belly of Leviathan, and return to the firm and real and living earth, and find again his reciprocity with it, uniting (as wise men always have) the universal reason within him with the objective universe outside him, into the poem of reality under the God of Things as They Are.

If our modern Jonah is to do that — and our hope is that you who are young will do that — he must rediscover himself, he must cultivate the garden of his own soul. Then he will rediscover his destiny (*i.e.,* his soul's destination), he will be reborn and he will find the world renewed with the orchards of Eden. He will be born again. And today, among men, only the twice-born find integrity.

Yet the strong, simple, real things of Nature that have not fallen so far from reality as has man today, still stand integral though they are not twice-born but once-born only. Integrity lies within all things real, as their destiny, their character. What is the integrity of the stone? — to be firm and solid, and so to bear the forest or city upon its shoulders. What is the integrity of the grain of corn? — to endure the darkness of the earth into which it falls, to use that darkness to fulfill its own destiny in the light, to digest the loam to nourish its own dream, to absorb the rain to hasten the beneficent heartbreak whereby its shell is rent and its meaning is born, to grow bravely toward the blade, the leaves, the good ears tossing victorious in wind and sun. What is the integrity of the eagle? — to break from the shell, to soar unshaken through buffeting winds, to stare unabashed into the very sun. What is the integrity of man? — to find the values that are the Word of his own meaning and to incarnate them in the use and beauty of his own work. The honor of you as youth is to consecrate your life — every inch, ounce, and atom of it — to the discovery of your Word and its incarnation in your work.

What does it profit a man to gain all the gimmicks and the gadgets of the world — to gain security and even affluence — if he loses his own soul? The essence of life, the joy of life, is to find what you essentially mean to be, and to realize and fulfill it, in defiance of poverty, or the gauntlet that the soul must run in this world, or wounds and bodily death. You, my son, will learn that the only thing that never fails and always sustains is integrity. You, as a genuine man, should so live that, when youth is made whole by age, you can say with Bunyan's Mr. Valiant-for-Truth: "I am going to my fathers, and though with great difficulty I am got hither, yet now I do not repent me of all the trouble I have been at to arrive where I am. My sword I give to him that shall succeed me in my pilgrimage, and my courage and skill to him that can get it."

So living and so dying, you will know integrity. You will find the integrity that comes when the subjective inner world and the objective outer world are integrated by the harmony of reason with reality. And your personal honor will demand that you seek that integrity, and serve that integrity, bearing the very sky on your shoulders that the stars may not fall from your soul.

II

IN SEEKING integrity, you must have the masculine virtue of militant affirmation. You seek not security but opportunity, not our false activism or our false passivism but vital affirmation. You must do; you must dare. You must not "adjust" yourself to the *status quo* of our present socialistic Establishment, but fashion life into the statue that expresses the reality that Life meant it to be. In that artistry and adventure, you will find the outlet for that dynamic of youth which is the best within you.

What is the essence of youth that is the best within you? It is your desire for adventure, for daring, for (O forbidden and forgotten word today!) — *romance.* The enemies of God and man today pervert that word by mocking it, by denying that it exists, by negating poetry and romance in the world. And we, your elders, who love you, have sometimes failed you too, by dulling your desire for daring, for adventure, for romance; we speak as if we wanted you dully to uphold some *status quo,* some bit of life preserved in a deep-freeze. We do not often enough tell you that we give you, rather, an ultimatum and a battle-cry, the trumpet that shall never call retreat, the fateful lightnings of a terrible swift sword. We forget the words of the young poet, Marchbanks, in that noble play (*Candida*) where Shaw (the socialist!) blows the social gospel forever to rags: "I no longer desire happiness: life is nobler than that."

Because we have denied you the trumpet-call and the battle-cry — the true romance, the real poetry of life — some of you in bravado break away to sow the *wild-oats*-of-poetry — drunkenness, drugs, lechery, the antics of Hell's Angels, the riots on street or beach, the beards of the Beats (and, on a different level, the grotesqueries of freedom-marchers and H.C.U.A.-baiters) . . . . All these are to true Romance what a painted woman of the streets is to Juliet.

I offer you something very different. I offer you the true romance — Alfred and Arthur, Roland and Oliver, St. Francis, David with his five smooth stones, the wisdom of Odin and the beneficent might of Thor, Hercules and his seven labors that he might become not a corpse but a constellation, and Don Quixote, the good knight who sallied forth to right wrongs and win glory. Too long have we seemed to say: "Make the world your oyster"; let us say what we always should have said, "Find within the oyster of the world the Pearl of Great Price."

Your naive reaction to our error — and the enemies of God and man have cleverly nudged you deeper into this — is to see romance in the dragon, the Pagans, the Philistines and the blue furnace of Dagon, the frost-giants and the misty hosts of Nifleheim that Thor and Odin fought. *Nostra culpa!* — the sin is ours. But the sin will be yours if you persist in such perversity; the hour has come to turn the eye of your soul toward light. We say, and you must see, that the true Romance lies not in frost-giants and the foggy hosts of Nifleheim, but in Thor and Odin; not in the Pagans, but in Roland and Oliver (avoiding Roncesvalles!); not in the dragon, but in St. George.

Your integrity will be real when you see where romance really lies — in wisdom, in creation, in the soldier-sons of God. You will find integrity when you work and fight not for quantity (today called "democracy"), but for quality and the Republic, for the magic casements opening on perilous seas, for the Pearl of Great Price, for the Holy Grail. If you wish adventure, join the great adventurers. Join St. Joan (woman militant when man failed to be man), giving her dead France life. Join Keats, when men become brittle with the philosophistication of wit and conceits, fashioning poems like stained glass windows into mystery and beauty, "Innumerable of stains and splendid dyes/As are the tiger-moth's deep-damasked wings . . . ." Join Jesus who, when Pilate made a jest of truth, and Caesar made a horror of the throne, shook the *status quo* of time with the *potentia qua* of Eternity.

III

THIS LEADS US, by inevitable logic, to *morality*.

There can be no personal integrity that is not based on the integrity of the universe. (This is where the existentialists, with their whim and caprice of solipsism go astray.) Integrity within you, the courage to create quality within you and around you, is not based upon the quicksands of relativism but on the granite of morality.

What is morality? Today's philosophisticates — relativists, pragmatists, nihilists — suppose that morality is only certain man-fabricated conventions and taboos and conformities, what they call "the mores," what they dismiss as "the folk-ways." (Often the folk-ways are an instinctive obedience to the imperative of reality, but morality is an even deeper affirmation of things as they are.) Morality is as basic as the truth that two plus two are four; that gravitation draws the falling stone and supports the standing man; that the seed grows toward the sun. Morality is a decalogue written in stone and star; it is not a conformity to illusion but a confirmation by reality.

Fundamentally, morality is simple — and inexorable. Whatever makes for death is immoral; whatever makes for life is moral. I do not mean physical death only — or mostly; physical death is often an integral part of life: I mean the death of integrity; the death of meaning and value and quality; the death of the heart, the mind, the spirit, the soul. Whatever decreases life in this sense and makes for death in this sense is immoral; whatever defeats death in this sense and augments life in this sense is moral. As Leithen says in *Mountain Meadow*: "What does my death matter if we defeat Death?"

Morality seeks to defeat death. Whatever cripples the mind, hardens the heart, dims the senses, debases the soul, makes for death; whatever enriches the mind, wakens the heart, makes the senses more sensitive, ennobles the soul, makes for life. Thus drugs, drink, lechery, treason, pornography, sadism, cruelty to men or animals, illusion, lies, falsity of any sort, all that detroys integrity, is immoral. You can judge your life this way: Do your choices and actions constrict and wall in and narrow your life into death? — then they are immoral! Do your choices and actions open your life into scope and area and growth and joy? — then they are moral!

Dante knew. He found Hell a downward funnel, where as you progressed into evil the walls grew ever more strict and cramping, and where you never could return, till in the last and lowest and narrowest circle you were frozen with the traitors-to-life in the pale constriction of ice forever. He found Heaven, on the contrary, the many mansions through which you could move at will, though one was especially your country and your home, and where your existence was forever enriched by freedom and growth into ever-augmented life and light.

Whatever makes for death in the widest and deepest sense is immoral; whatever makes for life in the widest and deepest sense is moral. That is reality. That is the inexorable logic of the soul within you and the universe outside you.

So today, when the work of the world must be done and should be done well, it is immoral to be interested most in pay day and quitting time. It is immoral to live like the hippie — slipshod, unproductive, a parasite on man. It is immoral to make truth the most convenient lie and right the most expedient wrong, like the collectivists. It is immoral, most of all, to throw acid in the face of beauty, as our pseudo-intellectuals love to do. It is immoral, beyond all else, to mock and murder quality, value, and meaning, and set upon the throne and in the temple the skull-and-cross-bones of nihilism.

Morality, on the contrary, means reality. It is moral to be like the dying tailor (whom Thoreau quotes), whose last words were: "Tell the tailors to tie a knot in the thread before they take the first stitch." It is moral to paint pictures, like Vincent van Gogh, that will still endure "even in the deluge." It is moral to bake bread that is good and to fry chicken well. It is moral to plow the field and plant the wheat. It is moral to say with the great Carlyle, "Produce, produce, though it be only a potato." It is moral to lift the bridge, airy-strong, across the chasm; to fashion a house that will stand up and take the morning across the centuries, like a tree or mountain; to build the cathedral like a frozen fugue of architecture; to bring water to a thirsty land in the aqueduct or span the miles with the Roman road. It is moral to build the better mousetrap. It is moral (as teacher or artist) to turn the eye of the soul toward light. It is moral to reverence love and to rejoice in its physical rapture and its spiritual joy. It is moral to serve the glory of God and to enjoy Him forever.

Morality means to bear the world on your creative shoulders like the good giant Atlas. It is moral, too, of course, for Atlas to shrug when the enemies of the world have corrupted earth with fungus and cobweb, and to shake such corruption off the globe. But the true function of Atlas, the eternal joy of Atlas, is to lift the world into life and light, into the free winds and the gracious sun, upon stalwart shoulders.

But remember always that you negate death and affirm life in the *essential* sense. Not physical existence but essential *life*! One of the worst horrors of the hour is its limited perspective that sees no farther than physical existence; this eventuates in the coward's cliché: "I'd rather be Red than dead." This stems from the secular superstition that physics and biology are a period after life, whereas life is a question mark after biology and physics. If we were Red, most of us would be physically dead, and the rest of us would wish we were. Even if we were physically "alive," what sort of "life" would it be under darkness all day long, in a pit-and-the-pendulum existence in the cells of 1984, amid the mindless, meaningless scurrying of hive or heap?

Without morality there can be no freedom, no poetry, no joy. Immorality leads to death — not only of the body but of the soul. Shakespeare (like all great artists) knew this. His Macbeth is a clear example. Macbeth chooses (like Fascist and Communist today) the road of immorality — truth as the most convenient lie, right as the most expedient wrong . . . the red road to power through treachery, betrayal, cruelty, murder . . . . He builds his power not on inward discipline and worth but on outward fraud and force. Inexorably that red road of the ruin of others leads to the ruin of himself. For him, as for Communism today, the judgment of Angus is the eternal judgment of morality:

> Now does he feel
> His secret murders sticking on his hands;
> Now minutely revolts upbraid his faith-breach:
> Those he commands move only in command,
> Nothing in love: now does he feel his title
> Hang loose about him, like a giant's robe
> Upon a dwarfish thief.

That is the inexorable verdict of a moral universe upon any immoral man or group. Macbeth himself, faced with the dead-end stop in that red road, reaping the death that he has sown, sees life inevitably narrowed into a funnel-trap. From that impasse he sees and says the truth: Life "is a tale/Told by an idiot, full of sound and fury,/Signifying nothing . . . . " From Macbeth's stance that is the only possible thing to say! Life, not in itself, but as Macbeth has lived it, *is* a tale told by an idiot. For Macbeth to have said:"Life is the sweet/Color and fragrance of fair honeysuckle/Delighting me . . . . "

would have been immoral. As a man sows, so shall he reap; down is not up; and two minus two are never seven.

The great artists are always moral . . . Aeschylus, Virgil, Dante, Shakespeare, Hawthorne, Melville, Emerson . . . . And so I say to you who are young, in order that you may find integrity, turn your backs on the conformity of the immoralists who trap life in the bottleneck of the downward funnel, turn your faces toward the open roads, the free winds, the ebullient sun.

IV

YET I BELIEVE — and hope — that you who are youthful will feel that something has still been left out, that there must be also the plus of beauty, the *play* of poetry and music and love and art, the fragrance in the flower, the sheen on the plume. And certainly this is so.

God might have created a universe of black and white. God might have thought that geometry was enough — and so have censored the spectrum out of the world. He might have traced earth not as a painting in oils, but as a lithograph. But He did not!

God so loved the world that he lavished on it and in it the plus that we call *beauty*. He knew that utility and sober existence are never enough: He added fragrance to the flower, color to the curve of the petal; He gave the bonus of many-hued plumes to the peacock, He gave the exuberance of song to the lark; He splashed the magic of the spectrum over sky and ocean and earth. He might have made a universe of geometry alone, an earth of the algebra of abstract x and y, a world of statistics and Kinsey Reports and Xerox computers. But He did not!

The Liberal Establishment naturally denies God, for it leaves beauty out of its world, and God affirms them. Socialism might be defined as the creed that negates the firm lines of geometry and seeks to censor the spectrum wholly out of the universe. Socialism is the creed that would reduce earth to a lithograph . . . . and that even abolishes the firm lines of black and white, because it says that there is no black and no white but only gray. Socialism is the creed which says: "There is no rainbow."

Socialism is the creed that hates the woods that are "lovely, dark and deep," and therefore launches the greatest lumbering expedition in history to reduce them to sawdust and the desert.

Socialism and "Liberalism" think that to become "civilized" we should become not Athens but Alexandria. Athens believed in imagination and art and creation and wonder and poetry; Alexandria believed only in analysis and pedantry and statistics — the husks and skeletons of men.

So today our "intellectuals," who are not citizens of Athens but of Alexandria, deny mystery, and wonder, and the magic casements opening on the foam, and the star on the horizon. They seek to degrade poetry into prose, art into algebra, creation into analysis, reality into statistics. Love to them is a Kinsey Report. Poetry to them is the dehydrated sawdust of John Ciardi or Langston Hughes or Karl Shapiro.

Shapiro, for example, writes: "We are gradually losing the line of demarcation between prose and poetry, and we are almost at the point of asking perhaps for the last time: what is prose? what is poetry? And we are almost at the point of answering: there isn't any . . . . It happens that prose for centuries has moved closer and closer to the conditions of human life and poetry farther and farther away. Now it also appears that poetry is also flowing in the direction of human experience and away from the ideal. Or so we hope." This nonsense, you should know, is standing life (and poetry) on its head; is it any wonder that the consequent rush of blood to the brain precipitates an intellectual tizzy? The trouble with life today is that it *has* flowed in the direction of a debased, dehydrated prose, and away from poetry. The "wonder and the wild desire," the "woods that are lovely, dark and deep," the "magic casements" and "The love that moves the sun in Heaven and all the stars," have been mocked, derided, denied. Is it any wonder, then, that today life seems the cold pancake that a zombie swallows?

Integrity in the fullest sense must include the renaissance of wonder, the resurrection of poetry. You who are young instinctively seek and vitally need the magic, the miracle, the immortal longings, the worlds unrealized, the light that never was on land and sea . . . the fourth dimension that is poetry.

What you need is not the "avant-garde," the "new ideas," the novelties (as of woman's fashions, as of the novelty-fanciers); you need not the *new* but the *renewed*. Reality is the sunlight that we forget we see because we see it so often . . . the song of wind and lark that we forget we hear because we hear them so often. The vision must be renewed, the sound must be renewed.

Sometimes I think that only if you become blind for an hour or a year . . . only if you become deaf for a year or a decade . . . will you be able to see, will you be able to hear. But I crave for you, thanks to the potency of your youth, that you may find renewal this side of such drastic therapy. You may renew the world by renewing your own selves — by seeing as if you saw earth as Adam saw Eden, by hearing as if you were Eve hearing the birds of Eden sing. If that miracle happens, and through your youth the youth of the world is recovered, then you will be poets and you will find the revolution that is resurrection, the re-creation of the world, the promise of God: "Lo, I make all things new."

At least I would assure you that you will never understand the earth unless you know what poetry is — the golden bird of fire that lies prisoned within the wood, waiting its hour to leap up and go dancing back to the sun, as love, as music, as art, as poetry . . . as *life*.

V

THIS I TELL you as my son, this I tell you as your father — man to man, mind to mind, heart to heart. I have done you the courtesy to speak; I ask only the courtesy that you should listen. I seek only to awaken you, to awaken myself, to break through the anesthesia of the hour, to renew the deep foundations that lie in the subconscious and the unconscious of the soul, to set free the buried fire. Genius, beauty, love, poetry — the present world of "Liberalism" and socialism hates these, and has done its best to reduce them through mockery to anesthesia, through "analysis" to coma, through unreasonable rationalism to death. But I believe that the *potentia qua* of God, the power whence all things flow, is about to open the foundations of the great deep again and restore the reality of life that we have lost. I hope that this will come through you who are young.

At least I would ask you again to dream and dare, and thus to ride again the stallion of manhood whose back is known only by those who with a brave heart grasp the mane of life and ride bareback and shouting even in God's thunderstorm.

Integrity:
What To Tell Your Daughter

IN the wisest book in the world there is an eternal symbol of timeless truth. In Eden, under the trees where the blossom of beauty and the fruit of use were simultaneous, the first conspirator against sanity and freedom — the primal nihilist — raised his philosophisticate head out of his sensual coils, and tempted the first woman to the world's fall. "Eat," the Serpent said, "of the fruit of the tree of the knowledge of good and evil, and you shall not surely die but you shall be as gods."

So today the snake in the garden, become largely the snake on the campus, still lisps his lethal lie. Now, as then, he directs much of his temptation toward woman — for woman is full of curiosity, desire for life, and sensitivity to a glamorous tongue; and woman, if she is tempted, can herself tempt poor fascinated man (through her charm and beauty) to an easy fall.

Much of the subversion of the soul, the ruin of values, the creeping death that afflicts us today, has come about because woman has been subverted by the Serpent. Woman is so important for life! — she is the vessel that transmits biological continuity across the generations in this world, she is herself the plume and song and hue and fragrance of the world, she is the very grace notes of life. She cherishes and transmits not only the physical child but the spiritual culture without which we cannot breathe, the embracing and nourishing nuance that is not an intellectual but an aesthetic and vital thing. If the Serpent can lead woman astray, man will surely blunder into disaster and stumble into debacle. So it is necessary to try to speak to our daughters, those loveliest of our children, and share with them whatever wisdom we have.

What, then, do I venture to tell my daughter?

I

To YOU, my daughter, since you are a woman, I do not know that I, as a man, can successfully speak. As woman, you know the world in a way that I cannot; you share ultimate fundamental secrets

196

that are hidden from men, like the dark side of the moon. Yet Artemis, goddess of the moon, loved Endymion, and I judge from the ancient story that he learned a great deal from her and about her . . . even about her dark and secret side. And if the fascinating dialogue of woman and man were not a sharing and communication, I could not speak to you and you would not even listen to me. The very differences – the delicious polarity – of man and woman are one of the reasons that men and women find it good to live, and, living, find their dialogue so fascinating a drama.

What, then, can I, as your father (and so a man) tell you, my daughter (and so a woman)?

Every thing and creature has its own fundamental destiny; each thing and creature – from the redbud tree rooted in the rich earth to the wild hawk in the wind-swept sky . . . from the kitten that you, my daughter, once named Aaron Purr, to the lion feral upon the veldt . . . from Eve to Emily Dickinson . . . has a destiny and a character that is the ultimate being and essential life of each. As Spinoza said: "Everything, in so far as it is in itself, endeavors to persist in its own being; and the endeavor wherewith a thing seeks to persist in its own being is nothing else than the actual essence of that thing." A destiny, a character! Success in life is to find these, and to incarnate them, and to set their inward essence free in outward experience and expression. This is the meaning of life, this the joy. And this is the only real freedom.

Freedom for everything and everyone, world without end, is this: To fulfill the essential, God-given, inherent being and meaning of its life. Freedom is not the "liberty" to exploit every casual whim and caprice and eccentricity and tangent that leads you away from your own causal destiny. Freedom means the liberty to realize ever more fully your own destiny and essence. Freedom is not the liberty to negate yourself, but to affirm yourself. And freedom is certainly not the unearned increment of bestowal from without, the garish lavishing on you of things that have no relation to what you do and are. Freedom is not the security that some abstraction like the state gives you, or the outward gifts poured from the cornucopia of a saccharine Santa Claus of welfare, or the acclaim that mob-voices like *Time* or *Life* sluice over you, or anything outside and around you; it is a feeling of increment and augmentation from within you, it is the growth of your power to become in existence what in essence you are.

Now you, my daughter, are essentially woman.

I read recently a fantastic ad for help in a mill; it said, "Wanted: Female Girls." Yet ridiculous as the ad may seem, the great need of the hour is for "Female Girls." Crazy "ideas," tangents away from the center that is reality, heresies from essential being, have afflicted women for some generations now. They are a sort of leukemia in the bloodstream of woman. "Emancipation of woman" . . . the "equality of the sexes" . . . "woman's rights" . . . these have enslaved women with the ideological fetters of cerebral abstractions. You, my daughter, still suffer from the backwash and undertow of a "freedom" that makes you the slave of the lie called "equality." D.H. Lawrence (whatever his other mistakes) was quite right in saying that the decline of the world today comes because we have bleached the subconscious (his "dark blood") into pallid mental abstractions and the anemia of "ideas" and "ideals." Ideas, ideals, cerebral abstractions (see Picasso's Guernica), ideological spiderwebs (see "academic freedom"), dehydrated propaganda against life (see most contemporary "literature"), have let our blood out and squirted our arteries full of embalming fluid. Western man and woman have lost instinct, the the will-to-life, the living reason (so much more than "ideas" and "rationality"!). Woman, while she is great and real, leaves "ideas" to Ph.D.'s — and other Alexandrines; she lives, rather, in Jerusalem and Athens. Remain always, my daughter, tangible, concrete, absolute — a "female girl."

What does it mean to be a "female girl"? It means that you are not — and do not want to be — a man. Does MacDowell's *To A Wild Rose* want to be "equal" to the line-splitting of Broncho Nagurski? To fill air with delicate sound is in itself an achievement and a victory. To crash the line like the greatest of fullbacks is in itself an achievement and a victory. But one cannot equate them, any more than one can equate honeysuckle and a hurricane. Discrimination, distinctions, differences, cannot be equated — and only a fool would want to equate them.

You are a woman. I thank God for that; you should thank God for that. But "emancipation of woman" in the modern world seems to mean emancipation *from* woman. To me, as a man, that is a great pity — and loss. A world without women would be like a menu without peaches and cream, an earth without music or the moon. Do you want to be "equal" to man — and so dig ditches and build subways in Russia? Do you want to be "equal" to man — and so disfigure your charming legs in blue jeans, as in Kokomo or Boston? Does Jeannie with the light brown hair wish to be "equal" to man —

and so let it grow scraggly and unwashed in helterskelter masculine similitudes? Do you want to be "equal" to man, so that you may be "emancipated" from the home beautiful, so that you may reach the ecstasy of a clerk at Montgomery Ward? Do you want to be "equal" to man and so share "modern man's" reduction of love to the absurdity of biological release, and a hygienic aspirin to quiet your nerves? If so, you will be just another "sexy" sexless "modern" who will augment the unhappiness of man equally with woman, and turn sex into the activity of corpses on leave from a mortician's.

The contemporary world, in the roots of its mind, has taken a wrong turning; and that has made all the difference. The modern world is unhappy because it is unreal. It supposes that "freedom" means the liberty to be anything that you do not mean to be, and cannot be without destroying yourself. It supposes that "freedom" means to negate and destroy your own being, never the freedom to realize what you mean and in essence are. It supposes that "freedom" means you must listen to the goons of Mao Tse-tung and Fidel Castro, when your destiny and essence is to be an American. The modern "mind" supposes that it is "freedom" for goldenrod to become an olive or an orangutan . . . that it is "liberty" for an orangutan to become a jumping bean or a bustard. This modern itch to be "emancipated" from a profound sense of guilt, a profound abnegation, a profound fear of a vacuum where a meaning ought to be. It leads to the "art" of Picasso, the "poetry" of Dada, the "philosophy" of Sartre, the "sex" of Dr. Kinsey. All such caricatures are the suicide notes the "moderns" write before they put the pistol to what they suppose are their brains.

But it is not so in the world of living Nature. Even the seed or the worm finds its freedom in realizing its own dream; in every change and metamorphosis, life follows the inner choice of its own destiny and essence — through crinkled quiet seed into the blazing trumpets of the nasturtiums, through oval quiet chrysalis into the gorgeous wings of the butterfly. Always while life is real, freedom means the liberty of the *I Will* to become fully the *I Am*. Freedom means the opportunity to become explicitly what you implicitly are. And you, thank God, are a woman!

II

Now if you are a woman — as you are — you have an inner destiny that is very different from that of a man.

Physiologically and psychologically your life will turn inward toward the child. This is so even if you never have a child. Thus in all you do and have and are, there will be an odd delicious quirk that is strange to men . . . a logic colored with personal intimacy . . . a female difference that is your fascination and your irritation and your riddle to men . . . a primal ferocity in affirming your *own*. Your living reason is so vital that it transcends the anemic abstractions called "rationalism." The logic of your feminine blood keeps you sane — and a woman.

Now thanks to this inward-centered, child-centered passion of yours, you desire — even more than man — *your own*.

You have an instinctive sense of property, an essential desire to cherish your own and create your own: *your* child, *your* home, *your* family, *your* man (or even *your* career). This is why, as Kipling said, the female of the species is more deadly than the male; she insists on possessing and defending her own. Man has this in a more prodigal way; he builds and creates, but not in so intimate and personal a fashion. Man strews his creations around, he tosses his work into the winds, he does not create within his own body. But woman does. Therefore she is fierce and passionate in her sense of her own; and she should be. She can be essentially happy (even if she has no children, even if she has only a career) only as she fashions her own personal beloved world, distinct and possessed. If collectivism decrees that her child is not hers but "society's," that her home is just a cubicle in the communal barracks, that *her* kitchen and *her* garden belong to every woman in the block or the ward, she is outraged in her essential being. You, my daughter, will never be happy in a world of impersonal communes where the human ants are all well scrubbed, sanitized, brainwashed, embalmed into a glazed somnambulism. Deep in the wisdom of your subconscious you know that, at the end of the turning the ants took, there lies the single queen ant who has neither the freedom of personal instinctive life nor the freedom of personal intellectual life. The queen ant is a mere mechanism of breeding — the apex and culmination of socialism.

You, my daughter, as incipient woman, as a "female girl," are born for the freedom of your own child (even if it is your career), your own home, your own property and place, *your own man*.

For, most of all, even more than man, you have the essential destiny of finding and loving and cherishing the one being amid the opposite sex (a "male boy"!) who will be most consonant and reciprocal with you. If you think of this, as typical "Liberals" do, as a mere lie-by-night function of biological necessity, as a mere casual titillation of "sex," you will be superficial in attainment because you are ignorant of essence. Sex is a splendor and a joy for love, but love alone makes and keeps sex a splendor and a joy. If "sex" is a precription by a psychiatrist, to be filled at the discount store of Dr. Kinsey, it is as bad therapy as benzedrine taken to bring health and vigor and joy. Only as love is present can sex be more than fireworks on the Fourth of July; only love can make and keep sex "immense in passion, pulse, and power."

One of the worst blows at sex has been the insistence on woman's "satisfaction" as something primal and unique. This has made too many men so self-conscious and so timid that they are often inadequate to provide that satisfaction. If woman would find – as she should – satisfaction and consummation, she must first be what it is woman's essence and glory to be – one who by joyous surrender and sharing *creates man.* Man, for all his blustering and self-conceit, is in need of that glad surrender, that joyous sharing; you, my daughter, as woman, will receive most by giving most, will be blessed most by blessing most. The man you love will be your supreme and greatest child. He will be the canvas for your masterpiece; the marble for your greatest statue. You, as the artist of love, can be more than Rembrandt or Michelangelo – for your work of art is a man of flesh and blood, a man whom you once more help to make a master – confident, joyous, radiant with faith and hope and love. Only you, as woman, can redeem the fragments that walk about and call themselves men today – the fractions of men that reckon themselves whole numbers (but know better) – and make modern man once more *man* with the sign of the nth power after the integer.

That will be your greatest career, your greatest child-bearing, your vital destiny. And if you succeed in this, the inbred sterilities and metallic evil of homosexuality, the dehydrated cruelties of Communism, the idiocies of "Liberalism," will fade and die. For man, thanks to woman, will be on the road to manhood again. And when man is man again, all these phantasmagoria of delirium will fade like miasmic fog before the sun.

Your greatest glory – and your joy, my daughter, will be to become woman again and help man to become man again. If with tact, humor, zest, *play* (never trying to make man over in his instincts, his work, his philosophy) – with a bounty as boundless as the sea, a love as deep, a sharing and reciprocity — you help man to be man, your reward will be great. He, in turn, will make you woman.

The contemporary "realists" (who are utterly ignorant of reality), the existentialists who do not even know that existence without essence cannot exist, the modern skater-bugs called "intellectuals" who move in spasms of futility over the deep waters they cannot probe, really do not exist. They are time-phantasms that reckon themselves real. They are monstrosities of ectoplasm. Their only relation to you, my daughter, is that (if you should let them) they would infect your mind with their own hollowness.

Remember, my daughter, that you will not find the fruition of love or of sex by finding a male — but only by discovering (and helping to create) a man.

And when you succeed, reverence his difference as man. Don't be fussy and bossy, don't subject him to a little domestic welfare state, don't "comb him all to thunder" as the Widow Douglas tried to comb poor Huckleberry Finn. Rejoice, my daughter, when man insists on parking his gun in the kitchen, or makes his study a horror of chaos (and a joy to him). Lest his subconscious seek a sick anarchy, allow him the wholesome freedoms of disorder in the house and a dog rather than a clean floor.

And always, my daughter, remember that man is a hunter and a soldier and an artist. You will risk your life to bear the child; man must risk his life to defend you, the child, the country. You should even insist that man does his militant risking too; you will not really love him unless he does. You should say to him, like that mother of ancient Greece: "Come home with your shield — or on it."

III

IF YOU LISTEN to the Serpent you will lose your instincts, the wisdom of your earth-rooted blood, the essence of yourself as woman. And then, your essence disfigured with acid, your being perverted into philosophistication, you will be an even worse destroyer than the worst man.

When you lose your essence as woman the preserver, you become woman the destroyer. The Vestal Virgins, turning thumbs down on the gallant but defeated gladiator; the terrible women of Paris, knitting dry-eyed as they counted the heads fall; the squaws amusing themselves with the prisoners the braves had taken; the Hell's Angels' molls rejoicing in mayhem and murder; the dusky Amazons crying on the dogs of destruction in Los Angeles . . . in these woman has turned upside down and inside out, till the power of her best sours to the lethal power of her worst. Hell has no gargoyles to surpass a woman gone wrong!

You, as woman the conserver and preserver, should know that there is nothing more disgusting — and ugly — than immorality, a-morality, evil. It is the vandal slashing the canvas, the nihilist smashing the marble. Woman become immoral or a-moral through philosophistication is the word *ugly* become flesh, the incarnation of death. But you, my daughter, remain always as beautiful as you now are — by reverencing your instincts, the living traditions of man and woman, the wisdom that sings in your very bloodstream, the Gods of the Copy Book Maxims, the timeless Decalogue. To love creation and organic harmony; to cherish the home, the child, the husband, the garden, the family, the nation; to be the High Priestess of Life, the Poet of Reality . . . such is to fulfill your essence — and to find your joy — as woman.

Therefore, my daughter, as woman, be inexorable against the mobs in the streets — and when they threaten your home, use a gun on them if your man won't; be contemptuous of the Bacchanals with vine-leaves in their hair: abhor the looters and rapers, the world-haters crashing the red lights of traffic, the nihilists. You will fulfill yourself as woman and your female destiny when you cultivate your garden . . . and have no mercy on wolf and rat, on cut-worm and tetanus germ, on Attila and Mao Tse-tung.

IV

IF YOU FIND this transcendent (yet implicit) destiny, no "career" will matter — whether you have it, or whether you don't.

Sometimes genius selects a woman, as it does a man. Then no one should try to advise, for genius is direct reciprocity with living Nature and God's transcendent immediacy, and any words of mine would be nets to catch the wind. If you are St. Joan or St. Theresa, Florence Nightingale or Emily Dickinson, go with God!

But this side of that sheer individualized genius lies the genius inherent in every woman. That, as I have said, is to seek her own and nourish her own; to be the *Alma Mater* of life.

Love is the sun; you are its planet. If you find, and have, and hold that sun, all these things shall be added unto you. Because you are in love with love, you will be in love with life, with the house and the housework; you will rejoice to keep your husband joyous and your country free. Yours to fashion a shrine of each patriot's devotion, even in this noisy, shallow, metallic-tasting age — a shrine that is a center of essence, an oasis of beauty, a nest for the bird of the heart. To fashion a place for beautiful pictures, noble music, great books, is to make your home a work of art. To love your rugs and your curtains, your dishes and your broom and your oven, to make all these servants of the heart's devotion, that is achievement and victory. Men will seldom appreciate this fully (or explicitly) — and you must never make housekeeping a fetish or a tyranny — you must always be willing to leave your broom to look at the redbud in blossom, or your dishes to look at the moon; but you can and should love all these. So you will fulfill yourself as woman.

And your love should include and embrace the nook of earth that you have chosen. The mountain view in New Hampshire, the rocks of Maine that joust with the ocean, the suave limestone levels of Indiana, the red-clay roads and romantic vistas of Mississippi, the sky-flung Smokies of Carolina, even the streets of "million-footed Manahatta" . . . these should be the furniture of your heart. You should love the land that is your land, your country and your man, your child, your house, your work, your ancestors and your descendents. Woman, by nature, unless she is ruined by the philosophisticates, is a patriot. So the redwoods of California should be no taller than your heart, the prairies of the Dakotas never broader than your love. Thus your life will be too rich, intense, and passionate ever to be bored — knowing that only the juiceless heart seeks escape. You, my daughter, will (I trust) find the essential genius of woman, and know that life is a miracle and romance so vital that not even death can write *finis*.

V

THERE IS something that every woman knows — though she does not often talk about it — if she listens to her own essence and genius. She knows that there is no "progress" toward an outward future; there is no regress toward an ancient past; there is only a possible growing realization and approximation of the timeless center that lies within. Light is the same light that shone on Eden and that will shine on Apocalypse. That is why it is — *real*. Birch-bark torches, beeswax candles, whale-oil lamps, gas mantles, Mazda bulbs and fluorescent tubes, are modes and approximations and relativities of light . . . but light in itself is an absolute that never changes. Love never changes, either; or the cherishing of the child nine months under the heart; or the miracle of birth and the equal miracle of death. Perspective antedated the first artist on the wall of the cave; it will post-date the last artist on the walls of the New Jerusalem descending out of Heaven. Modes shift and vary; essence endures and abides, it simply *is*.

The Serpent, my daughter, still tries to send Eve whoring after strange gods; but you, as woman, should know (even more than man can ever know) that woman touched her highest in the Annunciation and the Magnificat that proclaimed her most blessed when she bore the Son of God.

Integrity And Man's Work

THERE comes a time when only the audacity of a parable and a symbol can make the fact live as a truth. In a time like ours, when "realism" has largely destroyed our sense of reality, that is especially true. Therefore, to realize the integrity of man in relation to his work, let me dare to fashion a parable to be my symbol.

There was once a man who sought perfection in his work. He had no highfalutin ambition — for him perfection even in something minor was enough, if it enlisted his highest artistry. So he sought to fashion a ring of pure silver in which should be set a stone of pure turquoise, both so selected and blended and fashioned that the eyes that saw it or the finger that wore it should know in that one small ring the blessing of perfected beauty. He knew that the happiness of man does not come when he "kills time," but only when he makes time live. He knew the serene zest of the spirit that is willing to devote a lifetime to a single work, finding in such artistry the goal and the reward, beyond all payment or praise. So he sought over the world for the purest silver and the richest turquoise, forgetting the years and the decades and finding even the centuries brief, until around him the generations had passed and the fashions of the world had grown old and were gone. And when he had found the silver that pleased him, with the patience of a redwood forest that builds its height serenely toward the sun through the centuries, he melted the silver, and purified it, and hammered it and shaped it, till it seemed like a ring made out of the stuff of the moon. Then he set delicately and yet firmly in it a stone that was blue as a mountain lake amid mountain snows, a stone in which the sky was the willing captive of beauty.

And as he worked, he ignored death and transcended life, and so age looked over his shoulder, breathless with delight, and neglected to touch the artist in its absorption with the art. The decades and the centuries, in the mood of Eternity, became a part of the ring. Men who did not seek perfection, but merely pay or praise, completed their little works, and such works and workers faded. Only equal artists and arts — the Taj Mahal, the Parthenon, the cathedrals of Chartres and Rouen, the marbles of Michelangelo, the canvases of Rembrandt, the plays of Shakespeare . . . and the humble housewife baking bread with love and joy, or the farmer eighty years old planting new orchards over his hills — remained as his co-eternalists. The error of man's follies dissolved like shadows around him, for only beauty is truth, and only truth is beauty. And still the artist of the ring worked on, ageless, timeless, beyond pain or pleasure, failure or success, in the bliss of creation.

And at last . . . how can we compute the length of time, for he had entered a different dimension of being . . . he said, "All that I can do is done; the ring is at last a *ring!*" It was only then that he wondered if there were any finger to wear that to which he has given his love and labor. And he heard a Voice beyond all voices, and he saw a Finger beyond all fingers; and the Voice said, "Set it upon My finger, and I will wear it forever and forever."

That ring is now a new galaxy of suns and planets, shining in beauty upon the Hand of God.

I

THIS PARABLE suggests, humbly and far off, the integrity of man in relation to his work.

As I said in a previous essay, a man's life turns *outward*, objectively, toward his work, and becomes thus the outward incarnation of his essential inward word (*logos*). That work, no matter how humble it may seem, will give his life quality, value, and meaning — for it will fulfill his inner destiny — if it is a form of artistry that projects his inner aptitude into outer accomplishment. Man finds himself, man fulfills himself, in his work; man is happy only as he finds a work worth doing — and does it well.

In the greatest symbol we have of the beginning of the world and life, Adam is set in a garden, to dress it and to keep it. In that ancient story, the fundamental vision of life is this: Earth is a garden or a workshop or a laboratory or a canvas on which to paint or a page on which to write, and man is the artist of such labor and such artistry. Of course there should be spontaneity and freedom and joy in his work — the color on the plume, the song on the lips, the aspect of *play* but still this free spontaneity centers around a work that is serious, around the intense creation of a pattern that may perfect and incarnate meaning and validity. The integrity of man's life comes when he develops such art to accomplish such work.

The happy man is he who finds a work that he loves and expresses in it his own essential word. Only so does he find integrity. The kind of work will vary with the kind of man. For Corot it will be to surprise and incarnate the magic of Romance hidden like a Dryad amid misty morning trees; for Monet the white-and-gold waterlilies upon the Seine, lilac in the evening; for the artisan of the Toledo blade it will be to fashion a sword worthy for heroes to wear; for Johnny Appleseed it will be to plant apples in a land where before no orchards grew; for the housewife it will be to prepare "many-tasting food," or to make the bed with "the cool kindliness of sheets" that "soon smooth away trouble"; for Washington it will be to free the child of the Republic by the Caesarian operation of war. For the farmer, the businessman, the textile worker, the builder of jets, the architect, the mechanic, it will be to do the practical work of the world. For any true workman, the goal will not be the "rewards" of "success" but the accomplishment of his art. He will not ask what Carlyle called "praise and pudding" but he will be the artist of whom Kipling wrote:

> And only the Master shall praise us, and only the Master shall blame;
> And no one shall work for money, and no one shall work for fame,
> But each for the joy of the working, and each, in his separate star,
> Shall draw the Thing as he sees It for the God of Things as They Are!

Much of the unhappiness of man today comes because he has lost this essential characteristic of man the artist and artisan — "the joy of the working." Man speaks often of a "high standard of living" — but seldom (if ever) of a high standard of life. He works to heap up abundance and affluence, as if that were the real essence of work in itself; but men play with that abundance too often as pampered poodles play with their kibbles, and do not dance to the music of the spheres where the morning stars sang together in the morning of the world. Today our difficulty is that many men make a living — but few man make a life.

The greatest answer, indeed, to the contemporary Titans who would storm Heaven and lay waste the world — to the nihilists of "revolution" — to the traitors who betray and the Communists who enslave — is to restore to man the truth of vision and the essence of action. The renaissance of man, which is the only hope for man and for the destiny that God has set in his heart, is to renew in him the sense of integrity in his work.

II

TH E TWO greatest religions of the world have seen God Himself as a master workman.

To the Hindus, Brahma was the *potentia qua*, the power whence all things flow, the great I am perfect, and self-sufficient, and yet seeking to create out of Himself, like a dramatist or poet, projecting creation like a play or poem. Brahma in the ecstasy of creation blows the suns and planets like bubbles of light, and strews the colors of the spectrum through the worlds like a drift of peacock feathers. He rejoices in his poem.

To the Hebrews, and to the Christians, God is the *potentia qua*, the power at the origin of all things, who says of creation *Let it be*, and it is . . . and, later after Plato, the Word or *Logos* that is the beginning of all . . . . God is the Master of all Good Workmen, for He is Himself the Master Workman, the Creator, the Poet (*i.e.* "the Maker," as the Greek meaning is) of the Poem of Creation.

The great anonymous Hebrew seer told us that God looked upon His work and saw that it was good, which is the finest word in all the world about the joy of the artist in his work.

Especially to the good Hebrew and to the genuine Christian, creation is a thing of high seriousness, that extends through time and into that right-angle to time which we call *Eternity*. Ideas have consequences; actions have consequences. These consequences abide and endure; they follow us through this life and beyond this life; our works, for good or evil, abide and stand and follow us forever.* Our works, therefore, are of major meaning. They are a part of our metaphysical being, our essential *I Am*.

In the West, the Occident that was Europe and is also America, the Hebrew and Christian emphasis was dominant as long as the West remained dynamic and vital. To *be* is the great Hindu emphasis; to *do* is the great Hebrew emphasis; to be *and* do is the great Christian emphasis. Western man, while he remained dynamic and vital, was Faustian man; he was not to say to the moment, "Stay, thou art so

---

*To the good Hindu also, with a different and less concrete emphasis, these works determine our lives through all incarnations, as the Karma of our deeds that accompanies our being through all transformations.

fair!", but to seek in, yet through, each moment a creation that transcended it and fulfilled it only that we might seek a higher fulfillment beyond it. Goethe saw the nature of Western man intensely when he fashioned the active restless soul of Faust.

Therefore, in the great eras of the West, in the rise of the Dark Ages into the Ages of Light, in the splendid pageantry of the Middle Ages, in the Renaissance, in the creation of the architecture of the cathedrals and in the art of Leonardo and Michelangelo, in the *Divine Comedy* of Dante, the *Don Quixote* of Cervantes, the plays of Shakespeare, in the daring suppositions of the science that rereads the logic God first set in Nature, in the voyage of Columbus and the audacity of the Conquistadors and the Cavaliers and the Pilgrims, we see the West seeking the lightnings — or the sunlight — of great deeds. Western man, while he was vital and real, loved to create and to build, to find his inward integrity by fulfilling his destiny in outward action. Tennyson, in one of his finest poems ("Locksley Hall"), expressed the splendor of action, the mood of Western man tiptoe for fulfillment:

Men my brothers, men the workers, ever reaping something new;
That which they have done but earnest of the things that they shall do.

And he expressed the direction of that action superbly thus; man is to "Rift the hills, and roll the waters, flash the lightnings, weigh the sun." Even in 1835, not so long ago (as time in history is), that was still the vision of the West. Still man was Faustian.

We should notice that the essence of the Faustian spirit is to see the joy of the work itself as superior to the products of the working. Not products as a use, but production as a poem! As long as man found his fulfillment in the artistry of action he could safely enjoy the acquisitions that came from action, for he was constantly renewing creation as the peach tree or the wheat field renews the harvest with every year and season in the fruitful poem of seedtime and harvest. To Faustian man, the abundance of life is not a cistern of stored waters, but a fountain whence fresh waters ever flow from the heart of Earth. Never, "Stay, thou art so useful!", but "Flow, thou art so fascinating!"

Today our loss of integrity in work stems from our denial of the Faustian spirit. We are more concerned with affluence — the richness of the product, the wealth that is the consequence of work — than with achievement, which is artistry in creation. A sad sign of the decadence of Western man is his satisfaction with, and emphasis on, the "high standard of living" that capitalism provides, as if that were the real justification of capitalism. The distinction between capitalism and Communism does not lie only, or even chiefly, in the higher economic standard of living that capitalism provides. Of course that higher standard of living exists; of course that higher standard of living is an excellent thing. Professor John Kenneth Galbraith attacks "affluence" as something wrong, which should be drained off from private enjoyment into public use (this is collectivism), but I do not agree with him. The affluence that capitalism provides is excellent; we should be proud of it, and private man should enjoy it in private ways!

But capitalism itself is decadent and in peril if it ever emphasizes affluence as an end and not as the casual result of something vaster and more vital: *The artistry of work.* The affluence of our production will not long continue if we stress product and not production, if we emphasize the good things poured out of the cornucopia, and not the good workman who joys to pour those things into the cornucopia.

The emphasis today, in capitalism when it decays, is on "60,000,000 jobs" – and not on man's delight in his work. "Jobs," in themselves, may mean little; does man do those jobs with integrity, does he create with joy, does he *love* his work and find his work a destiny? We loose a "war on poverty" – as if, in itself, it brings a wealth of life. We think that men can be happy, and that "the Great Society" will come, if we make every man an economic king by subsidies and unearned affluence, with no realization that a man must be a king in a work that he loves to do and in a creation that gives him a sense of pride and mastery. And then we wonder that men are unhappy, and restless, and that they say: "Give me more – but ask me to do less!"

If capitalism justifies itself only by its "high standard of living," it will not enlist the soul of man; it will not even long preserve its "high standard of living." Capitalism, at its best, seeks risk, adventure, freedom to strive and compete, daring, creation – and it must make man happy in the work he does, it must give him a true "joy in the working." Other ages did not bring so much affluence; but they did preserve more artistry.

Unfortunately, in our decadence, we often seek the wrong way to achieve the right goal. Our goal should be life at a higher voltage, life "immense in passion, pulse, and power." Our means to this too often, today, is to seek to get more for doing less; to see in the products of work the meaning of work, or in the profits of work the reason for work. Many of our labor unions, it seems, are mostly concerned with pay day and quitting time; with more reward for less production; with more fringe benefits, more dollars in the pay envelope, more pudding and pie, but less perspiration — and no inspiration. I do not intend to delve into the false economics of this: I wish here to discuss the fallacious psychology of this. The real flaw in industrial capitalism is not that the worker gets too little of the product, but that the worker finds too little fulfillment in the production. He *should* say: "Let us together, management and labor, somehow find a way of making work more significant, more interesting, more personal, so that once more a workman can find the pride of an artist and artisan, so that once more he may find the joy of fulfilling himself in the product he makes." If he should say this and if (with management) he could bring this about, in the end he would find his production increased and so his share of the product greater. But meanwhile, and more important, he would find again his integrity in the work itself, and so his happiness as a man.

Of course Communism, socialism, and welfare "Liberalism," compound all that is bad in capitalism, making it worse to the nth degree. They add a *greater* emphasis on the "satisfaction" of economics with less economic product to provide for that "satisfaction"; they bring *in* (necessarily) the coercion of the State to take the place of the motivation of profit; and they make man unhappier than ever before.

Communism hypocritically promises to make men free, affluent, and happy by collectivizing the farm and nationalizing the industry. But the creative genius of man is stifled and dehydrated and unhappy on the "collective farm" or the Chinese commune, or the State-ruled factory; it registers that rebellion and unhappiness in doing as little work as possible, like a canny mule refusing to pull, so that the collective farm will never feed the population and the nationalized industry willl never supply the human need. But the same mulish recalcitrants will do a wonderful work if they are allowed their own little backyards of independence and private property, where they can be "every inch a king" and express their destiny by raising cabbages and tomatoes to their hearts' desire. Collectivism performs a lobotomy upon man, so at best he works like a slave in a coma or a zombie with a hoe. The result is no production to speak of and an apathetic distaste for the artistry of work.

Socialism sentimentally promises to make men free, affluent, and happy by assuring their "security" and making them drowsy little guinea pigs in a cosmic featherbed; but there is always something forgotten — and rotten — in the state of Sweden, and a tinkle of rats' feet over the prophylaxis of the soul.

"Liberalism" tries to wage its "war on poverty" by seeking to domesticate man into a cozy clam. The planners and regulators, as Robert Frost wrote long ago,

> Swarm over their lives enforcing benefits
> That are calculated to soothe them out of their wits,
> And by teaching them how to sleep the sleep all day,
> Destroy their sleeping all night the ancient way.

Taylor Caldwell has told us, in her pungent great inimitable fashion, how Appalachia* is to be uprooted to agree with the "Liberal" myth; I cannot tell the story half so well. But you know it already — and it proves my point.

In all these unnatural — or anti-natural — ways, collectivism ignores or denies or seeks to destroy the essence of man in relation to his work, which is that his artistry in individual work is the joy of life.

So we return to the essential question: The integrity of man in relation to his work. Until that question is answered and that destiny fulfilled — until we rediscover the ancient and unchanging truth of things and the root of the matter — we shall perpetuate our present adult delinquency. That is the worm at the root of our life. That is the cause of the decline of the West, of the apathy and unhappiness that lead us to help the West commit suicide.

The mischief of all this lies, as always, in a false philosophy. A "realism" that knows nothing of reality, a dehydrated prose that knows nothing of the full-bodied and full-blooded poetry of life, an economics and an anemic scientism that usurp the role of the spiritual — these destroy the essence of work and the joy of life.

We need men who understand the parable and symbol with which I began; men who will shatter the falsity of economic determinism

---

*"Appalachia," *American Opinion* for March, 1966, Pp. 73-80. Included also in Miss Caldwell's delightful autobiographical book, *Growing Up Tough*, Devin-Adair, 1971.

with the truth of vital determination. If even only a million men over all the world would say: "Our immortal souls are too valuable for us to lose them by gaining the whole world of affluence but abandoning the real world of artistry. It is better to perish than to continue doing a work that means nothing to us, and we refuse to do it any longer." Then at last the history of the world might become noble once more — then at last the resurrection of man might begin — for then at last Atlas would shrug.

III

THE BEST THING about the industrial revolution has been that it increased the affluence of man; the worst thing about the industrial revolution has been that it decreased the artistry of man. A sense of destiny in the individual, a sense of talent and initiative, a sense of craftsmanship that makes one proud — all this has decreased. Men on the assembly lines of industry too often come to seem to themselves mere utilities and appurtenances and half-conscious dummies, not artisans and craftsmen and masterworkmen. Compare them with a silversmith like Paul Revere or an artisan of furniture like Duncan Phyfe! And men, in the too often blind reaction of their distaste for this, have tried to compensate for it by the wrong solutions — by falsely calling themselves "wage-slaves" and by demanding only less hours and more pay.

Now there is no easy solution. The expanded populations of the world will necessitate mass production if their needs are to be met. Therefore the assembly line will have to continue. The coarsening of work that is inseparable from mass production will have to continue. The lessening of individual significance in mass production will therefore continue. The question, finally, must be raised out of economics and into the spirit; it will be this: How, in the nature of modern production in industry, can man find some spiritual motivation or mood which will give him again a sense of integrity even in the worst phases of modern industry?

There is always going to be some work that has less interest for men than it should. Upton Sinclair, in his sentimental *The Jungle* sees this even where it doesn't exist, in the preparing of food and the washing of dishes in the home; and, like all collectivists, he sees the solution in "co-operative" kitchens that will do the cooking for everybody, or "communal" dish-washing machines that will do the job for everybody. How much he and his like miss! The real problem does not lie in dishwashing — which can be quite interesting work, where you can cleanse beloved china, "ringed with blue lines, clean-gleaming," while another member of the family reads Dickens to you; or in cooking, which is an art and a love. The real problem lies outside the home. Garbage will have to be removed. Subway trains will have to run in Manhattan. Coal will have to be mined or oil barrelled. Nuts will have to be tightened on bolts. Stenographers will have to take dictation (a much less artistic work than cooking!); check-out girls will be necessary in supermarkets. Such is the way of all flesh. No automation is going to abolish such work, though it may (I hope) mitigate it. How, then, can we find integrity in such chores of life?

I say flatly that only a religious meaning in life will make us happy and integral in *some* of the world's work. An old inscription, surely Christian, reads: "Lift the stone, or cleave the wood, and I am there." A knowledge that for the organic life of the world certain unpleasant work must be done, and a consecration to that work for the good of man and the glory of God, will alone bring integrity into some of the world's drudgery. While the West was still Christian, George Herbert wrote:

> A man that looks on glass,
>   On it may stay his eye;
> Or if he pleaseth, through it pass,
>   And then the Heaven espy.
> A servant with this clause
>   Makes drudgery divine:
> Who sweeps a room as for Thy laws,
>   Makes that and the action fine.

A workman who has that spirit, and feels in his work a divine meaning, can do any work that is sound in nature and necessary for the organic good of the world, and find his integrity in the work. He will work to meet the needs of man and to serve the glory of God, and in so doing he will make "that and the action fine."

But today the men who most insist on the industrial process to provide affluence are often spiritual nihilists who do all they can to scorn or wreck and destroy any religious conception of life. How, then, can they compensate for the bleak unhappiness of man in mere industrialism, in the assembly line, in production without individual artistry? How will they get the affluence, if men are no longer happy in their work and ask ever more of the product with ever less production? Where will they get the products to pour out in subsidies if men no longer have interest in doing the work that alone can provide the subsidies? If there is no spiritual meaning, and if the work has to be done willy-nilly, the only possible answer will be the answer the Communists give: brute compulsion, the goon squad and the bayonet, slave labor and the concentration camp, the fiats of the omnipotent State, the world of 1984.

Always, till the end of the world, the only way of making some of the world's work a thing of quality, value, and meaning, will be the religious sense: *"Lift the stone, and cleave the wood, and I am there."*

There is a second answer, akin to the first — for it also is spiritual. It is the answer that poetry, philosophy, art in the individual soul, can give. It is the way that some significant minds have found, and that more of us — that *any* of us — could find. Spinoza made his daily bread by grinding lenses, and did that work faithfully and well; then, having made his living by a lesser work, he made a life by a greater work — by fashioning a majestic philosophy. Thus man can live his life on dual levels — and if workmen use their leisure, which they are right in seeking, for something significant in itself — writing poetry, painting pictures, raising roses, fashioning bird houses and feeders to bring birds to their yards, having a vegetable garden, building a library of their own, learning a foreign language, fighting Communism, *etc., etc.*, they may find integrity because they both make a living *and* a life. It is best if your vocation is your avocation too; but if that cannot be, do your vocation well so that you may be free to develop your avocation richly.

In North Thompson, Connecticut, we trade at a store excellently run by a man and his wife, who do both the planning and the work, a store which is eminently successful. Mrs. Pauline Godzik, the wife, is a most efficient member of the partnership. But she has also discovered in herself that "one talent which 'tis death to hide." She has within her the destiny to paint, and she developed in herself that destiny to a degree of splendid accomplishment. The walls of the store have become the walls of an art gallery, hung with scores of paintings that she has fashioned with love and skill in the intervals of a busy life. If I know anything about art — and it is one of my major studies and interests — she is an artist of worth and distinction. She will not sell her paintings, though she has been offered high prices, because she loves them. This avocation of hers has not hurt her vocation, but helped it; her vocation has not interfered with her avocation, but helped it. And she has found more meaning in life, more happiness in living, more fulfillment of destiny, than most people I know. But, even in a lesser degree, many others could find her way to make not only a living but also a life.

I know a man who runs a motel — his own — and runs it well. He does the world's work faithfully, as we have to do it, and does not try to evade or avoid it. But his parallel interest, the center of his life, is the writing of poetry, and to that avocation he devotes the plus of his energies. In that he finds the central happiness of his life.

When one thinks of all the nihilists, the "rebels" who run amok after illusions, the rioters and rapers who let loose the grudge and hate in their own sick false narrow hearts, one pities them for their sterile waste of energy. One wishes he could say to them: "Produce, produce, if it be only a carved peach stone!" One wonders how, in this life, they will find a way to enter joyously into the life to come; one wonders how even the Master of All Good Workmen can put them to work anew, when they have said "no" to work and to life itself.

If there *is* work which no vital man should do, and in which no sensible man can be happy, then let such men be creative rebels — let Atlas shrug! I cannot myself believe that the proliferating bureaucrats under the "Liberal" Establishment — the tax collectors (the Gospels spoke of them as "the publicans and the sinners"!), the snoopers, the chiviers of farmers, the urban renewers, the wheels within wheels — can ever be happy in their nonsense "work." And I'd like to hear them all say: "Better perish than make a 'living' by losing a life! I'll run a motel, I'll scratch a subsistence living out of five stony-lonesome acres, I'll gather cypress knees and sell them, I'll live like the young Robert Frost on four-hundred dollars a year, I'll wash cars or run a filling-station, I'll raise earthworms, I'll make little brass cannons and sell them, but I won't be a well-paid functionary in the Circumlocution Office." If they only would so speak, as men should, the "Liberal" Establishment would end like the soap-bubble it is — pricked by the pin of integrity.

In this connection, one should remember the destiny of the good soldier. He certainly makes a meager living and he may make a gory death. But if he is the man he should be, he will feel in the defense of his country, in the war with the perpetrators of darkness at noon, a destiny and a meaning. And that will give him integrity that will make his skill and his courage a quality and a value. He will, even if he dies, live.

There is one more thing to say. In our lives, and not only in our work, the value subsists not in the *fact* but in the *truth*, not in the *realism* but in the *romance*, not in the prose but in the poetry. What this false and petty age of the "Liberal" Establishment most lacks is the poetry of life. We have forgotten that a "fact" is *not* — a truth. The "fact" is that even the best violin is a concatenation of wood and catgut; the truth is that a man named Stradivarius touched it with his genius, and so it is a magical treasure-house of beautiful sound. The "fact" is that Emily Dickinson lived in Amherst, was a member of the species *homo sapiens*, weighed so many pounds and ounces, and was so many feet and inches tall; the truth is that she wore the sandals of the sun and wrote the greatest poetry of any woman in America. The "fact" is that the farmer raises so many bushels of potatoes or wheat; the truth is that he is a co-worker with the rain and the sun and the loam, and with God who said, "Let there be light." The "fact" is that some adolescents are juvenile deliquents; the truth of vital boyhood is the vision of Keats: "A laughing schoolboy without grief or care,/ Riding the spring branches of an elm." The fallacy of the modern, from Edgar Lee Masters and Lincoln Steffens to Dr. Kinsey and Le Roi Jones, is to enthrone the "fact" and betray the truth.

The wisest of the world have always known this. William Blake wrote: " 'What!' it will be questioned, 'when the sun rises, do you not see a disc of fire, somewhat like a guinea?' 'Oh no, no! I see an innumerable company of the heavenly host, crying "Holy, holy, holy is the Lord God Almighty!" ' I question not my corporal eye, any more than I question a window, concerning a sight. I look through it, and not with it." Only as man, in resurrection and renaissance, again sees not *with* but *through* the eye, shall we raise the temporal fact into the eternal truth. Then we shall live once more, and know reality once more, for we shall live by poetry, by romance, by the *nth* power of reality, and rise from the *status quo* into the *potentia qua*. Then we shall find quality, value, and meaning, which will bring integrity back into our work — and into us; and we can say: "My name is Lazarus — for I live!"

IV

TO FIND integrity in our work let us cease to look toward the reward and let us look toward the work. Usually in the history of the world those who have done the greatest work have received the least reward: But what of that? They have been the most blessed of men, and from the life beyond the world not one of them would change his destiny.

What reward, in "praise or pudding," came to the great anonymous benefactors of man who discovered fire or fashioned the wheel? And in later days and years, think of the master workmen of the world: Remember Browning's question, "What porridge had John Keats?"

Cervantes discovered and incarnated the soul of Spain forever in Don Quixote, the very crown and apex of that great land; but he lived and died a poor maimed soldier, a poet ignored or ridiculed by the fashionable of the day — Lope de Vega and his clique — he was falsely sentenced to prison, and at the end he was considered so negligible that he was buried in an unmarked grave that is lost forever. Which is just — for he was so great that all Spain is his grave and his memorial! Don John of Austria, "the last knight of Europe," took weapons from the wall and rode to the sea; he hurled the headlong Turk backward at Lepanto; but the politicians feared his brilliance and his genius, and muffled him in the shadows, and let him eat his heart out in inaction till he died forgotten.

Giordano Bruno called himself "The awakener of sleeping souls," and went through life like a sword of the sun; but his reward was to be burned in the physical flame that is the parallel of the spiritual flame. General of the Armies Douglas MacArthur won the war in the Pacific, and returned to the lost lands to restore the honor of America, and would have overthrown the fire-ants of China, but the politicians dismissed him from command and relegated his genius to inaction in a time that supremely demanded action.

Too often the few great teachers who (in the Greek phrase) "having torches themselves, hand them on to others," seem nothing to the educational hierarchy, and are tossed aside at the very height of their powers. Columbus, the symbol of the discovery of the New World, lived his last years in chains, and the rabble cried while he still walked the streets, "Behold the Admiral of Mosquito Land!" The bravest and wisest anti-Communist in America is traduced not only by his enemies, but sometimes by those who should be his friends, and has to stand like a mighty headland buffeted by blind tides. But what of all that? As Kipling's explorer says:

> Have I named one single river? Have I claimed one single acre?
> Have I kept one single nugget — (barring samples)? No, not I!
> Because my price was paid me ten times over by my Maker.
> But you wouldn't understand it. You go up and occupy.

The integrity of man lies not in the reaping of the harvest — but in the sowing of the seed. Only in his joyous work does man find his destiny and his being; he does not have to "go up and occupy," his integrity is to "hear the Whisper."

A contemporary "realist" once — knowing "the price of everything and the value of nothing" — asked an acorn: "Why grow?" The acorn, being the realist of Eternity, answered: "To incarnate my destiny, and to fulfill my dream, and to realize my artistry in the century-enduring oak that scorns the lightnings and the winds, and lifts its leaves into the sun, and gives the violet and the little rabbit shade."

What To Tell Your Children About Sex And Love

ALWAYS "Liberals" try to drag the Twentieth Century, kicking and screaming, backward into the Nineteenth. "Liberalism," of course, was and is a fallacy of the second half of the Nineteenth Century, and does not belong to the realities of the Twentieth Century at all. The dry brittle bones that support the cadaver of "Liberalism" are clichés that lost their marrow long ago. But still "Liberalism" asserts the "right" to be wrong, and ridicules the responsibility to be right. Still "Liberalism" ignores the inexorable objectivity of the universe that affirms "It is this way," and asserts the subjective controverse of "I want what I want when I want it." That is why "Liberalism" in the Twentieth Century must be recognized as an antiquity and an anachronism if man is to endure and thrive and come to be Man.

One of the casualties of "Liberalism" is sex. Whimsical and petulant, "Liberalism" demands the license to turn sex into exhibitionism, and to degrade the glowing experience of physical love into "freedom" (as one of them says) to have sex experience with a "lamp" if you want to. And just as the Soviets claim to have invented everything from the oesophagus to the Edsel, "Liberals" seem to claim that they have invented — or at least discovered — sex. They treat sex to an intellectual strip-tease and assert that when we have removed the last Bikini, and (as one of them said) have come to the point where "we would not qualify freedom by demanding responsibility,"* man will at last be happy, healthy, and whole.

This "Liberal emancipation" of sex began in the second half of the Nineteenth Century. All sorts of Madison Avenue pre-view boys began a publicity campaign for "sex." H.G. Wells, Grant Allen, Frank Harris in his fleshly aspects, Havelock Ellis, W.L. George, Krafft-Ebing, Freud (certainly in his effect), and such birds of a feather, proclaimed that perfect "candor" about the "facts of sex" would

---

*From an article called "Campus Encounter," *United Campus Christian Fellowship*, the campus movement of the Christian Churches, Volume III, Number 4.

deliver us from repressions and lead us into complete health and total happiness. Their slogan was (to paraphrase Byron): "On with the prance, let 'sex' be unconfined!" The "obscurantism" of the "Puritan," they told us, had condemned us to complexes, neuroses, mental illness, hypocrisy; it had made literature tepid and stale and senile; so our duty was to lift the "sex-basis" of life into the light, and we would become *"Integer vitae scelerisque purus."* Then literature would be real and joyous; then life would be healthy and happy. Men and women would be as gods under a lidless sky; Mr. and Mrs. Everyman would have a holiday of perpetual fun and games; all men and especially all women would kick up their heels like little calves in a cloverfield of biological release and psychological titillation. "Love" would at last be "real."

The "Liberals" had their way. The last Bikini is now removed, the exhibitionism is complete, the physical processes of sex are detailed in the raw, and reiterated and exploited in paperbacks sold all over the land for a price even teenagers can pay. Yet, though "Liberals" keep insisting that now we are free and happy and whole, the apex of joy refuses to arrive. The "literature" that was to be so joyous is dismal with despair, pessimism, boredom, cynicism, and the botch of weary blues; the "joy" of sex set free has become the dull monotony of omnisimilitude, or a tepid regimen of biological hygiene; life, the "sophisticated" think, would be impossible without drink, drugs, and psychiatrists. There are no more magic casements opening on the foam, and "We'll to the woods no more,/The laurels all are cut / . . . "

Yet the "Liberals," congenitally unable to face reality, do not admit their reduction to bathos, and say that if we only had *more* exhibitionism and *less* Bikini we would at last come to the country of Sex Fulfillment and live happily ever after.

The trouble with "Liberals" is that they are fall-guys for that first con-man, the Serpent in Eden. They are pitifully credulous of abstract theories; they are pitifully impervious to concrete realities. As Malcolm Muggeridge wrote, the egghead "buys every gold brick because, imaginatively, its glitter is convincing. When, however, he goes to sell it he finds it worthless. And quite often he has it thrown at his head for his pains."

The "Liberals" in relation to sex, bought a pretty, glittering, surface-only brick of fool's gold — and turned their backs on the mines where the real gold of love lies beautiful and rich for the patient and skillful miner. That was their fallacy of sex. Today you can, in Zenith or even in Gopher Prairie, buy *Fanny Hill, My Life And Loves, Lady Chatterley's Lover, Tropic Of Cancer*, and (far worse than these "classics of sex") their imitators and vulgarizers — the hundreds of fly-by-day volumes that detail physical acts and describe in monotonous clichés the biological mechanics of "sex." The total effect is like picking fair, blue-misted plums from a proud ravaged garden tree, and passing them raucously from hand to hand down a street of rioters, till they are bruised and dirtied and are plums no longer. And then we eat them and say: *"That is fruit!"* The proud and free and wise, however, now as always, love to preserve the sky-blue fruit of the tree of joy by reverencing it and cultivating their own garden, and savoring it in joy by themselves. Wise men seek a reality of private experience and not a public caricature of exhibitionism. And they realize it as a poem — they do not tear it into verbal tatters as the statistics of pseudo-science.

Man's noble delight in the poetry of fulfillment has thus become the physiological computation of "orgasms," fussy "scientific" statistics, sex-in-the-head (which is not the place for it!), the phallic become the anemia of cerebration, the reduction of love's mystery and the glory of love's consummation to "ideas" about it . . . such is the disorder of the day. The result is the almost universal and complete destruction of sex by our prevalent surfeit of "sex."

This culminates in a power failure, because the "Liberals" have cut the high voltage lines of life. In this situation we need a return to the dynamos — or rather an *advance* toward even greater dynamos — which create the currents of power and glory that flow into love and life from the metaphysical. This can be done only if we tell our children the truth — that sex is so real and joyous that we should institute a renaissance of the joy and glory of sex in its relation to *love.*

I

ALL CONTEMPORARY collectivisms — "Liberal" or totalitarian — put a hex on sex.

Communism, so far as we can judge from this side of the iron-curtained voiceless vacuum, does not have the *same* problem of sex that is posed by the "Liberals," but a variation on a theme. This is natural. Communism is our "Liberal" materialism and collectivism carried to the extreme — to the point where the dead-end street of economic determinism leaves us huddled meaningless under the sign "Abandon hope all ye that enter here." Communism asserts that economics, sociology, matter and mechanism, *etc.*, are the end as well as the means of life. Sex, if it is considered at all in their a-philosophy, is strictly business; it is to provide children to be workers in the ant heap or soldier-ants for the conquest. Communism censors romance, poetry, and the psyche out of life; it cares nothing for the magic of love and the joy of sex. Such private ecstasy (Communists think) is bad for public business and Chairman Mao.

But "democratic" socialism and the Welfare State are like this in kind if not in degree. Scandinavia, Great Britain, America, are today equally credulous of the centrality of economic satisfactions: They provide more of the "satisfactions," but they make them equally material and equally central. Our "Liberal" welfare-mongers give their hearts (such as they have) to "Civil Rights," to "urban renewal," to "medicare," to the "war on poverty," to the "peace corps," to "revolution," and to all the kinks of "reform" that are all they can see with their myopic and honey-coated eyes. They give their "hearts" to these, and so they regard sex as a "kick" along the march, or a conformity to the urges of biological necessity, or a mode of being "revolutionary" against "tradition." Sex is, to them, a thing really minor and unimportant and casual — and therefore a thing that can be engaged in by everyone, everywhere, everytime, without any supreme commitment or any major glory. How could it be otherwise? If life is only a transient episode disturbing the nullity of a finite, meaningless, temporal world, where social amelioration is the best we can do, why regard love as an exception to the rule? To the welfare-mongers, sex is only a phase of the trivia experienced by that latest of the ephemera, man. And so, in the end, they urge that it be swallowed like a cold pancake and wonder why there is mass indigestion.

Too many of our contemporary "psychologists" are no better. The dominant psychologists of the Establishment, save for Carl Jung, are fundamentalists of materialism. To them, sex is as material, as blind, as meaningless as the flung pseudopodia of an amoeba with a libido. Their way of treating it is to italicize its biological urge, and to advise its gratification to free us from "repression." They reduce psychology to an ideology by deleting the *psyche* and making the *logy* irrational: They are thus traitors equally to reason and to the psyche.

Against the background of all these assorted materialists, it is no wonder that too many men and women today are confused, frustrated, miserable, perverse, joyless, or that they feel driven to fantastic destructive escapes like L.S.D., suicide, riots in the streets, psychiatrists, and the promises of "the Great Society." All great conservators of value could — and did — prophesy such results. And one chief cause of such a debacle is the degeneration of sex into "sex" and the betrayal of love into biology.

The reality of life is never material, it is always spiritual. Without spirit and psyche and mind, machines will rust into rubble, cities (as Omar saw) will soon be habitations for the lion and the lizard, Nature will bury man under the trees like the Mayan cities or the ruins of civilizations in the jungles of India.

All collectivisms, in their emphasis on mechanism and materialism, degrade sex into "sex," and seek to satisfy the immortal longings of man with the mortal "satisfactions" of physical being. As Leopardi wrote even in the Seventeenth Century: "But the lofty spirits of my century discovered a new, and as it were divine counsel: for not being able to make happy on earth any one person, they ignored the individual, and gave themselves to seek universal felicity; and having easily found this, of a multitude singly sad and wretched they make a joyous and happy people." This irony applies even more today. And it applies because our ideologists ignore all concrete realities — like the poetry of love, the destiny of individuals who seek to fulfill their private *I Am*, the creative concrete work of individuals — and seek abstract ideologies and *isms* that lead men into quicksands of illusion and fallacy. Especially when our "Liberals" caricature sex into "sex" they hasten the decline of man into mass and escalate the degeneration of the West.

II

LET US MAKE CLEAR what we conservators of value criticize and what we seek to create. We conservators of life and love are not "Puritans." We are not against sex — we are only skeptical of "sex." We do not seek to deny, repress, or censor the love of the body; we simply affirm life and love in their essence, as God made them. God made us male and female; he made us man and woman; he blessed us with opposites and contrasts that provide us with the delicious polarity of sex. He made our bodies to be the opposites that unite, the contrasts by which we become most intimately one. Ours the great parable of Eden. There God made Adam and Eve innocently joyous in the poetry of sheer being where they wore not even a fig leaf. It was the eternal "Liberal," the footless, rootless egghead, the snake in the Garden grass, the side-show barker costumed as the Serpent, who sold us intellectual gold bricks. He sold Adam and Eve a bill of goods — that they would "not surely die," but "become as gods"; that they would "know good and evil" *(i.e.,* analyze, discuss, argue about, turn into a "dialogue," and mentally disintegrate good into evil). It was *after* this degrading of concrete reality into abstract illusions that Adam and Eve sought out fig leaves. It was *after* the Serpent fractured Eden into Academe that man and woman dislocated sex into "sex." But we conservators, who refuse to eat any longer the fruit of the forbidden tree, still enjoy the innocence and glory of love.

The good Greeks or the great Elizabethans were conservators of reality. Aeschylus and Shakespeare, Homer and Spenser, were conservators; and, as such, they had more freedom of sex and of love than a truckload of Freudians or a Pan Am jet freighted with Dr. Kinseys. Equally, we conservators today are lovers of the joyous miracle of sex, of man as essentially man and woman as essentially woman, and of the magical blending of the two which is the physical side of love. Therefore, naturally, we prefer the great passionate poem of sex and love, "The Song Of Solomon," to all the posed "sexy" artifices of *Playboy,* or the arid pages of the *Kinsey Report,* or the erotica of the "sex"-fanciers. We renew our life and our love by the great verse: "Who is this that looketh forth from the windows of the morning; clear as the sun, fair as the moon, terrible as an army with banners?" We do not glaze our love into artifice with the self-consciously posed "sexy" nudes exploited by the slick pages of "sophisticated" magazines.

It is the "sex"-fanciers who destroy innocence, polarity, vital consummation, the torn page of man and woman made whole so that we may read the poem of love. It is the "Liberals" who go witch-hunting after love and torture it into "sex." We conservators, on the contrary, rejoice in the eternal Eve and the eternal Adam, and seek to restore them to Eden — the place of joy and freedom and innocent bliss. We wish to renew the mystery and the wonder of sex, its atmosphere of poetry, its plus element and its Nth power.

Only as we renew in ourselves and (we hope) in others the blissful seat of Eden, can the world regain life and love and sex and enter the Twentieth Century. That is why we need to consider what to tell our children about sex in its glowing and joyous and innocent reality.

III

Most "sex education" is a blunder because it abstracts sex from its context in love and in the orbed organic cosmos of life and the world, and so strips it of its wonder, its magic, its infinite variety. Emerson supremely expresses what happens when you remove any individual aspect of beauty from its context in Nature. In "Each and All" he wrote:

> The delicate shells lay on the shore;
> The bubbles of the latest wave
> Fresh pearls to their enamel gave;
> And the bellowing of the savage sea
> Greeted their safe escape to me.
> I wiped away the seeds and foam,
> I fetched my sea-born treasures home;
> But the poor, unsightly, noisome things
> Had left their beauty on the shore
> With the sun and the sand and the wild uproar.

A perfect parable of contemporary "Liberal" procedure!

"Sex education" is today designed to be primarily "scientific"; yet sex is *real* only when it is mostly *poetic*. If it is "scientific" in the limited, unscientific, arid jargon of the hour, it will be *only* informative, factual, functional – and so will leave reality behind it, with the sun and the sand and the wild uproar. The contemporary fallacy is conventionally to conform to what "science says," which is – in contemporary jargon – to abstract a fragment of life from the orbed cosmos of Life. Unless poetry is also there to give life and love in their context – the pebbles and shells of life on the shore of the concrete (and infinite) ocean – we have only a dehydrated fragment of love.

Today, specifically, the late Dr. Kinsey is still supposed by the pedants of the hour to be "scientific" – but they always call anyone "scientific" if he has a degree from a University and if he explains the nature of man by studying the habits of monkeys. The "Book of Judges" records the words of Samson:

> With the jawbone of an ass, heaps upon heaps,
> With the jawbone of an ass have I smitten a thousand men.

But not even Samson slew so many men with the jawbone of an ass as did Dr. Kinsey with his! Kinsey supposed that to catalogue the "sex habits" of American men and women told us the truth about the essential realities of sex. One might as well catalogue the "habits" of American drivers to tell us the essential reality of great driving; or make tape-recordings of the words of a hundred haphazard men in the street as a criterion of great style and logical thought. This is a part of the fashionable fallacy today known as egalitarian "democracy."

A wise and brilliant friend, whom I love to quote as he always reaches the root of the matter, writes: "The ladies' magazines are full of articles by psychologists and sociologists and pyschiatrists and other phony test-tube sorts with barrels of statistics and social measurements, but they don't know what it's all about. They think our children are the counterparts of Rhesus monkeys, and that love is business and sex is 'science.' The score and music of life has become a gadgety lesson in high-school physics . . . the union under the Morning Star has become a mechanical tranquilizer . . . the Unicorn has been harnessed to the computer. What is thrilling and noble and beautiful has been made to seem dully functional — and yet somewhat 'sophisticated,' and city-smart, and science-struck."

Love is not a science — it is an art. Just imagine George F. Babbitt (in his contemporary academic incarnation) making a statistical study of pearls from Japan — as a mode of reaching the Pearl of Great Price! Just imagine Jeremy Bentham appraising the Magic Casements Opening on the Foam as quite irrelevant to "the greatest happiness of the greatest number"! Just imagine a hygienic laboratory specimen of the *annelida* (which includes the common earthworm) appraising the High Sierras with his "scientific" worm's-eye view!

Before we give our children a knowledge of sex we must ourselves be awed and humble before the mystery and wonder of man and woman, and the bounty of love that is as boundless as the sea. We must know (with Browning) "the wonder and the wild desire," we must gallop the hills with the centaur, we must stare into the sun with the eagle, we must reverence the unicorn, that legendary beast as immortal as Camelot and the Happy Isles. And we must be like children, wandering with the great Newton the shore of an infinite ocean, gathering a whorled shell here, a wreath of seaweed there. We must know that sex can never be abstracted from mystery and miracle, from the ecstasy of our infinite longings and the anguish of our finite limitations.

IV

WHAT SHALL we tell our children about sex?

The physical processes of conception and birth should be told naturally and quietly, with no fanfare, with reverence, when the age seems fitting and the time right, by the parents. Most children today know these things in skeleton by a kind of osmosis from the age — but do not know them as a beautiful mystery and a noble wonder and a living soul. They should be told without shame or pedantry, as part of the magical, miraculous processes of life — as something beautiful like the chrysalis wherein the caterpillar becomes the butterfly. This is hard for some parents; but it can — it must — be done.

In this essay I would go beyond that. I wish, rather, to speak philosophically to those who are older than children, and yet younger than they think they are — to those who have had little opportunity today to hear a philosophical view of sex. What we lack in the Western world today is someone equivalent to what the classical Hindus call the *guru*, or spiritual teacher. The *guru* speaks objectively from the soul; he speaks as the sun speaks, giving the objective light whereby you can see not only geometry but also the spectrum. He pours the light over the world, like the sun, and says, simply, "See!"

I am not a *guru*, and I cannot so speak. But beyond pragmatism there is eternalism, where the sun shines on the good and the bad and the rain falls on the just and the unjust, and truth lives to complement fact — truth founded in the objective universe and the inner reason. If I were a *guru*, and if I could transcend pragmatism and reach essentialism, I would try to speak the objective truth in some such fashion as this:

"The glory of youth is that it is curious and eager and passionate, and that it seeks pure integrity. The mistake of youth is that it supposes youth is something which it alone has experienced, and that there is no valid growth by which one can become wise through age yet remain splendid with youth. It is a part of the gallant exuberance of youth to suppose that, by haste and immediacy, it can today touch the star that is beyond the last tomorrow of the world. But haste may destroy and immediacy may nullify. If I give my teenage son, immediately, a Savage .300 and not a .22 rifle, I not only make him a danger, but I deprive him of the long-savoring, patient, beautiful experience of rifles. If I give my seventeen-year-old daughter, immediately, a Jaguar, I not only make her a menace on the road, I deprive her of the delight of eventually winning for herself, through years of patience and growth, a great car. If I make the mechanics of birth-control available to children once they reach puberty, and bid them to be casually experimental and hastily promiscuous, I blunt the Damascus blade of love, I destroy the power and the glory of sex by vulgarizing it with the cheap and the hasty. Easy immediate gratification destroys the hard eventual glory. All great things are far, difficult, and rare; they lead us over the horizon of time into the fields of Eternity. The anonymous authors of the Bible knew sex passionately, and knew the power and the glory of it; so in 'Genesis' we read: 'And Jacob served seven years for Rachel; and they seemed unto him but a few days, for the love he had to her.' But today, in *Peyton Place*, the girl says: *'Hurry, hurry, hurry!'*

"Our generations of the hour are too often insulated from the reality of Nature. Else they would know that all that grows and genuinely lives must long do so in mystery and the dark, in the unconscious and the silent. The tulip bulb does not analyze its processes, or detail its growth in a hurlyburly of talk spilled over the pages of a paperback, or lift its unconscious destiny into a dialogue with test-tubes or even with the sun; it grows in silence and the dark, so that its splendor of crimson and gold may break gorgeous out of next April's loam. The sober bud of the caterpillar's chrysalis lies silent in the chemistry of its Inner Kingdom, its sojourn with its own destiny and the grace of God, in silent and unspied-upon secrecy — so that it may be born 'innumerable of stains and splendid dyes.' One does not ram forceps into a bluebird's egg, or pull a puppy apart with a boathook to find how it lives, or drag genius into the laboratory, or thrust Juliet from the balcony into the fraternity necking-parlor. All that is alive and beautiful and free and great demands privacy and silence and the seal of mystery. What sort of child will be born if he does not lie in secrecy and silence and the dark for nine months under the mother's heart?

"What sort of love — what sort of sex — survives when you talk about it, analyze it, finger it, and turn the private glory into the public blatancy? Lovers should loathe it when the 'sex'-hucksters turn their beautiful privacy into a public parade, with seventy-six trombones, and press-agents ballyhooing it, and the Madison Avenue boys making it as cheap as a TV commercial. Only an age of collectivism, where everything is made 'public like a frog,' could tolerate such intolerable invasions of the secret and the sacred.

"Above all, youth is cheated today by being sold a bill of goods.

Young men and women are brought up to conform to the superstition that sex is but a biological function, a fleshly must. Thus sex is made to seem a sort of mechanical pill to gulp, a release of tensions, a mode of hygiene; and so sex becomes increasingly a disappointment — and a tension. We destroy the infinite miracle of sex when we make it the finite medicine of 'sex.' We are born with immortal longings and we are restless till we rest in them, but we betray and ruin those longings most when we treat them as urges of the libido that can be 'solved' by 'gratifying' them in simple physical easing. We are restless till we find the great chords of Beethoven, but we betray and destroy that longing if we dunk our hearts in the dishwater of the Beatles. To geld the centaur with conventional 'sex satisfactions,' to break the unicorn's horn and bid him gallop the hills of morning so despoiled, to clip the eagle's wings and tell him that is the way to enjoy the winds — surely that is modern, and surely it is impotence!

"We lose the joy of sex if we exploit the 'pleasure' of mere 'sex.' The meaning of the sexes lies not in 'pleasure' but in joy. And that joy — the wonder and the essence that we seek — is to know sex as a beautiful mode and means of becoming utterly and essentially *one* with the contrast and the opposite whom you *love*. The truth of sex is that we become one in body that we may become more fully one in soul. The embrace of lovers is a transcendence of the finite by a consummation of the infinite. Lovers say, when sex is real, 'Let us become more truly *you* and *I* because we are no longer, *I* or *you* . . . but *us*. The sundered halves of diversity become the fused integer of unity. The torn page is made whole and the poem is fulfilled for God to read — as well as for lovers to read. Here is the sacrament of love. The wine of love and the bread of love are for our nourishment, our delectation, our fulfillment. The immortal longings have led us to the mortal rapture.

"If you cannot understand this, you need to be born into the psyche as once you were born into the flesh. The Nineteenth Century (and, so far, the Twentieth) has had a pathetic faith in the flesh, and so it has made the flesh petty and miserable. The Twentieth Century — if it is to *be* — must set its faith in the infinite psyche, so that it may regain and enjoy the finite flesh.

"The age of positivism — secular, collectivistic, existential — is the age when men deny quality and affirm quantity. It supposes that if you have fifty 'sex experiences' you have experienced sex. It supposes that if you divorce nine wives and have the tenth coming up you have experienced marriage. But that is quantitative nonsense. Because you are unable to find the quality of woman, you turn to the quantity of women. Because you are unable to experience marriage, you try to compensate for your fallibility with marriages. You fail, and so you think that failure is the only way to succeed.

"Youth is not a quantity — age is not a quantity. Whether you are eighteen or eighty is unimportant: The true question is, *What quality does Keats give to twenty-six years, what quality does Goethe give to eighty-three years?* The quantity of our years means nothing; the quality of our years means everything. And if we have quality in our years, whatever our age, we shall make sex a quality, and we shall live (as Blake said) 'in Eternity's sunrise.' "

V

So FAR the *guru*. But finally let me speak in my own right. I would say to youth, as I would say to age, that sex is great because it contains multitudes and transcends itself. Color and song, the plume on the bird's wing and the music in the bird's mouth, the splendid canvasses of the painter, the magnificent sounds of the composer's music, the words that march across the poet's page like Roman legions in crimson and in gold, all these are a part of sex. Play (that is so essential a part of life), the rhythm of the dance that the stars and the planets keep, the riot of bloom over May's apple trees, the intimations of immortality that disturb us with more than this world — all these are parallels to, and aspects of, sex . . . as sex is parallel to, and an aspect of, them.

And man and woman, if they are to know sex truly, must find it, beyond themselves, in the living objective universe. Man the sun with his center of light and strength — woman the planet, with her fertility and her answer to the power of light with the gift of life — are born to be joyous in the organic integrity of the universe. They must rejoice in their own differences and opposites and contrasts, because these are a way *to* unity — and also a part of the essence of life. They find themselves in the attraction and the repulsion of the negative and the positive poles of electricity, in the point and counterpoint of the seasons, in the seed they set within the dark loam so that it may become the bright blossoms, in the work of man and in the child of woman. Our deprived generations in megalopolis — deprived of Nature and natural life, censored by skyscrapers and concrete and subways — naturally know little of sex, and suppose that they know a lot of "sex." For sex is immediacy with the wheeling sun and the fruitful earth, with the *yin* and the *yang*, with the life that runs like a flame through the arteries of the universe. Two who know love — the eternal Adam, the eternal Eve — partake of the transcendent life in which they live and move and have their being. And in this greatness, they leave the abstract world of "modern ideas" and enter the concrete being of the living universe that is beyond time.

In this truth of sex, man, like the sun, holds woman, the planet, forever in his embrace of fire; and woman, the planet, asks only that the embrace of fire shall never end.

For Sons:
On How To Choose A Wife

OUR battle is against the Communist Conspiracy outside us, and also against the intellectual heresies and the spiritual decay that fester within us. If the Communist Conspiracy were utterly defeated in the outer world, and yet the inner debacle of intellectual rebellion and spiritual nihilism remained within us, we would still inhabit a world of chaos, sickness, and death; and we would still fall short of a better world and a fairer life. So, while we must resolutely rally our minds and souls for the war against outer Communism, we must also strengthen and purify our minds and souls against the forces of intellectual error and spiritual decay that lie within us. We need most, *in ourselves*, integrity, harmony, wisdom, insight — and joy.

Especially we must strengthen the individual and the family: If these are as they should be, Communism cannot prevail in the world. And one of the bases of the joyous individual and the harmonious family is what Shakespeare called "the marriage of true minds" to which no man should "admit impediments." That is the integral and happy union of the man who loves and the woman who loves equally. To this end it is most important that each of us, as man, should choose wisely the woman he marries; and (as we shall see in a later essay) that each should choose wisely, as woman, the man she marries.

How may we, as man, wisely choose the woman who is to be our wife?

I

IT IS EVIDENT that today, in the world of the Liberal Establishment and of nihilism rampant, man often does not choose a wife wisely nor does woman choose her husband wisely. That is proved by the flurry of divorces that occur, or the sullen unhappiness that often is as painful as proud flesh when divorce does not occur. How can there have been wise choices when a man and woman marry on March 13, 1967 — and separate on May 13, 1967? Or even after longer intervals? This does not mean that divorce is not sometimes right: it is. But it does mean that men and women should choose by wisdom, principle, values, vital intuition and philosophical insight, so that more often their choices may be right and their marriages may be lasting. They should choose as if the dawn of their love, like the dawn that forever moves unchanging around the world, *is forever.*

But today, too often, the choices that are made are not very wise; so the lovers, overnight or overyear, turn haters. In my book *Ulysses To Penelope*, wherein I wrote at length about one of the great marriages of the world, I described briefly the false marriages of the many-too-many:

> I do not mean the marriages we see
> Often around us on the sorry earth —
> Lovers grown haters, whose proximity
> Destroys, in either, joy, and chance of worth,
> And kindness of the heart. There is no blight
> So terrible as love too false to last! —
> Each lies and listens in the lonely night
> To hear the other breathe, and is aghast
> To know the other lives . . . . And worse are those
> Who make Love's dancing star a hearth-fire dying,
> Whereby they slumber blear and comatose.
> Love must forever be a white star flying!

Of such marriages Nietzsche wrote: "Your love to woman, and woman's love to man — ah, would that it were sympathy for suffering and veiled deities! But generally two animals alight on one another." The hit-or-miss marriages, the merely biological unions, the conjunctions of the immature or the unawakened, the marriages of sudden lust or sullen "convenience," these are caricatures of marriage. They occur when man or woman chooses without wisdom. Do not misunderstand what I say: I believe in love at first sight — if it is also love at first insight; but it must be based on more than biological affinity, or pride of the eye and lust of the flesh; it must be also a marriage of true minds. Much of the lie of marriage today comes from the sex habits of the "Liberal" hour, of which a decent rabbit would be ashamed. What can you expect of marriages if choices are largely confined to something akin to shopping around in a used car lot run by Dr. Kinsey, the Smiling Irishman of "Liberalism"?

Of course our enemies, the Communists and the collectivists and the nihilists, rejoice in the used car lots, the divorces, the lovers turned haters, the unhappy mis-marriages, and do all they can to foster such insurrection at the elemental level. But do not blame them only; blame ourselves even more. Blame our false philosophies, our petulant frivolity! Gore Vidal somewhere — I think on television — spoke of the impossibility of staying in love with the same man or woman for sixty years; and of course — if you are incapable of staying in love for sixty minutes — it *is* impossible. If, like a well-known "Liberal" justice, you are hell bent on trading in a wife on a new model every few months or years, it is hardly likely that you are capable of staying in love for sixty years with anything but your own sick psyche. But there is a love which such "Liberals" as Mr. Justice Douglas know not of — a state in which it is possible to love for sixty years or sixty aeons — and that is the marriage of true minds. There *can* be such marriage based on quality, value, and meaning. It is akin to the intellectual union that occurs between the human mind and a work of art, from which divorce is incredible: No true mind would ever wish to be divorced from Shakespeare, from Velasquez, from Bach. But divorce is inevitable — *if* the mind is true — from Arthur Miller, Allen Ginsberg, Grace Metalious.

In our mortal lives there are immortal occurrences. To see Zambesi Falls with Ian Smith, to come to know George Washington, to stand silent upon a peak in Darien and see John Keats, to watch the dawn rise over the surf in Maine, to know the *Symposium* of Plato, to read *King Lear* or *The Trojan Women* (in the translation of Gilbert Murray), to walk the flaming autumn woods with your two dogs, to meet the first pussywillows upon the boughs of late March, to see suddenly your destined love "across a crowded room" — these are immortal joys amid the mortal woes of life. High among these, as I suggest, is that love at first sight and first insight which leads to the marriage of true being.

How, then, may a man recognize the woman who is his by fiat of destiny?

II

FIRST OF ALL, a man should fall in love only with a woman. I am not here as obvious and crude as "Liberals" will suppose me, and am not warning against the sick inbred perversity that disfigures so many men in this petty "Liberal" hour. I mean something much subtler and much more fundamental. The unhappiness of too many men today is largely due to the "equalizing" of the sexes, which is misinterpreted to mean the homogenizing of the sexes. To be happy, to be real, man must be drastically man, woman must be drastically woman: Men who wear long hair, women who wear trousers and would sport beards if they could, are worms in the apple of joy. Choose a woman who is not merely biologically female, but who is also psychologically feminine. Choose her only who *loves* to be a woman, who is a female female, who has all the sometimes infuriating and always fascinating quirks of the feminine, who rejoices in the polarity and the destiny of her sex. Then she will be for you adventure even in rest, peace even in passion; the fruitful paradox of the fire upon the hearth and the star upon the horizon.

Such a woman is difficult to find today, because the fashion of the hour is to make woman only a mannequin in a store window, modeling a plastic miniskirt. The kind of female you see posing in *Playboy* or *Cavalier* would deceive only a "modern"; they are not women, but *things* — flashy, fashionable, cold-eyed, with a martini where blood ought to be and a psyche as cold as the Ice Maiden's. Any man who would marry a *Playboy* woman should expect a divorce; a marriage of stature with such a woman is absurd. She is thin, shadow-spun, two-dimensional, lacking especially what D.H. Lawrence describes as the *fourth* dimension: "This is the state of heaven. And it is the state of a flower, a cobra, a jenny-wren in spring, a man when he knows himself royal and crowned with the sun, with his feet gripping the core of earth."*

The modern sex-fancier doesn't want to marry a "frigid" woman; and he is right, though superficial and immature and partial. A woman who is quite capable of physical response, sexually, may be quite incapable of psychical response spiritually; she may be frigid-eyed and frigid-souled; she may be no more capable of giving or receiving love than a plaster mannequin in Macy's window. The swinging chick, the "sex symbol," the biologically acquiescent modish demonstrator of concupiscence, the worldly-wise purveyor of sensation, the *Playboy* female, may on command give the body of sex — but she can never serve the soul that holy communion which is love. No man who is a connoisseur of Heaven would marry such a woman! Who, after all, wants a plastic zombie outfitted by a Parisian couturier?

---

*D.H. Lawrence, "Reflections on the Death of a Porcupine."

Stephen Vincent Benét's William Sycamore knew the woman to choose —

> Till I lost my boyhood and won my wife,
> A girl like a Salem clipper!
> A woman straight as a hunting-knife
> With eyes as bright as the Dipper!*

Of course the Liberal Establishment doesn't breed such women today; such women don't go to finishing schools and get finished; such women don't graduate from Vassar to become members of the League of Women Voters. They will be hidden and rare; you may have to search in Appalachia or the High Sierras or the farms of Indiana, or in Punxsutawney, Pennsylvania, where the groundhog sees . . . or doesn't see . . . his shadow. Wherever you find her, she must live outside the conformities and fashionable cliches of today; she must be as simple as the sun and as timeless as the moon; she must be like a tree planted beside the rivers of God, that brings forth her fruit in her season, and whose leaf does not wither, because she finds the waters of life.

D.H. Lawrence, at his best, wrote: "To men, the sun is becoming stale, and the earth sterile. But the sun itself will never become stale, nor the earth barren. It is only that the *clue* is missing inside men."† The man in whom the clue is not missing will seek the woman in whom the clue is not missing. And if they both have the clue, marriage for them will be possible, for the sun will be forever a magic flame, the earth forever a seedbed of miracle, and life an adventure in mortal woe and immortal joy. But if she continually vivisects sun and earth with the scalpel of "discussion," "dialogue," debate, and such, pass her by as you would an ambulant corpse that reckons itself real. She is not for you!

One thing no genuine living man can ever choose to marry is the modern "rebel," the contemporary "revolutionist," the usual "mod" or "hippie." Imagine marriage with Bettina Aptheker! Imagine marriage with a veteran of the Berkeley student wars! Imagine marriage with an acidulous, smart, know-it-all, stringy-haired *thing* — with a walking buzz-saw, a wasp's nest in a teakettle, a rattlesnake with

---

*Stephen Vincent Benet, "The Ballad of William Sycamore."
†D.H. Lawrence, "Reflections On The Death Of A Porcupine."

insomnia, a tarantula with an obsession and an ideology! One can imagine no nightmare more terrible than marriage with a Carrie Nation of Civil Rights, equipped with a hatchet become a Molotov cocktail! In my hyperbole I imagine the kindest fate you could expect in such a union would be to wake up early enough to hear her whisper "Burn, Baby, burn." But perhaps she would leave you and the children, before that to go driving around the Alabama night with a "companion." The only nightmare equal to that would be marriage with a "sex-symbol." As Samuel Butler once wrote, "O God! O Montreal!"

You, as genuine man in search of genuine woman, will seek her who from birth to death is essentially *woman*. Swedenborg rightly saw, in his mystical insight, that in every life and in every world, man is man and woman is woman, life without end, life everlasting. If she denies this, she is subverting her essential life, and will make all associated with her miserable, because she is making herself miserable by denying her destiny and being; if she affirms this, not consciously but subconsciously and superconsciously, she is a center of womanhood and one of the creators of human bliss and glory. Seek her and find her, woo her and win her, and say (as she says), "This dawn is forever!"

III

WHAT ARE some of the ways in which a genuine and living man may know the living and genuine woman that he should choose? How will he recognize her?

I assume that such a man will have imagination, humor, a heady zest for living. So he will wish to find a woman who also has poetry of being, a rich sense of the laughter of earth, a heady zest for the adventure of life; that is, he will seek a woman who is gallant and gay. How wise Nietzsche was! — "In the true man there is a child hidden: it wanteth to play. Up, then, ye women, and discover the child in man! A plaything let woman be, pure and fine like the precious stone, illumined with the virtues of a world not yet come. Let the beam of a star gleam in your love!"

Never choose a woman who does not comprehend, who does not *love* play, imagination, humor, the joy of adventure. How can you know whether she does or not? You can test her easily: Does she enjoy naming a kitten . . . Purry Mason, Aaron Purr, Mr. Anonymous, Tinker's Dam, Willie Scramble? Does she, like you, believe that your car is not really yours till you name it? — The Royal Goldfinch, The Flying Unicorn, Rozinante the Third,* Touch-and-Go, Ataboy, Lord of the Road? (If she had rather compile statistics and compute vectors, she is not for you — unless *you* had rather compute vectors and compile statistics . . . in which case, of course, she *is* the woman for you!)

Choose a woman who, by temperament and essential being, dislikes what you dislike — the "wit" of Dwight Macdonald, vodka, the "poems" of Allen Ginsberg (that beard in search of a poet), Twiggy, "modern" translations of the Bible, and canned grasshoppers. Choose the woman who, by temperament and essential being, loves what you love — broiled swordfish and roast young duck, coffee, Alfred Noyes' "The Highwayman," the water-colors of Winslow Homer in the Chicago Art Institute, the little crescent moon flung like a child's boomerang across Heaven, dogs and cats, *guns*, "The Song of Solomon," the great prose-epics of J.R.R. Tolkien. Of course you will differ about details; you will fancy your coffee sweetened, she will prefer it unsweetened — to each his own! — *but you both will like coffee.* Never choose a woman who loves to dissect and argue, who has to psychologize everything into explanations, who has to find *why* and *wherefores*, who must analyze and "discuss" everything, who tortures the subtle and direct into the abstruse and the difficult and the ideological. Choose a woman who has an intuitive hatred of Commissars for the Suppression of Wild Flowers, of bureaucrats and income taxes, of sociological computers; who says with William Blake, "Damn braces, bless relaxes!"; who loves to conserve and enjoy simple natural things like fish fried on the shore whence you caught them, the first salt smell of ocean as you drive East, the iris in her garden like bluebirds joyously poised ever for flight. Choose the woman who is Eve reborn and born wiser; who hates the serpent (that first con-man, old when the world was young); who longs to find in all things *the mood of Eden.*

Choose the woman who is happy to be with you every hour (as you wish her), yet who loves you enough to let you alone. Choose only the woman who understands your destiny as man; who knows that you must do your work always, that you must be free to do your work in your own way. She should know that a true man is a

---

*"The Third" because surely somebody has already named his car "Rozinante the Second"!

sun; he must follow the inexorable destiny of light: She should know that a true man is an eagle — he must never be deflected from the free flight of pinions that seek the buffeting winds. The farmer, setting his wheat-fields like a golden flag across the earth; the soldier, charging the enemy when the bugle blows; the saint, justifying the earth by his vision and his consecration; the poet, restoring Eden to the earth — such are the destinies of man, and unless a woman comprehends and accedes to this, she cannot make man happy or be happy herself. Choose, therefore, only the woman you can trust to seek in you the master, the artist, the free workman; the woman who loves in you the man you were born to be, the statue within the marble; choose only her who loves you so much that she can let you go your own way. She must never be fussy and bossy, she must reverence in man the Huckleberry Finn, she must never be a Miss Watson, that "tolerable slim old maid, with goggles on," who seeks to comb the Huckleberry Finn in man "all to thunder" and "civilize" him into a slave of the Liberal Establishment.

Choose a woman who is capable of the dainty balance between realism and romance. Choose the woman who is romantic where she should be — in the poetry of experience, in the rich involvement in the rich emotions of senses and heart, in the delight with the glory of sheer being. In choosing a home, planting a garden, enjoying surf or moonlight, taking an auto ride, making love, she will seek the four-dimensional bliss of romance. "Facts," statistics, the two dimensions minus the third of depth and the fourth of meaning, will seem to her what they are — thin abstract unrealities, the husk around the wheat. The living germ of the wheat itself — nourishing, succulent, rich — will be to her the reward and the reality of life. She will be that non-conformist today . . . almost non-existent today . . . the romantic. Yet she will also be, as conservator and woman, the realist where and when she should be; she will have a sense of form, limits, bounds, foundations; she will be what today's "realists" seldom are, *practical.* She will have a sense of time and timing. When the hour of romance is over, she will know it; she will not sentimentally prolong the hour. She will have a sense of form and need; and she will *be on time*! If she has no sense of the necessary and the inexorable, of the practical needs of keeping an appointment or washing the dishes, of the necessity of getting the bills off on time or seeing that the dogs get their supper, take the first boat for Bali Hai. But if she thinks that "house-cleaning" is more important than making love, that a study in order is more important than a poem written, that your "duty" to call on a neighbor is greater than your destiny to attend the Rally for God, Family, and Country, take the first *jet* for Bali Hai! She is not for you!

If she is the woman you should choose, she will have her own destiny as woman. Whether she ever has a child or not, her deepest instincts should cohere about the child she bears beneath her heart; she should cherish the child in all things; she should seek to be the mother of that child in whom earth is reconciled with Heaven, even as Mary was. A kitten lost and wandering alone, a dog abandoned and astray upon the world's bitter roads, larkspur to protect from weeds and to nourish in the rich earth, genius harassed by mediocrity and needing the great word of appreciation, our land betrayed by idiots and traitors and needing loyalty and love, all these, to her, are aspects of the child she bears beneath her heart. And the man she loves will be the child beneath her heart; she will comfort and renew him in her arms and upon her breast, even as she does the child. Hers will be tenderness for all that deserves tenderness — for all lovely and gracious things and creatures, for the watercolor and the flower and the butterfly and the poem and the moon now threatened by astronauts and the commissars of cosmic imperialism, for the egret in the Everglades and the golden eagle upon the mountains, for the privacy of a man's own vine and fig tree, for the child's freedom to read the Bible and to be shielded from the pollution of psychological tests. Conversely hers will be a good anger for all that threatens the lovely and the gracious; the lioness is more terrible than the lion when her cubs and her kopjes are threatened. She will be like Deborah mustering the hosts of Israel when Sisera invades the land and tramples down her garden and threatens her people. Choose *only* the woman who has these natural instincts, follows them inexorably, is centered about them; avoid any woman whose heresies deny her own destiny — her home, her children, her country, her traditions, her eternal and absolute values — avoid her, distrust her, shun her, for no true man should mate with one of the deracinated of earth. The random, the rootless, are not for you. But if and when you find the woman deeply rooted in reality, and she is lovely and gracious and yours by fiat of destiny, when once you have found her, *never let her go.*

For such a love and marriage is the foundation of being. It is the union of the two halves of being, sundered by birth and reunited by the drama of life, the rediscovery and the reunion, the reaffirmation in the physical world of the metaphysical reality. Polarity, tension, difference between the sexes is the secret of harmony, congruence, union between the sexes: The peace that lies in passion, the adventure that lies in rest! Such is the secret of life; the secret of love; the secret of marriage. As D.H. Lawrence says, here is "woman in all the mystery of her fathomless desirableness, man in the fullness of his power. . . ." Here is our Lost Eden become Eden Regained.

IV

HERE ARE a few specific hints, which will be wasted on "rationalists" but which will speak to men of Reason.

In any marriage of true minds, both man and woman feel that they knew each other before they met. You recognize her as the one you knew before you were born, and are born to find again; she is the picture you always carried in your heart, even before you had a physical "heart." The Buddha once said: "Some souls are bound together in lives past; meeting again, they know." Plato said that all true knowledge is remembrance. True love demonstrates this; we remember and we know; she is ours, she belongs to us, for we *recognize* her.

In a true marriage, two who love — if they have been separated for an hour, a week, a year — will meet and know that they have never been separated. They will not have to adjust, to become reacquainted, to reestablish harmony; they will not have to waste time on questions and reacclimatization, they will be one like the twin halves of the torn page that fuses again so the poem may be read.

Also each will bear, like a tape recording on the heart, all that the other has said of immortal wit and value. Such a marriage will not be one of the pseudo-marriages in which each partner speaks a foreign language and can communicate only through an interpreter. Each will be a richer "I" because he or she rejoices in the richer "you," and because both *I* and *you* are lost and found in the perfect *us.* If you can understand this, you are capable of marriage; if you cannot, you are destined for the divorce court or a joyless union legalized by the police. Only the mystic of marriage is fully capable of Marriage; only the poet of marriage will ever know the poem of Marriage, and only if marriage is a poem is it Marriage. And a true marriage is the great basis for a stable and joyous society, for joyous and stable individuals. The chaos, the rebellion, the restless rootless inanity of the many-too-many in our minor day, is largely the misery of the vacuum of the soul that afflicts us because we have not found the marriage of true minds. We not only "admit impediments" to true marriage, we fabricate and import impediments — impediments of false philosophy, of existentialist lies, of rationalistic destruction of Reason. Our battle against Communism and collectivism and nihilism will be won by those who find the reality of harmony and joy in marriage.

The marriage of true minds must be the incarnation of the word *love*.Cyrano de Bergerac, speaking out of the night to Roxane upon the balcony, says it best:

> We are alive;
> We thirst — Come away, plunge, and drink, and drown
> In the great rivers flowing to the sea.

And Cyrano adds a secret that we should note. If we have found the right woman, then:

> I never
> Look at you, but there's some new virtue born
> In me, some new courage. Do you begin
> To understand, a little? Can you feel
> My soul, there in the darkness, breathe on you?*

If she is the one woman, then she does indeed inspire in you "some new virtue, . . . some new courage." She is the magnet and the star, the bugle's reveille, the dawn of resurrection. And she will italicize this because she will never notice and accent what is *wrong* with you, she will see and say what is *right* with you. She will encourage and praise, she will perceive and enhance the hero in your soul, the excellences in you that bring you meaning — and that bring her joy. If this be so, then she is the woman for you.

In my book, *The Way Of All Spirit*, in the chapter called "The Windows of the Morning," I discuss this in detail, and note:

> Yet how shall we surely know, here and now, amid the inertia and lethargy of the flesh, amid the lies and shadow shapes of the world's illusion, that love is come to us . . . ? Thus we shall know the authentic presence of love

---

*Cyrano de Bergerac, translation by Brian Hooker.

herself: When "the world" dies — and the world is born; when we love one against the world, and, careless of the world, yet fall at last in love with the world; when propinquity seems too great a distance — yet distance only brings us nearer; when one is a dearer self — yet dearer because she is not ourself but another; when the bread that one eats feeds two; when one added to one makes two — and also infinity; then indeed does love look from the windows of the morning — even upon us.

How important this is in our battle with the commissars, the bureaucrats, the revolutionists! For when we find such love, we wish to *conserve* it — as quality, meaning, value; we would not "seize the sorry scheme of things entire" and "shatter it to bits," but we would preserve and fulfill and enjoy the Eden that love has restored to us. We have come "beyond the ice, beyond the North, beyond death." We dwell where the Hyperboreans dwell. And that blissful world we would defend with our lives — against the commissars and the bureaucrats and the revolutionists — against the nihilists and the No-sayers and the destroyers of the morning — because it is our *life*.

When we find the one who is life and love for us, as I wrote further in *The Way Of All Spirit*, then "The world itself is like misty air after a rain, monochrome, neutral; love is like the white sun across the mist, wakening it to rainbow." Does she, the not impossible she, bring you the sun and the rainbow? If so, she is yours to marry. And once you have found her, never let her go!

V

ONE FINAL WORD, which, like all my words, is in head-on collision with, and absolute contradiction of, the clichés and conformities of the hour: The woman you marry should be a *good* woman.

The cliché of the hour says that only the off-beat, the eccentric, the heretical, the rebel and denier, is interesting and dynamic. It is the old sentimentality that Swinburne once put into the worst verse he ever wrote:

> Could you hurt me, sweet lips, though I hurt you?
> Men touch them, and change in a trice
> The lilies and languors of virtue
> For the roses and raptures of vice.

That is the old contemporary sentimentality, supercharged by "Liberals," that sees the bawdy house, the gambling den, the sniffing of airplane glue, the trips on the jets of L.S.D., the riots in the streets, the whims and petulancies and perversities and selfishnesses and lusts and greeds and postures and fashions and cruelties and negations and nihilism, as interesting, thrilling, dynamic — "the roses and raptures of vice." It supposes that the lonely consecration of Michelangelo on his masterpieces, the dedication of St. Joan to the service of her France, the love of Dante for Beatrice, the genius of Milton making his whole life a poem, the passion of Christ that made the Cross the throne of victory, are only the "lilies and languors of virtue." It thinks the sun a "languor" and the neon lights a "rapture"!

Actually, there is nothing more usual, more boring, dull, crass, and mean and cheap, than "the roses and raptures of vice" — the woman emancipated from her family and driving around in a "Civil Rights" junket with a young hipster of a different race, the acidulous Carrie Nations of Berkeley "rebellions," the shrill harebrained harridans of conventional "free-love," the avant-garde experimenters with drugs and Dada, the tossers of flame-bottles of gasoline, the breakers of "traditions," the Gadarene swine who trample values. They are a dime-a-dozen; they are the destroyers of roses and the disintegrators of raptures; they are things (not men or women) to make the saint, the poet, the hero, the creator, yawn with the only ennui that can affect the great.

The good woman, of course, is not the "good" woman. She is not a goggle-eyed Miss Watson chivvying poor Huckleberry. She is not the upholder of mechanical rules and regulations. She is not the cousin or the aunt of the commissar. She *is* the woman gracious and gallant, compassionate yet never sentimental, light-loving and life-serving, inexorable to subordinate quantity to quality, enemy always of the weed and the tarantula and the man-eating tiger, friend always of the sun and the wheat and the lion born free on his own kopje, seeking organic form because it alone creates, saying *no* to the temptations of the ever-present death that so easily besets us, saying *yes* to the challenge of life that requires of us strength and courage and faith and labor and creation. Wherever the good woman is, there is a center of harmony, of beauty, of creation, of life, of love. She has integrity. You can trust her with your life, she is loyal and will not betray; she has a self so genuine that she is not selfish; she is like the true gardener who has the green thumb, so wherever she comes, earth is a garden where life grows; she is a source of inexhaustible joy, like the pure spring from the deep earth. It is joy to be with her, it is life to be near her, it is an intimation of Heaven to know her. She does not have to go off the deep end to be interesting, for she has the depths and the living angels within her, and the infinite variety that comes only when your roots go down into God.

These lines from one of the finest of modern poems, Rolfe Humphries' "The Angels," describe her well:

> For they are Being's perfect revelation,
> Whose very essence is Becomingness,
> Intense existence, pure illumination;
> They more than heal, they bless.*

The good woman is a source of "intense existence," a center of "pure illumination," and wherever she comes she not only heals — she *blesses.*

All things respond to the good woman. A wise gardener once told me: "Flowers know who loves them." *Everything* in life that is genuine knows who loves it; the cat and the dog, the furniture and the dishes, the trees that shade your lawn and the daylilies that open like petalled stars in your garden, the friends who share and grace your life, the husband who finds her blessed among women, all these thrive and bloom where the good woman comes. In choosing your wife, know first, last, and always — that she is, in the sense I mean, *a good woman.*

In all great ages of the world men know that the great — and the interesting — are the good. In the great ages of the world, the Hydra, the Gorgon, the Philistine Giant, the dragon, the witch-Queen, the acidulous stepmother and her hateful daughters, are abominable and detestable; but Hercules, Perseus, David with his sling and his five smooth stones, St. George for Merrie England, Snow White, Cinderella, are figures of shining honor and glamorous delight. Among women, who would not give a million Cleopatras for one St. Joan or one Emily Dickinson, or a dozen Helens launching a thousand ships for one Penelope (to me the greatest of women)? And Snow White, Joan of Arc, Emily Dickinson, Cinderella, Penelope were *good women*, women vital as well as vivid, with the power of the gracious and the gallant and the good. They are the daughters of Light, the daughters

---

*From *Forbid Thy Ravens,* by Rolfe Humphries, Charles Scribner's Sons, New York.

of God; they are the children of Heaven and therefore they are the creatures of eternal beauty and joy. Choose a woman of that sort to be your wife — and pray God that you may somehow, somewhere, find her!

For Daughters:
On How To Choose A Husband

AN essential fallacy of Communism, and also of Socialism, is the illusion that happiness depends on economics, on the material factors of life, on the outer world and not on the Inner Kingdom. Thus it is the great opposite and enemy of Christianity.* That is why Communism and Socialism produce a world of unhappiness, wherein man first seeks "escape" in revolution and destruction, and then in a Utopia wherein no vital instincts are satisfied and no psychological needs are fulfilled. Both Communism and Socialism generate a world of inorganic unhappiness, which is why wise men say of them both, as Voltaire said of another human mistake, *"Écrasez l'infame!"*

We who seek to free ourselves from the Collectivist Society, seek the opposite. We seek the organic world of integral harmony, the reality which alone makes for the only happiness man can find in this world — a harmony of the tension between the mortal grief that we all must bear and the immortal joy that we may win.

As I said in my essay on choosing a wife, one great organic happiness is the harmony of man and woman in the marriage of true minds. Communism never even seeks this: It promises woman "freedom" to be a carbon copy of man and the slave of the State; it promises her the "equality" with men which deprives her of the true equality with man — which is to discover her destiny as woman as he discovers his destiny as man. It makes her automatic, sexless, neuter, and as feminine as a saw-horse. What any vital philosophy should seek and elucidate is woman's freedom to be woman, and woman's equality to be not a copy but a creation.

If man is man and woman is woman, both may be happy again in the joyous tension of difference, and so become organically one. Man, to attain this, must choose his wife with integrity; woman, to attain this, must choose her husband with integrity. I have already written about man's choice; today I wish to write about woman's

---

*Christianity says: "The Kingdom of Heaven is *within* you." It knows that out of the heart are the issues of life.

choice. How, then, should woman choose the man who is to be her husband?

I

FEW DRAMATISTS have known less about woman than Bernard Shaw. The women in his plays are as feminine as a pamphlet on the policies of the A.D.A. and as much like woman as sawdust is like a living tree. Robert Louis Stevenson in one of his letters said of Shaw (I do not quote exactly, but this is the substance of it): "But, my God, Archer, what women!" One idea of Shaw's, however, even though Shaw said it, is illuminating. He said that it is the woman who chooses, it is the woman who takes a husband rather than the man who takes a wife. This, though exaggerated, is partly true — and almost wholly right; for woman should seek the one man who is the answer to her need and dream, who is the completion of her otherwise uncompleted life.

Marriage, the child, the family, the home — the preservation of race, country, culture — the survival of quality on this earth — is the destiny of woman. That is so important that a true woman, sound in instinct and clear in intuition, wishes to choose, and should wish to choose, the one man who most fully completes her being and fulfills her dream. Man is to be the father of her child. Man is to continue, through her, so far as this earth and life are concerned, the nation and the family and human culture. Man is to fulfill all that she dreams as the consummation and meaning of her life. Can she, therefore, leave the choice wholly to man? Of course not! To be true woman, she must seek and see and win the true man who is the answer to her most vital question.

So far as I am concerned, I would never choose a woman unless I were sure that she had also chosen me. I could not love a woman unless I felt in the depths of my being that she also loved me; I would wish her to seek me even as I sought her; were she not mad to have me I would be tepid to have her.

If woman is vital woman, moreover, she does not choose merely rationalistically. Joseph Conrad speaks of "the obscure inner necessity" of the artist, that bids him create; in true woman there is an "obscure inner necessity" that unites the subconscious, the conscious, and the superconscious, into a living wisdom. Woman is more primitive than man (in spite of "Genesis"); she is closer to the deep sources of being; she is less misled by the externality of "rationalism" (unless she has been to Hunter College and joined the League of Women Voters and the Book-of-the-Month Club and like conformities). She may not fully *understand* the reasons why she chooses as she does, but she *knows* in the depth and height of her being. Her choice is deeper and higher than utility and rationalism; it is as deep as the protoplasm and as high as the soul.

To integral woman, the creation of genuine men and women, children of vitality and talent and even genius, is the basis of her being. She wishes to create in her husband and in herself and in her country the qualities that make for life and life ever more abundantly. So she intuitively seeks that man who is, in himself, worth something; who can build and be; who is not just another ambulant shadow-shape but a four-dimensional reality. She wishes a man who is something and somebody; who counts and is, who means something in and for the life of the world.

If hers is to be a fruitful and abiding marriage and a vital union, woman must be able to honor and reverence *her man* as a being of quality. This does not mean that she must seek a V.I.P. A man who can till a small farm or succeed in a small business; a man who can live in the obscure glory of genius all his life like William Blake; a man who can fight a great fish and win like Hemingway's hero in *The Old Man And The Sea*; a man who can make a dog love him and a child laugh with him, is a man — a great and vital man. She wishes to see in her man something sound and affirmative, something creative and fruitful, something not Mephistophelean (the spirit that denies) but Faustian (the spirit that creates). She knows that Goethe was right: It is the Devil that says *No*; it is God that says *Yes.* If she seeks only biological union, pragmatic support, a marriage of either lust or convenience, she is a woman of no worth, and I would not bother to talk about her. The true woman, first and last, seeks in her husband the true Adam who delves in the Garden and who brings into being the living Apples of Eden.

If a woman seeks in marriage only pleasure, a "kick out of life," a sexual caper, she can choose any handsome and healthy playboy for the playmate of a minor hour. But if she seeks value and quality, she is akin to Columbus, finding Passage to India, and even of Mary, the Mother of God, who bore the Child who reconciled earth with Heaven.

Therefore woman should choose only that man who sees in life and seeks in life something beyond life, something that partakes of

Life. I am not overly laudatory of the late James Branch Cabell as philosopher and artist, but his *Beyond Life* was a wise and noble work. In it he wrote:

> And so it comes about that romance has invariably been the demiurgic and beneficent force, not merely in letters, but in every matter which concerns mankind; and that "realism," with its teaching that the mile-posts along the road are as worthy of consideration as the goal, has always figured as man's chief enemy.

Woman should choose the man who relegates "the mile-posts along the road" to their proper subordination, and who sees the goal as supreme — not as a silly Utopia, nor an equally silly myopia, but as a star to steer by, the City not Made with Hands, the gleam of Heaven. A lasting marriage will be possible when men and women unite in earnest expectation of the sons of God and serve something that is more than themselves — beauty, truth, and goodness — country, family, God. If they see the physical as the symbol and the metaphysical as the reality, not the existential but the essential, not the transient but the transcendental, they may attain a unity of being that is abiding and real. As Cabell goes on to say:

> It is only by believing himself a creature only a little lower than the cherubim that man has by interminable small degrees become, upon the whole, distinctly superior to the chimpanzee. . . .

And he well concludes:

> And it is this will that stirs in us to have the creatures of earth and the affairs of earth, not as they are, but "as they ought to be," which we call romance. And when we note how visibly it sways all life we perceive that we are talking about God.*

Unless in marriage woman — and man — recognize and reverence that metaphysical transcendency that is God, there will be no marriage — only a partnership for biology and business, legalized by the police and easily dissolvable by divorce. Let woman, therefore, seek the man who is somehow touched with that light from beyond the world which is the shadow of God. That is the meaning of the noble saying that marriage is made in Heaven.

Beyond Life, by James Branch Cabell, The Modern Library, Boni and Liveright, New York.

II

BUT GOD WILLS — thank God! — that genuine creatures, and His true sons and daughters, should never become overly solemn. God wills the bird to sing her heart out on the blossomed trees, the chipmunk to scurry in delight over the gray stone-wall, the otter to slide in play down the clay-bank into the silver shock of water, the tree to express the rapture of life in sun and wind by the toss and gloss of blossoms. Our God is a God of joy!

Let woman choose a man capable of *joy*. Any woman who chooses a man incapable of going a little mad under the full moon is a fool. Let her choose a man who can shout when his favorite Colts score a touchdown; who loves to be cushioned soft and rocked in billowy drowse of Rhode Island breakers; who will notice the dimple in her chin. Never choose a man who will not grow articulately lyrical when you roast a young duck and bake a cherry pie. Choose a man who loves the rich ardors and appetites of life — the lilt of the car on the superhighway, the feel of a kitten's fur stroked into little bubbles of purr, the giant miracle of seeds shouldering aside the loam, the sound of music and the sight of painting, the rich delights of the senses fulfilled by the interpretation of the soul. In these things, *in the Inner Kingdom*, lies the harvest of being, the realization of life.

If more men were that way, we wouldn't have the bleak puritanism of the Communists, the unhappy bitterness and grudge of rioters in the streets, the dismal solemnities of hippies abandoning the poetry of earth for the caricatures of drugs and beards. I say to every woman: Choose a man who loves life in its rich sensuous (not sensu*al*) details, who finds in simple things earth's most subtle realities, who can hold infinity in the palm of his hand and Eternity in an hour.

And let a woman choose no man who hasn't a sense of humor. Humor is to see sanely the incongruities of life that alone make life congruous. There was (they say) an old Greek philosopher who laughed himself to death at the sight of a donkey — that delightful creature, eating his breakfast of hay like the whiskers of earth, his ears like prehensile exclamation points, his voice raised every now and then in the lyric of a bray. The only thing wrong with this was that the philosopher laughed himself to *death* — he should have laughed himself into *life*! Laughter is the great critic of the pretensions and solemnities of the bureaucrats and the commissars, reducing man dressed in a little brief authority to Stevenson's "bubble of the agglutinated dust," and so seeing ever more clearly by ridiculing the incongruities of man in his temporal secular lapses, the congruity of man set only a little lower than the angels in the will of God.

Laughter is a grace and a gift always (unknown to Socialists, Communists, and "Liberals") that tells us it is useless to put a pinch of salt on a sunbeam to coax it out of Heaven, but that we should love and enjoy the sunlight of God without planning or ideologies.

No woman can safely marry a man who has no sense of humor. She and he must share a sense of the rich incongruities of being, and find in them much of the salt and savor of life. One of the loveliest women I know — she happens to be my daughter — had a little dog that she loved and who loved her. He used to put his head on her shoulder and talk to her in little dog decibels. And she would tell her children: "Clifford isn't very bright, but I love him dearly. He keeps telling me that the world isn't round but square, he is sure it's square. But I don't tell him any different. I don't want to hurt his feelings, so I just let him keep on believing that the world is square!" Now if a man doesn't like and understand a charming fiction like that, and if he doesn't find in it the salt and the sunlight of life, he isn't a safe man to marry. For he would be no fun. And he would be too dull to be wise.

Because a true woman loves the poetry of life and the humor of living, she finds the joy of life not in the acquisitions that lie without but in the delights that lie within. The joy of life, she knows, lies in the emotions and in what Stevenson called "the Kingdom of the Light Imaginations," and in the weather of the soul. She will, therefore, seek as her husband a man who delights, with her, in the first shrill frogpipers in the springtime pools, the dip and sway of the returning swallows playing tag in the azure day, the glory of Alfred Noyes' "The Highwayman," the shared zest of a coffee-break, the pages of *Pickwick Papers* read aloud, the *Orfeo* of Gluck, which even Bernard Shaw described as "the Elysian fields . . . the Good Friday . . ." of music, the perennial magic of *Huckleberry Finn*, the mood of Mendelssohn's *A Midsummer Night's Dream*. She will never choose a man whose novocain-calloused being is closed to a kitten making a holiday with strings or the sunset of Emily Dickinson (that supreme woman) where ships of purple gently toss on seas of daffodil.

Woman should know that she cannot be happy with any man who does not fulfill something of Joseph Conrad's words about the artist:

> He speaks to our capacity for delight and wonder, to the sense of mystery surrounding our lives, to our sense of pity, and beauty, and pain; to the latent feeling of fellowship with all creation — and to the subtle but invincible conviction of solidarity that knits together the loneliness of innumerable hearts, to the solidarity in dreams, in joy, in sorrow, in aspirations, in illusions, in hope, in fear, which binds together all humanity — the dead to the living, and the living to the unborn.*

She should feel, at first sight and last insight, that her man is one capable of such rich realization of being. And she can test him by a ripple of fancy, by a flash of humor, by quoting a great lyric; and if he remains obtuse to the bubbles winking at life's brim, if he does not laugh at Sam Weller or Huckleberry Finn, if he is allergic to the lyric, he is not for her.

Always she should feel perfectly *at home with him*, as if she had known him before time began and will know him after time ends; she will be the perfect feminine tune for his perfect masculine words, fused in the song that marries words and music into a beauty that sings in the world's heart.

III

YET THOUGH such grace-notes of life are essential for true marriage, a woman must seek for something else in her husband — especially in this grim day when the bugles blow for battle. She should seek, also, in her husband, the qualities of the good soldier.

What are these qualities? Courage, loyalty, obedience, discipline, the will to fight (always with the mind and potentially with the weapons that are the final ultimatum), the ability first to *reason why* and then to do or die. Today no true man can escape the call to be the good soldier. I do *not* mean that he must be the *professional* soldier. I do *not* mean that he must be in the *army*. Today, of course, in several countries like Argentina, Brazil, and Greece, the army is the last bulwark of civilization. Yet to be a good soldier means more than that. Perhaps the best example of what I mean is given us in the character of Captain von Trapp in *The Sound Of Music*: If we had more men like him, of invincible integrity to fight the Communists taking over the world as he fought the Nazis taking over Austria, we

---

*Preface to *The Nigger Of The Narcissus,* Joseph Conrad.

would be nearer sanity and freedom today. Let us remember always, also, that it was the good soldiers in the German army who tried to overthrow Hitler; that it was the most brilliant of Russian Generals, Vlasov, who turned against the Communist horror, and the Cossack soldiers during World War II who "deliberately slaughtered their political Commissars and put up a tremendous fight before they were overwhelmed, disarmed, and marched off to the Bykovsky-Peresov detention camp."

Only a decadent woman could choose a pacifist or peacenik. The pacifist is a low type of man in any day — deracinated, unreal, without reason or tradition, futile. And, perhaps because pacifists are so rootless, they are the most bellicose, arrogant, hating and hateful "men" you can find. While I was teaching at Earlham College, the present head of one of the peace groups (now centered at Voluntown, Connecticut) was my student. The matter of defense of person and country came up in class; this "pacifist" became virulently militant there, and stayed half an hour after class to argue militantly still; he accused me of being a "coward" because I said that, if threatened with violence, I would kill (if necessary and possible) to defend my own life, which I said I considered more important than that of a murderer. He also wrote the President of Earlham, asking that I be forbidden to write for any college publication, because I had publicly reviewed and endorsed General Bonner Fellers' book on air-power. Today he and his like "march" from Montreal to Havana, display arrogant and insulting slogans, attack their country as always wrong and her enemies as always right, and are more bellicose than a cobra that has been smoking marijuana. No woman with sound instincts and clear intuition would tolerate the pacifist as her husband.

But the good soldier, yes! The qualities of courage, loyalty, discipline, the subordination of petulant whim to the valid authority of eternal values and transcendent quality, the will to fight the enemy outside the walls and the enemy within the door, the brilliant intelligence that reasons why and then fights to the death for its convictions, these a man should have; no woman should choose a man who does not possess them. Choose in your husband the good soldier!

This is the more necessary because, thanks to the pacifists, the appeasers, the coexisters, we face a world of militant war for perhaps the next century. The late H.L. Mencken, in his penetrating study of

Theodore Roosevelt ("Roosevelt: An Autopsy"), said that Teddy lived just long enough to see his notions take on life, but not long enough to see them openly adopted. Mencken wrote: "However unpleasant it may be to contemplate, the fact is plain that the American people, during the next century, will have to fight to maintain their place in the sun." Even so!

We shall have to fight, also, to maintain our republic in our own cities. This is an increasingly dangerous world, where, if you wish "security," you should refuse to be born. It is a world where it is dangerous to be born; where enemies without plot in a worldwide conspiracy to bury us; and where enemies within plot in a nationwide conspiracy to burn us. Courage, discipline, authority of mind and will, are the only way to survival of the body and creation by the spirit.

Any women who prate of "peace," who would rather be Red than dead, who would surrender all that makes life worth living and compromise everything that makes life great, betray the essential nature of woman — which is to create and conserve life and the values of life. Woman has her own daring, which is child-birth; she must demand of man his own daring, which is the courage of the soldier standing between his country and wild war's desolation. The flesh desires "peace" but the spirit enters time to trouble the sleep even of the granite or the marble and to burn it into the beauty of the statue or the glory of the cathedral. The spirit does not bring peace — but a sword. Let woman always seek in man, and enhance in man, the hero in his soul.

IV

I WROTE that the woman a man chooses should be a *good* woman. Even so, the man whom a woman chooses should be a good man. What does that mean? It means that the man a woman chooses should be on the side of order, harmony, cosmos; that he should stand for qualities and values; that he should seek to build and create and preserve and conserve; that he should follow (though, in his human fallibility, far off) the God who says, "Let there be light." Our God has blessed Creation: That man is good who smites the random weed and sows the fruitful grain; who fashions the good steel for plow and sword; who graves on tablets of stone the commandments of reason which are the will of God; who loves the beauty of the rose in the garden or of the roadside aster; who makes two blades of grass to grow where there was only one; who stands armed between the lamb and the wolf; who fashions and guards a space of light and grace where woman and child may flourish.

In all sane ages the hero is honored, and the hero is *good*: Hector, who dies that Troy may live, Odysseus, enduring the ten years' wandering that he may again reach the rocks and the gray windy olives of Ithaca . . . and the Penelope whom he loves and never forgets; Perseus, rescuing Andromeda from the sea-monster; Cervantes, like his own great Don Quixote, dying a pauper – and a lord of life; Cyrano de Bergerac keeping his white plume unstained by the world's corruptions; George Washington, refusing the crown that the Republic might live; Chiang Kai-shek making Taiwan the garden of Asia and the home of free men; Douglas MacArthur standing though the skies fall; George Washington Carver, living in humble obscurity and using black genius for the world's life, white or black; the quiet unsung citizen who does the work and keeps the world's faith amid the frothings of "Rap" Brown or Stokely Carmichael and the aberrations of the hippies; these are the heroes, these the good men. Let woman choose only a man who, in the infinite variety and fascination of the possible creations that lie within the Providence of God, is such a man.

Then let woman, by her passionate love and her flaming loyalty, strengthen that man – giving him ever new hope, new faith, because she gives him ever the greatest of all her feminine gifts – her love as woman.

Integrity And The Family

THIS, we are told, is the space age. And the central image of man today, to small boys who seek adventure and to small men obsessed with "science," is the space man. Now I have only admiration for the brave and efficient men from our Army, Navy, or Air Force, who swing in nonchalant and gallant orbits around the Earth and walk on the alien surface of another world: Honor to them! But the "space man" as an ideal, the space man as an idol-image of the age, the space man's orbits around Earth or his safari to the moon as a profound discovery about the nature and meaning of life — all this is inept and shallow. We tend to see the space man as far more than he is — or ever can be. The space man is just an interesting fellow helmeted in a goggle-bubble of glass, who lies prone in a silver arrow shot from a bow of flame at the bullseye of the moon, or who orbits the launching-pad of the Earth, thus extending the range of human reach (*not* of man's wisdom). The mischief of this is that the space man is seen as the apex of human advance, whereas he is only a gaudy tangent to it — not a destiny but a decoration.

Such is the obsession of the age in which we live. This collectivist, secular, "Liberal" age of ours does not explore the metaphysics of *time* but concentrates on the physics of *space*.* And space means, to the present age, the external, the exterior, the extraneous, the extended; it means a geometrical world where extension is seen as the possibility of action and the field of motion on the *outer* plane. If the cosmos were a piano (and that is a realistic image for it), the space men would be concerned not with the intricate subtlety of the keys, or the latent discovery of music, or the fruitful time-intervals of the notes, but rather with the extension of the keyboard and equally with the extension of space around and above and below the instrument. The space men are curious about the exterior, but

---

*The secret of life certainly lies not in space but in time. Time is our way of perceiving the fourth dimension; it leads us toward meaning, it has a great deal to do with the nature of immortality, it is the field that most needs exploration. But only a few choice minds, like J.B. Priestly and the largely unknown philosopher, J.W. Dunne, dig into it today. We are space men — not time men!

callous to the interior; concerned with the extraneous, but careless of the essential; compulsive about the extension of existence, but oblivious to the intention of being. Bergson's critique (in *Creative Evolution*) of the rationalistic, geometry-loving intellect — as opposed to intuition — applies to the space men. Bergson showed that the narrowed intellect is the geometrician, the action-obsessed analyst, the mechanistic pseudologician who sees matter in terms of lines-of-action. So the space-minded always! But beyond action and motion lie essence and meaning.

This means that the space man, in his philosophy, moves away from the essence that is the center, out toward the existential circumference and the film-surface of things. Space-age philosophy is concerned with extension, extension, and ever more extension, through which to move and in which to act. Space-age philosophy never knows (or cares) whence it comes or whither it goes; but it is always on its way . . . to the nowhere or everywhere, by speed through space . . . .

The crux of the mischief is that the space age applies extension to everything — even to the interior, the metaphysical, the spiritual, where it cannot apply. Politics is made a field for extension, and so is collectivized; sociology is seen only as a field for extension, and so is not vital but ideological. Living relationships that do not extend in space but are things of continuity in time — individual destiny, the family, the nation, man's relationship to God who made us for Himself so that we are restless till we rest in Him . . . are not spatial, and so they are either ignored today or misunderstood if they are noticed. Our space-age compulsion is applied to non-spatial fields — we seek, in the world of the mind and the heart of the soul, a world spatial, extended, spread out, and thus made tenuous and unreal, thin and circumstantial rather than introstantial. We shun the center; we seek the circumference and the surface: Thus we move away from the *potentia qua* of the individual, and toward the *status quo* of the collective; away from the family, and toward "society"; away from the Constitutional Republic, and toward "world government." We betray the concrete man, and seek the mass and nebulosity (which exists only as a concept) of "humanity." Thus the inner world is corroded, dissolved, or subverted, and we enter the new lunacy of rockets to the moon — inwardly as well as outwardly, as if we could travel to Heaven in Apollo XV!

In every age we most need a criticism, *sub specie aeternitatis*, of the temporal credulities and somnambulisms of the age. We need always a return to fundamentals, a renewal of vital radicalism in the root sense of that distorted word — *for to be "radical" in the true sense means to return to the roots of things.* That, we conservatives alone do today. The needed contemporary critique is a criticism of the space men in their insect-shaped bubbles of fantastic spatial madness, and a renewal of the eternal verities and vitalities and values of things as they timelessly and absolutely *are*, above and beyond space. And for the moment I wish to concentrate on one facet of this — the family, that space-transcending reality, and on the integrity of that life-centered unit of human relationship. What is the integrity of the family, without which we shall perish from the Earth, exchanging spirit for space? It is time to return to the *Lares* and *Penates* — to the household gods!

I

THE ADVOCATES of extension through space, of course, hate the family and wish to destroy it. We all know the ant-heap communies of Communist China, the collective farms of Soviet Russia; but the "Liberals" in America are equally against the family. Characteristic of their hatred of the family are the questions they insinuate into the minds of our children in their psychological "tests" and "questionnaires." There they are the acid-throwers of education, tossing acid in the face of the family. They ask our children to check — suggesting that they *should* check:

186) I don't like my home.
191) I wish I didn't have a brother.
195) My mother is too bossy.
196) My daddy is too bossy.
201) I wish my mother liked me more.
203) My mother and daddy often fight.
215) I'm afraid of my mother.
216) I'm afraid of my daddy.*

Now in every close intimate relationship of us fallible human beings there will be hostilities, difficulties, tensions. That is the way of all flesh! But to exaggerate their centrality and importance, to

---

*This is taken from the section called "About Me And My Home," in the test published by the Science Research Associates entitled "Junior Inventory — Form A." It is cited in the *Congressional Record* for August 13, 1958.

stress and italicize them, to omit the over-all harmony that surrounds and transcends them, is unnatural, abnormal, malicious, sick. It is a deliberate short-circuiting of reality, so that the lights burn out in a dangerous blackout. The space-obsessed do this deliberately. For they know that they can destroy the harmonious and the vital, and bring in the collectivistic and the positivistic, only if and when they destroy the family. They wish the way of all flesh to destroy the way of all spirit.

Again and again in the world today these acid-throwers seek to disintegrate the family. In the *Ladies' Home Journal* for October of 1965 we find the case history of what happens when they succeed. The article is entitled: "How America Lives." The author, Betty Hannah Hoffman, tells the miserable story excellently, though she does not fully explore why this sort of thing occurs, or just how sinister (in both the English and Latin sense) it is. Her heading to the story reads: "She comes from a fine home and used to be a Young Republican. Yet, at 22, brilliant Susan Druding has a jail sentence and lives in protest against the morals and ethics of her parents and professors [*sic*!]. A very personal story of a student's search for identity." The last sentence reveals the author's hypnosis with the clichés of the hour — "a student's *search for identity.*" The story proves that the student broke her roots to reality, and so is like a young apple tree that tears up its roots and goes wandering off on the fractured stubs — not toward "identity," but toward conformity to the temporal mores . . . toward sterility, a loss of all peace and meaning and joy, a nullity of any blossomed, fruit-bearing self. I once wrote a poem about this sort of thing, foreseeing prophetically the contemporary creed that we human beings should be like trees that demand apples before they have even grown boughs and produced blossoms, trees that wander around in fantastic search for fruit:

> Cyclones and suns, lightning and ache of snow —
> Toward these I go.
>
> I must not be the earth's green scaling-tower
> Till I have power.
>
> Apples hung five feet off my boughs in air
> Till I come there —
>
> Not thus, not thus the rugged fountains grow
> Whence apples flow!

That is eternal truth. But students like Susan Druding, hypnotized by the clichés of "Liberalism," seek "identity" by pulling their roots up and wandering around in petulant search for the apples they do not have the wit or wisdom to *grow*.

The story — you should look it up and read it — is typical of our illusioned time. Susan Druding was an excellent student, daughter, and person until, somehow and somewhere in her "education," she had her roots severed and went hobbling off in haywire safari. She went first to Oberlin College (it seems to have begun there), she wandered through Michigan and on to Berkeley, until she has "a prison record, her name is on the FBI files, and her relationship with her family has become one of anguish and continuing frustration." Now she shuns cosmetics and make-up, disfigures her limbs with blue jeans and boy's sandals,, and scorns her family. She thought she found reality at Berkeley by self-consciously and deliberately rooming with a black, by saying of our forces in Vietnam, "Imposed democracy is horrendous and immoral" (notice the big word and the advocacy of morality — which in general she detests — and notice especially that, by implication, she seems to suggest that imposed *Communism* is quite right).

She sought a "commitment" to some "cause" outside herself that alone could give meaning (she supposed) to what in itself seems to her sort to be a meaningless existence in a valueless chaos. She also, as extra-curricular and extra-commitment activity, has had "three great loves" since she was nineteen, and engages occasionally, it seems, in minor casual (but, she claims, not "promiscuous") "loves." Her attitude toward the family as a unit is best given in her own words: "If I ever feel the need for children, I can always adopt them." That is, to her, the family is not a creative unit of continuity and consanguinity, but a casual adjustment of expediency and artifice — a mere extension in space. She sought her "identity" by the extraordinary means of swallowing "quantities of Dexedrine tablets and staying awake all night brewing coffee and discussing life."

Susan Druding is a typical conformist to our cliché creed of extension and existentialism. She is — her mother put it perfectly — one of those with "a high I.Q., low common sense. . . ." She is another contemporary apple tree that pulls up its roots and goes on a search for apples!

Somehow, somewhere, Susan's "education" deprived her of taste and critical intelligence — so that she came to take Mario Savio for her ideal; he had (she thought) "magnificent integrity" and an "almost Christlike air." But her father, who is a good craftsman and earns an honest living by doing the world's work, is (like all adults) a square and lives "in a phony, artificial manner."

Such is the sad⹁nonsense story when the continuity of the family is fractured!

To change the figure and to illuminate reality still further, the extentionists of the space age are inorganic and partial. They never understand the paradoxes of the laws of Nature. They split life into fragments and italicize one fragment at the expense of the organic and orbed whole. Thus they italicize centrifugal force but erase centripetal force.*

In Nature there is always the interplay of these forces, in the harmony of reciprocal tension; this, and this alone, makes possible the movement of the wheel or the rotation of the Earth. God has willed that in Nature there is a tension and balance of the force that would hurl things *from* the center and the force that would hold things *to* the center. Both, in fruitful paradox, cooperate to make it possible for the wheel to revolve and the Earth to rotate. But the nihilists of the hour are partialists, fragmentators, extremists — the *avant-garde* of death: They deny centripetal force; they idolize centrifugal force. They are rebels against the noble tensions that add up to harmony; they are revolutionists against reality; they are the-half-is-the-whole people. They see only the centrifugal, the center-fleeing force; and without the compensation of the equally potent centripetal force their lives fly off into space-flung splinters, fragments, and flying saucers. They are, in the root meaning, eccentric, *i.e.,* off-center.

And they never listen to the inner life, the Inner Light. They never hear the Daemon of Socrates that bids them, "Look homeward, Angel!"

II

In all creation, whether by direct fiat of God, or by God's gradual artistry through the process of creative evolution, the secret and center is — *continuity*.

G.K. Chesterton said it best in his *The Victorian Age In*

---

*"**Centrifugal force,** the force outward exerted by a body moving in a curved path . . . ."
"**Centripetal force,** a force acting on a body, which is directed toward the center of a circle or curve, which causes it to move in the circle or curve." *American College Dictionary.*

Literature: ". . . . real development is not leaving things behind, as on a road, but drawing life from them, as from a root."

Any true development of the life of the individual is like this too — not an abandoning, as on a road, but a drawing life from, as from a root!

In Nature life is always a process of continuity. The flower and fruit grow, in living continuity, from the root and the seed. The butterfly, that gaily staggering pinnace of the air that leans in ecstasy upon the breeze, grows only by living continuity from the worm and through the chrysalis. Rome, that once noble Republic that (in Virgil's phrase) was to spare the vanquished and war down the proud, grew in greatness until it lost continuity and succumbed to the partiality of the centrifugal. England was great and real only while it kept continuity with *Beowulf* and Chaucer, with the action of Alfred and the legend of Arthur, with the seamen that harried the Armada to destruction, with Milton and Shakespeare and Blake, with Bunyan and Thomas à Becket, with the King James Bible and Magna Charta. "Ripeness is all," said Shakespeare in what is probably the apex of England's wisdom; but there can be no ripeness without continuity and centrality.

Great popular arts, like the dances, the music, the lace and rugs, the arts and crafts, of peasant culture, are great and living because they never lose continuity and centrality through time and the generations. In all eras of fine craftsmanship, as of silversmiths, makers of Kentucky rifles, architects of Colonial houses, creators of beautiful furniture, *etc.*, the secret of excellence was continuity. At one time certain monks worked with silver so beautifully that they fashioned what is still known as "sainted silver" — a craftsmanship so delicate, so subtly simple, that it seemed impossible that silver could ever have been worked to such finesse. But its perfection came through centrality and continuity. So in one of our few people-based and nation-centered popular arts today, the fashioning of floats out of flowers for the Rose Bowl Parade, there is growth and change and advance each year only because within and beyond all change there is a living continuity that draws sustenance from the root of the past and the timeless tradition of essential meaning.

(On the contrary, a capable but rootless writer like John Steinbeck has no living continuity or centrality. From book to book he jumps here, he jumps there, seeing life unsteadily and in fragments, never growing from the root of his people or himself. And so a Tennessee

Williams, though he has a diseased root in his own sick self, has no root in tradition and the living center, no continuity with the soul of his people, and so fashions only a circumstantial art. And so an artist who technically has a genius for painting, but who has no roots in life or himself, Picasso, jumps like a Mexican bean from style to style, and vision to vision, without continuity, in terms of mere extraneous extension. Naturally he is the idol of the space age!)

The family is closely akin to all true creation because it has continuity and centrality. In the genuine family (how few we have today!) there is passionate love between man and woman, that — since it is *love* — seeks permanence and continuity; out of the passion of that love the child is conceived and born, as what Euripedes' Medea beautifully called "my flower of pain." The child is not a spatial extension, but a temporal continuity. It is formed and nourished for nine months under the mother's heart, it is not fabricated like something tossed off a centrifugal wheel in the compartment of a space-ship orbiting the Earth or targeting the moon. And when the child is born, if the family is real, he is equally a child of continuity in blood and spirit. The home that surrounds him is a place of continuity with the culture and the soul of his country and his race — a place of continuity with the pictures, the music, the books, the faith, the philosophy, the religion that are the outward and visible sign of an inward and invisible grace. The child absorbs from his earliest years a reciprocity, a consanguinity and a cultural communion, a mutuality that continues in him a life that transcends him. This must come always as an unconscious sharing, not as a sociological "adjustment"; "togetherness," "tender loving care," and all the conceptual ideologies of spatial and mechanical fabrications and artifice, ruin the growth of life. (That is as if some fussy planner should thrust his fingers into the chrysalis to "adjust" the butterfly!)

In a genuine family the child grows upward in an atmosphere of organic *unconscious* harmony, absorbing faith and love and philosophy from every chime of the clock and every morsel of food (prepared with artistry and love and joy) and from the natural music of the spheres that is the rhythm of his home. And let the child have intimate contacts with the wise good animals, our elder brothers, in terms of reverence for *their* natures and lives — with kittens, with puppies, and (if it is possible) even now and then with colts and horses and chickens and cows. And let the child be assigned his fruitful and happy place in the work of the world and the chores of the home; let him know inexorably that there are dishes to wash, and bait to dig, and errands to run. Always the father should be the center of authority; he should be obeyed and honored that our days may be long in the land (though you may, as a child, call him affectionately "the Old Man" or "the Jolly Old Moke," *etc.*). The father should be a central figure of *strength* — the central figure who earns the food, who drives the car when the family goes on a long safari, who has the gun for hunting and the rod for fishing, who makes the fundamental decisions and whose word is as objectively final as the showdown in poker. He should have the authority of inward strength and wisdom.

The mother should be a figure of grace and charm — the central figure who makes food delectable, who binds up the cut finger (bidding you not to pay too much attention to it, because you are a *man*), and who initiates you into romance and beauty as she reads you *The Wind In The Willows*, and *Through The Looking Glass*, and *Huckleberry Finn* and *The Jungle Tales* and *Treasure Island* and the poetry of Keats and Kipling, and who is herself your beloved image of gaiety and charm. The word for wife and mother is: *gallant and gay*. And the house should be the child's cave and nest (in the poetic sense), his refuge and castle and workshop and playground, his chrysalis in the pupa stage, his lustrous center of being. The child should have a fierce pride in his home and his family. The family, he should unconsciously know, is his fountainhead and source of being. Here is his unique, and consanguineous, and beloved home, that he loves as the bird loves its nest and the woodchuck its burrow — only with the wider grace and love that comes because he is a many-splendored human being. With his father and his mother, his brothers and sisters, the living unit that his vital and mysterious continuity of life has given him, he should have a rapport that transcends all tensions. Out of such a family alone can come a life that is sound and sane, a life that is natural and happy, whereby the child may grow in wisdom and stature, and favor with God and man.

And out of such a unit can come generations of talent and even genius, as in the Edwards family that produced not only the great Jonathan, but generations of other figures of eminence and power. Always the truly wise and living family wishes that wife or husband shall choose husband or wife in terms of a purity and nobility that may add to its blood-stream only genes that enhance and advance power and courage and integrity and wisdom. This is suggested — this pride in noble choice and unity — in the beautiful Spanish custom of naming the family by uniting the name of the wife's family and the husband's family by a *y* (or "and") between the names. Zarathustra has well said: "Thirst in the creating one, arrow and longing for the Superman; thus doth it cause thirst for the Superman; tell me, my brother, is this thy will to marriage? Holy call I such a will, and such a marriage." But, as Zarathustra knew and we see today even more, of modern man we must too often say: "Or doth the animal speak in thy wish and necessity? Or isolation? Or discord in thee?"

Out of the latter marriages come our juvenile delinquents and child-monstrosities. Out of the will and the marriage that is "holy" come the children who have integrity and grace and beauty and wisdom. And they come essentially from the family that is closest to tradition and the roots of things. Chesterton, in his magnificent *Tremendous Trifles* ("Humanity: an Interlude"), describes such a family: "I thought of a low and lonely house in the flats, beyond a veil or film of slight trees, a man breaking the ground as men have broken it from the first morning, and a huge gray horse champing his food within a foot of a child's head, as in the stable where Christ was born." How much more real than the "modern" home of gimmicks and gadgets, of radio and television and streamlined cars, of prophylactic isolation from basic reality! Even amid our many inventions, what we need is a family and a home that reverences and still remembers the simple fundamental realities — the *Lares* and *Penates*, the household gods!

III

THIS integrity of the family is most possible when you remember and reverence the continuity of the family through time and beyond time — in the generations that were, in the generations that shall be. The family must include all these. The family, as mere space men think of it, is a kind of atomic fragmentation — a brief concatenation of individuals discrete like ball-bearing atoms, not a continuity of the living root with the living rose. To them it is a hit-or-miss, helter-skelter thing of "Mom" and "Pop" and a population explosion of little wiggly-worms and tangents known as "children"; to them it begins with the "living" existential generation and ends with the "living" existential generation. But the ancient Hebrews or Greeks, and the classical Chinese, and the genuine races of the once dynamic West, knew better.

The family is a continuity of metaphysical unity that extends outward in space but (even more) inward in time — a continuity that binds the living dead with the living unborn. Frank Harris (in one of his wise moments) wrote: "We are immortal when we die: it is the dead who steer the living." So with the family! The strong stern noble face in an old daguerreotype; the still living inscription in a family Bible centuries old; the old, old letters that bring across the centuries the notation of the eternal human heart; the memory of the noble courage and love of your grandmother (now dead), who when she was ninety-three went alone with you into the country to take care of you when you were convalescing from the edge of death and had to get away from the influenza that was sweeping the country, and when no one else could go;* all this noble river of heritage flowing from far-off mountain peaks and still making glad City of God. . . all these are a part of the family in which you are another incarnate symbol in the present moment of time.

The integrity of the family comes from remembrance and pride and anticipation, from the reciprocity of your ancestors with you, from your mutuality with the descendants that are an integral part of the family though they have not yet been born. Your continuity with the ancestors who came before you, your continuity with the descendants who shall come after you, form the psychic or spiritual reality of the family. This depends partly on the consanguinity of inheritance, partly on the psychic continuity of a search for the same high stars. George Meredith wrote in one of his finest poems:

> Our life is but a little holding, lent
> To do a mighty labor: we are one
> With heaven and the stars when it is spent
> To serve God's aim: else die we with the sun.

That speaks the very soul of the genuine family. The family is more than our individual selves; it is the concentrated continuity and meaning of which we are a vital and contributing and continuing part, not so much extended in space as continuous in time (and Eternity). From the family, if we give to it what we should, we receive the life

---

*I know that this is true, because it was my grandmother who so cared for me.

that we need — the power, not ourselves, that makes for our own true *I Am.* To sever one's continuity with the family in order to "find one's own identity," is like the idiocy of a trout that should seek to find itself by abandoning water, of an eagle that would find its wings by repudiating air, of the man who lights a candle in order to see the sun.

One reason why the family today has degenerated into sociology, why "Mom" is too often today both bossy and possessive *and* saccharine and sentimental, and why children have become too often brats and nuisances, is that both parents and children have lost the integrity (i.e., *wholeness*) that comes only when we know that the family is more than the present members of it. The family goes backward to Eden and onward to Heaven: It is a metaphysical reality, it may be a mystical part of the body of Christ Himself, a living victory that partakes of the dead, the living, and the unborn. It is a time-transcending reality that flows ever on through time and stands ever in God's Eternal Now.

The great Greeks, in epic and drama and life, had a deep abiding sense of the continuity of the family — for evil and also for good. We should become good Greeks! Each member of a family should have a fierce pride in the family as a whole, a reverence for and a reciprocity with the family as a whole, a loyalty to the family as a whole. The horrible habits of Chinese Communist "families," or Soviet "families," or "families" in *1984* — where children spy on, and betray, and accuse parents, or vice versa, is the destruction of integrity. The family itself enhances loyalty, honor, integrity, meaning — that is, *life*: It gives life a higher voltage. And thus its loyalty serves other living aspects of the soul — individual destiny, one's country, one's God.

As one seeks to honor one's family he will seek to protect it, affirm it, preserve it. He will be the inexorable critic and enemy of all the acid-throwers who seek to disfigure its face into a burned slag of hideous flesh. He will criticize and fight the politicians who, in their own greed and for their own power, seek to destroy the family by communes and collective farms and barracks in China and Russia, or by the progressive and exorbitant income tax and inheritance tax in "Liberal" America. He will seek to affirm private property, to enhance and increase private property, to build up the ancestral acres and estate, for these are the concrete foundations of the family triumphant and enduring. Here he will agree with the Distributists in

England and Canada — with Hilaire Belloc and G.K. Chesterton — who saw and see the roots of the family nourished by the distribution (*not* by government but through energy and individual initiative) of more and more private property in the hands of more and more individuals, families, local groups, and less and less in the hands of the Soviet, the State, the Big Corporations, and the financiers.

For these material reasons, and far more for the psychic reasons of freedom, creativity, and faith and hope and love, we who revere the family will be the mortal enemies of all collectivism — of Socialism, Communism, "welfare Liberalism," and all their alien corn. We revere the family as a unit based on continuity of blood and purpose and meaning, on a spiritual culture, on a psychic entity. Therefore we of the family oppose all wire-tapping, mail-opening, state-imposed regimenting and ticketing and numbering and alphabetizing, all public invasions of the private soul. Thus the family, in its integrity, is a chief fortress for our God, against relativism, pragmatism, existentialism, and the collective tyranny of the State — or of the "democratic" mass.

Members of the genuine family will stand like a star above all the shifting tides and veering winds of the hour. The attempt of the space men to spread life thin, the "Liberal" idiocies of fractured roots, the world homogenized into egalitarian mediocrity, will find an inexorable enemy in the family. The family is the Ark, preserving the seeds of life, the seeds of time, against the new flood, against the "waves of the future" that would drown man under mass. The family alone brings creative revolution — which is creative renewal. This is the true revolution of our time — a revolution that is renaissance and renewal, a return to the root and so a restoration of the rose.

The family! — May it endure like the central and life-giving sun in heaven, around which the fruitful planets revolve! May it be the deathless root within the earth whence blossoms the immortal rose! May it endure always like the central fire of earth that, as the foundation (under the granite) of our cities and our society, still keeps the heart of Earth a *star*!

In The Beginning Was The Word

Books To Encourage Children To Read

THE schools will not do it. The colleges will not do it. You, the parents, must do it or it will not be done.

What am I talking about? I am talking about the communication of a living culture, a literature of beauty and wisdom, an ozone of the soul, that is to children what clean air, pure water, the radiant sun are — what the green living forests are, absorbing carbon dioxide and breathing forth oxygen — a climate of health and life so natural, so inevitable, so unconsciously absorbed, that we do not know that they are there, until we fall sick because they are not! Given that once more, our children will be too naturally wise and too radiantly joyous to seek the lethal substitute of drugs, the gaudy caricature called "protest," the deafening cacophonies of rock-and-roll, the smart-alec "sophistication" of talk-show wise guys, and all the synthetic phony artificialities of the hour.

I am talking about the books, the wise and beautiful books, that should be the life ever more abundant in which children may live and move and find their being, because they are the very climate of God.

What books should your children read?

One of the fine young men I know once asked his father the question: "What shall I read?" And the wise answer was, "Read the classics!" Yes, read the classics! Of course. But there must be grace notes of explanation, and codas of warning, and names to be named, if we parents are to know what the classics for children are.

In suggesting books for children I would urge you not to be narrow or stiff — not to uphold "propaganda" even for reality — I would refuse to set the right content above the right art. I would have you suggest only books that are so fine in artistry that they cast their own magic spell over the child, and so are a living joy to read. I would suggest only books that in my own still living childhood (for time is an illusion and the child forever lives on in that eternity that is our timeless life) spoke to my own condition and nourished my own being.

I still remember sadly how *on Sundays* my beloved father (who was a minister) allowed me to read only books from the Sunday School Library of the church. That was wrong, for many of the books so permitted were quite mediocre, and made me feel that "good" books were dull books. And that is contrary to the will and Providence of God, in whose triune being is the Holy Spirit that is the fountainhead of *genius.* At the time, though I was less than ten, I wanted to read Poe's tales and Charles Reade's *The Cloister And The Hearth* . . . neither of which happened to be in the Sunday School Library. And so I not only wasted my time, but I also thought my parents had the false idea that I must read "good" books rather than great books. I am sure that my father, in that wider unimpeded world that transcends this, knows now why I say this and forgives me, but I would not make his mistake; I would not have *you* make his mistake.

So first of all let me say this. None of the books I list or suggest will be suggested because they say the right thing *unless they say it in the right way.* And the right way is the way of art — the way of genius, the way of beauty, the way of magic. All books for children, because young unspoiled children are very close to the wonder and the wisdom of God, must be things of magic and joy. They will never be heavy, they will never be dull; they will be moral (as the universe is moral), but never "moralistic" or dogmatic. Jerry Rubin and Timothy Leary are immoral, but they are very "moralistic" and dogmatic. They are always preaching at us to kill our parents, or to destroy ourselves with revolution and LSD. They never let life speak its own magic, because they are too eager to speak their own little screed from their ugly variant on the Sunday School Library!

I suggest only books that children will *love.* I suggest only books that will be a *joy.* I want books for children to be like the seashells whorled with enamel, and the pebbles rounded by the ocean into magic, which the child loves to pick up and play with on the beaches of the world where the great waves crash and roll. I want books for children to be like the fascinating wildflowers that children gather because their color and their fragrance say: "Here is joy!" The books for our children should be, of course, those that say *Yes* to life, that see life as it is, not in a two-dimensional world (which is the "modern" world), but also in the depth and the height of the third dimension . . . and the transcendent hint of the fourth and fifth dimensions which surround and fulfill this lesser world of ours. They must never be mean and low and cynical, and therefore false.*

The living values must be there. (They are really there even in *Gulliver's Travels*.) But they must always be communicated with the fine art of magic. They must always be the living flowers whose roots go down into the living earth, and not cut flowers in a vase or plastic flowers fashioned as lifeless artifacts.

What, then, are some of the books that your children may read?

First, when children are very young, repeat to them or read to them the Mother Goose Rhymes. I know that the sentimental "Liberals" (who uphold hurling cobble-stones at policemen or Molotov cocktails into buildings) call them "bloody" and "violent" and "savage." I know that solemn "scholars" dredge out "historical" sources of them. What does all that signify? St. George and the Dragon are primal realities in life, and the sooner children know it, the better. Mugging and murder on the streets of our cities are corollaries of "Liberalism," and the sooner children know it the better. That Jack falls down and breaks his crown, that Jill comes tumbling after, are facts of life. That the farmer's wife cuts off the tails of three blind mice with her carving knife . . . that Mary, Mary, is quite contrary . . . that Jack must be nimble and quick to jump over the candlestick . . . that Jack Sprat would eat no fat, his wife would eat no lean . . . that pussy-cat went to London and frightened a little mouse under the queen's chair . . . that we ask "Baa, baa, black sheep" if he has any wool . . . such are facets of life that delight the soul. And if "Liberals" say these have no sense, let us remind them that generations so brought up had the sense not to be "Liberals."

Children when very young should learn a lot of sensible nonsense, to cleanse their souls with innocent laughter, and to know what the great Chesterton calls "the giant laughter of Christian men." Children brought up on Mother Goose will be too sound and sane with nonsense to listen to Jerry Rubin's nonsense telling them to go home

---

*Whatever you may think of Oscar Wilde's perversions, it was he who wrote the masterly words: "The cynic is a man who knows the price of everything and the value of nothing."

and kill their parents, or to Edward Kennedy's nonsense telling fantasies about Chappaquiddick. And, most of all, children should know the nature and fate of bureaucrats —

> Humpty-Dumpty sat on a wall,
> Humpty-Dumpty had a great fall . . . .
> And all the King's horses,
> And all the King's men,
> Couldn't put Humpty together again.

That too should be a part of their heritage of wisdom!

And Grimm's Fairy Tales, and Hans Christian Anderson's wonderful tales, should be as natural as mother's milk to children. For in the Fairy Tale you find reality, you see life as it is, and you nourish children who will know what George Orwell calls "the basic freedom" — the freedom to say that "two plus two are four." Above all, you will let your children love the hero, the champion of good and God, the soldier of Eternity. G.K. Chesterton (in *Tremendous Trifles*) speaks the truth superbly:

> "Can you not see," I said, "that fairy tales in their essence are quite solid and straightforward; but that this everlasting fiction about modern life is in its nature essentially incredible? Folk-lore means that the soul is sane, but that the universe is wild and full of marvels. Realism means that the world is dull and full of routine, but that the soul is sick and screaming. The problem of the fairy tale is — what will a healthy man do with a fantastic world? The problem of the modern novel is — what will a madman do with a dull world? . . . In the excellent tale of 'The Dragon's Grandmother,' in all the other tales of Grimm, it is assumed that the young men setting out on his travels will have all substantial truths in him; that he will be brave, full of faith, reasonable, that he will respect his parents, keep his word, rescue one kind of people, defy another kind . . . . Then, having assumed this centre of sanity, the writer entertains himself by fancying what would happen if the whole world went mad all round it, if the sun turned green and the moon blue, if horses had six legs and giants two heads."

But your modern literature takes insanity as its centre.

And again (in the same book but in a different essay), Chesterton says:

> Exactly what the fairy tale does is this: it accustoms him [*the child*] for

a series of clear pictures to the idea that these limitless terrors have a limit, that these shapeless enemies have enemies, that these strong enemies of man have enemies in the knights of God, that there is something in the universe more mystical than darkness and stronger than strong fear.

And therefore, at the earliest possible hour, even before the schools have subjected him to the mumbo-jumbo of primer drool about Ida and little Sam watching the garbage man doing his "social duty," read your children these great tales till they have been soaked into their subconscious, beyond all the efforts of the "Liberals" to dislodge them.

And be especially sure your children know the marvelous Hans Christian Andersen tale about "The Emperor's Clothes" . . . where only the child had the wisdom and the courage to say, "He's naked!"

And do not omit poetry. Before your child knows what poetry is, read to him or her Stevenson's *Child's Garden Of Verses*. Here is the key to Arcady, here is the doorway into the real world — a world of joy, of wonder, of delight that will help a man or woman in the dark and lonely hours with the remembered sanity of the child's joy. Here is "The friendly cow, all red and white" — the "shadow" that goes in and out with you — the river that is dark brown over golden sand — the holes your wooden spade digs on the sea-shore where the sea comes to fill every one — the greater wonder of *not* "living abroad," because you are "safe and live at home" — the heady joy of the swing in the garden — the whole duty of children:

> A child should always say what's true
> And speak when he is spoken to,
> And behave mannerly at table;
> At least as far as he is able.

Even John Dewey cannot pervert children whose soul is melodious with such poetry of the wonder of the world! — with the sanity of the world! Not even such a human mistake as Jerry Rubin!

And, oh, for the sake of your children's souls and their wisdom and delight in life, read them — read them from their earliest hours! — Rudyard Kipling's *Just So Stories*! This so they will learn to laugh like the sunlight that dances down the sky, and to know the secrets of being as the flower knows them and the cow knows them (the brown cow that eats green grass and turns it into white milk) and as the child knows them (before he has been to a modern school and got all curdled); and to play with the stars for marbles, and to know the universe as a Miracle Play for living souls . . . . Read them (even before they can read), "How The Whale Got His Throat" and "How The Camel Got His Hump" and "How The Leopard Got His Spots" . . . and "How The Alphabet Was Made" . . . and about "The Cat That Walked By Himself" (as all cats do). And these will be always the salt of the soul to keep it sweet, and the sun of the soul to tease it toward Heaven . . . and the wonder that will lead you through the valley of the shadow of death to the Unimpeded Life that lies beyond . . . . This is one of the great books of the world — for children and for grown-ups who are not grown down. So one reads:

> In the sea, once upon a time, O my Best Beloved, there was a whale, and he ate fishes. He ate the starfish and the garfish, and the crab and the dab, and the plaice and the dace, and the skate and his mate . . . . and the really truly twirly-whirly eel. All the fishes he could find in all the sea he ate with his mouth — so! Till at last there was only one small fish left in all the sea, and he was a small 'Stute Fish, and he swam a little behind the Whale's right ear, so as to be out of harm's way. Then the Whale stood up on his tail and said, "I'm hungry." And the small 'Stute Fish said in a small 'stute voice, "Noble and generous Cetacean, have you ever tasted Man?"

Read this — and all the others — and enter into the joy of the world. And remember always that only a Master (as Kipling was) can lift you out of time into wisdom.

Read, also, Kipling's *Jungle Tales* — those stories that fashion the soul to love adventure, to worship courage and loyalty, to be courteous to Baloo the Bear and fearless before Shere Khan the tiger and Tobaqui his jackal. Once you read *one* of these to a true child, you will have to read *all*; once you have read them *once*, your child will read them all his life . . . as you do. Here is the center of character, as when Kaa the rock python says, "A brave heart and a courteous tongue, they shall carry thee far through the Jungle, Manling." Here is the glory of battle for the right ("Red Dog"), and the immortal ache of the heart that drives Mowgli back to man, and the wonder of the moon over the wonder of the world.

And let no child of yours grow up without the company of the Water Rat, the Mole, and Mr. Toad, in that delectable classic,

Kenneth Grahame's *The Wind In The Willows*. Adventure, the joy of life, humor, loyalty, love of home and country and friends, reverence for the Friend behind All Phenomena, these are here to be found. So that the child who reads of them never need be "A stranger and afraid/In a world he never made." It is one of the great books — for children, and for the undying child in all real men and women.

A little more esoteric, yet great and good, is George MacDonald's *At The Back Of The North Wind*. Not all children today will like it, but some will; and all should be given the chance to find out. And if you can only get if (you may have to search it out in England), read Richard Jefferies' *Bevis: The Story Of A Boy*. You surely can get Thomas Bailey Aldrich's *The Story Of A Bad Boy* — a lovely and delicious book; and (if nothing else) it will give your child a hint of the world before "Liberals" smogged it up, the world that was free and exciting and true and good.

And don't forget William Blake's "Tiger, Tiger" from *Songs Of Experience*; and "Little Lamb, who made thee?" from *Songs of Innocence* . . . . And, above all, read the Bible — the great and true "myths," the stories; read about Samson and Delilah, and David and Goliath . . . . Don't insult and degrade the child by supposing that he cannot understand these! He can. And only as you offer him the best will he rise toward the possible.

As your child grows older, read to him Longfellow's *Hiawatha*; and even better, Longfellow's "The Saga Of King Olaf" (from the stories in *Tales Of A Wayside Inn*). And, of course, as my wife wisely reminds me, Coleridge's great "Rhyme Of The Ancient Mariner," and (at least) "The Feet Of The Young Men" (from Kipling's *Collected Poems*):

> Who hath smelt wood-smoke at twilight?
> Who hath heard the birch-log burning?
> Who is quick to read the noises of the night?
> Let him follow with the others, for
>   the Young Men's feet are turning
> To the camps of proved desire and known delight!

Read your child, too, *The Arabian Nights*. Here is love that endures; here woman and man are born for each other and find no peace till they find each other. Here Sinbad the Sailor carries free enterprise into the dangerous places of the world, and brave Princes and passionate Princesses hold the impossible dream through separation and years of waiting. Here the great standards go into battle, and loyalty and courage live in the hearts of men. Here are Ali Baba and the forty thieves (with no Supreme Court to save them!); and Aladdin and his wonderful lamp. It is a book that will nourish the joy of life in the heart and the glory of love, too.

Here, in "The Story Of The Three Sisters," Prince Bahman, for his sister's sake, goes on the perilous quest for the Golden Water and the Singing Tree. He meets a wise old Dervish, who warns him of the invisible enemies he will meet. "As you ascend you will see on your right and left a great number of large black stones, and will hear on all sides a confusion of voices, which will utter a thousand injurious threats to discourage you and prevent your reaching the summit of the mountain. Be not afraid; but above all things, do not turn your head to look behind you; for in an instant you will be changed into such a black stone as those you see, which are all youths who have failed in this enterprise."

How truthfully that speaks to our condition — to those of us who also seek the Golden Water and the Singing Tree, and who hear a confusion of voices and a thousand threats which, if we turn to listen, will change us also into blackened stones by the side of the perilous road!

And read your children that beautiful modern classic, *The Incredible Journey*, by Sheila Burnford (Little, Brown & Company, Boston and Toronto). For here the bonds of love between children and animals are made articulate and strong, and the faithfulness and love and courage of our elder brothers, the creatures with four feet, are made a joy forever.

A bit esoteric, but beautiful and good, is the late Lord Dunsany's *A Dreamer's Tales* (John W. Luce & Company, Boston). Lord Dunsany was always a romantic, the foe of all the stuffy mediocrity of the "modern" world, the critic of preoccupation with the economic and the "social" and the "political." In his poignant tale, "Blagdaros," he writes of the old worn-out Rocking-horse in the waste land, who says:

> "I am Blagdaros . . . Alas! for the great days that are gathered, and alas for the Great One that was a master and a soul to me, whose spirit is now shrunken and can never know me again, and no more ride abroad on knightly quests. I was Bucephalus when he was Alexander, and carried him victorious as far as Ind. I encountered dragons with him when he was St. George, I was the horse of Roland fighting for Christendom, and was often

Rosinante. I fought in tourneys and went errant upon quests, and met Ulysses and the heroes . . . . Or late in the evening, just before the lamps in the nursery were put out, he would suddenly mount me, and we would gallop through Africa. There we would pass by night through tropic forests, and come upon dark rivers sweeping by, all gleaming with the eyes of crocodiles . . . . Then I would wheel suddenly, and the dust flew up from my four hoofs as I turned and we galloped home again and my master was put to bed . . . .

But his master "began to grow larger in his body and smaller in his soul" – he went to Progressive Schools, that is, and was subjected to the Department of Health, Education and Welfare – and "then he rode more seldom upon quests." This is a book, I think, that can save your child from becoming a Flower Child . . . because it makes him a Child of the World's Wonder.

I cannot imagine any child – or boy, at least – growing toward the shining glory of true life, unless he has read *Treasure Island*, with its romance, its adventure, its glory of living dangerously, its loyalty and courage. Or unless he has read *Robinson Crusoe*, and the endeavor of the individual. When I wish to rest and convalesce, I read that *now*, and as a boy I read it with delight in the secure cave, the mighty wall, the loaded muskets, the goats and the parrot and the dog, the faithful Man Friday. Here is a book to dwell in and find the strength of the soul. Read it to your children!

And be sure, too, that they grow up on the older Mississippi, with Huckleberry Finn, and old Jim, and Tom Sawyer – absorbing the river and the sun through the naked hide, "haggling a catfish open" and frying him on the shore, discoursing under the night sky about King Solomon – or the stars . . . . This is a great book out of the American psyche and *for* the American soul, and children who read it as it should be read will grow up to be Americans forever, even in Heaven.

Be sure, too, that your children know the knightly splendor or *Ivanhoe*, and "The Lady Of The Lake," and "Marmion," and all that they can of Sir Walter Scott. Here virtue and courage will become the shining substance of the soul; here all that is good and great, all that is absolute and eternal, will be sunlight in the very bloodstream. And as children grow older, try to incorporate into the family life a reading of Charles Reade's *The Cloister And The Hearth* and Charles Dickens' *Great Expectations* (my own favorite). And do not forget Cooper's *Deerslayer* and *The Last Of The Mohicans*.

Under the saccharine sentimentality of John Dewey and the "Liberals," the sentimentality of most of the "modern" mind, we are told to water the difficult down into the easy. Children are supposed to need the high and the hard turned into the soft and the low. The Bible has to be turned into the vernacular; the classics have to be diluted with barley water. How stupid! Children need to be treated as if they had minds — challenge them, act as if they were athletes of the brain.

I remember when the late Countee Cullen, the fine Negro poet, was visiting at our home my step-son, then seven or eight, immediately got out his volume of Chaucer and discussed it with Countee and man and boy were equals. I remember, too, that when I was five or six my parents were reading me the poetry of Milton and Dante (in translation); that when I was only ten I found, for and by myself, most of Sir Walter Scott, and all of Longfellow, and the plays of Shakespeare (including "Troilus And Cressida" and "Measure For Measure"), and read them through. Children, if you don't treat them like little victims of pernicious anemia of the mind, *can* read great books — and *should*. Don't stoop *down* to them. Act as if you expect them to reach *up*.

Within the last year, I read to the three lovely children of my friend Scott Stanley, Alfred Noyes' "The Highwayman," and from Robert Frost, and my own "Unicorn," and they sat entranced and appreciative. His charming daughter, Leslie, was at the time writing a report on "Unicorns" for her teachers. The minds of children, the souls of children, unless "Liberals" get hold of them, are capable of the high and the difficult and the great. But most schools cater to them as if they were little morons; and on the silver screen the networks suppose they have the I.Q. of a mudbank clam.

If it is impossible to return to reading, our culture is no longer a *culture*. Such a Wee One as Marshall McLuhan writes against the printed page (often in three hundred printed pages!), and in sentimental praise of the silver screen. He may or may not know what he does, but he does it. And what he does is to seek to destroy the abiding and eternal bases of beauty, of life, of wisdom, and to uphold the ephemera of the hour. Our labor of love is exactly the opposite; we would nourish the Inner Kingdom, the contemplative soul, the life that has become art, in our children by the books they read.

One of the great sources of joy and wisdom in my own life was the family practice of reading aloud together — and even in this age of superficiality and nonsense and the silver screen, I think it can be done again. It may be hard at first, it may require firmness, but I have faith enough in children to believe that they will answer to beauty and magic as the living seed answers to the sun. Most of TV (not all, thank God!) is ephemeral; and none of it is distilled into abiding form, only a hand's reach away, as Stevenson and Dickens and Cervantes and Shakespeare are. Books partake of the miracle of the Incarnation — the Word that has become flesh!

Therefore I would hope that all your children, very early, will read (or have read to them) Cervantes' *Don Quixote*, and *Romeo And Juliet* and *King Lear* — or at least *The Tempest*, the novels of Sir Walter Scott and of Charles Dickens, and *Cyrano de Bergerac*, and the one great novel of Thornton Wilder, *The Bridge Of San Luis Rey*, and John Buchan's *Mountain Meadow* as well as *The Thirty-Nine Steps*. And also *The Forest Lovers*, by Maurice Hewlett, and *Green Mansions*, by W.H. Hudson (one of the great books of the world), and Mary Johnston's beautiful *Prisoners Of Hope*.

There are for us all — for the children who are more mature than we sometimes know, and for us who are more childlike than we sometimes admit — books that are friends forever, books that inhabit what the wise Australian aborigines call "the great dream time"; books that are the immortal soul of the West — *of the world*. The things that are really ours, consciousness and character, are things of the Inner Kingdom; they dwell in books; and books in their essence are immortal and eternal, and wait for us in the Libraries of Heaven. Books are the treasures of the soul, radiant and rich as the gems of Ali Baba's famous cave; they are the true treasures of the earth.

God's Book:
The Soaring Beauty Of The Bible

IN our justified and noble reverence for the Bible as religion, we sometimes forget or neglect it as literature. And if we so ignore the Bible as literature — as the greatest single book of literature in the world — we lose much of the power and glory of the Bible. Here is a great work of art; here beauty that is "fair as the moon, clear as the sun." Here a *readable* book.

And if we read it as we should, the lilies of the field have splendor greater than Solomon's; and rainbows fill the skies like a drift of peacock feathers; and lightnings dance upon the hills. Seeing this, feeling this, we are never the same: We have shared the supreme expression of supreme experience. We should *read* the Bible because it is so *readable*; because we *love* to read it, just as we love to walk in the sunlight — not as a "duty" but as an aesthetic experience.

Scientific "explanations" of the world are here today and gone tomorrow. They are mere facets of time. But the Bible is the whole diamond of Eternity, giving us all the facets of life and also the whole and organic gem. Secular "literature" or "science" has its place and use for a day, and then is swept into the dustbins of history. The Bible transcends all the brooms of time, and grows younger and deeper and richer *in saecula saeculorum*, as immortal as beauty, as timeless as Eternity.

The Bible is invulnerable to all the weapons of time. It never grows old; it *can* never grow old. It lives in the only "Now" generation — *in the Eternal Now of God.* It is true in every age, because it transcends every age. It is primal, but never "primitive"; it is ancient like the sunrise, like the way of a man with a maid, like the wings of the eagle; and therefore it is never old. "Man is born to trouble as the sparks that fly upward" . . . "Seven years seemed to him but a few days, for the love he had for her" . . . "I sleep, but my heart waketh" . . . "The stars in their courses fought against Sisera" . . . "Before Abraham was, I am" . . . .

Turn where you will in the Bible, you find the wisdom that has become beauty; the beauty that makes wisdom potent in the world.

Here (in the King James, or the Authorized, or the Douay translations) you find literature that is life immortal, *in saecula saeculorum* . . . .*

I

ONE of the primal modes of the Bible is what foolish moderns
deride as the "myth" — that greatest mode of conveying reality.

Nowhere else in the world can you find such a "myth" to equal
that of Eden — in truth, in beauty. It is the key, and the only
complete key, to all that afflicts us today. There we see the primal,
unspoiled, and integral being of man fractured and ruined by rationality; by the gadgets of artifice and the knives of analysis; by the lie
of that first great con man in history, that we shall become as gods!

All that D.H. Lawrence saw through a glass darkly (honor to
him!), is here seen face to face. The segregation of mind from soul,
the cerebration and sophistication that are the leukemia of the mind,
all these are seen and said in that supreme and eternal "myth." Here
is the beginning of wisdom, the reality that should be at the basis of
all education. And the beauty of it! — of that immortal Garden
"eastward in Eden"! The truth of it — of man and woman — is
superb and timeless; "Therefore shall a man leave his father and his
mother, and shall cleave unto his wife; and they shall be one flesh."

And the other "myths" that are the substance and the essence of
reality — of Cain and Abel, of Noah and the ark, of the Tower of
Babel (that preview of modernity and the U.N.!), of Lot's wife —
looking backward and being frozen into the pillar of salt! To find
modern reality — *and to understand it* — one should turn to the great
ancient timeless "myths" that are truer than all the "facts" of
empiricism.

The Bible is both true and beautiful because it never quibbles with
the lie called "relativism"; it is categorical, absolute, final; it laughs at
Supreme Courts and political ideologies, for it is itself the Court of
Last Resort and the Book of Judgment Day.

Its authenticity is always based upon the one thing that cannot
end or change: *"In the beginning God . . . ."* Every philosophy based
on "In the beginning man," or "In the beginning matter and mechanism," or "In the beginning the amoeba," forever fails because it is

---

*Do *not* read Phillips, or Moffatt, or the most recent abomination: They are not *literature*
at all. Always what a man or a book says is true only in the *how* by which it is said.

forever and obviously false. The only abiding and living philosophy is based upon the Absolute — hence, *"In the beginning God."*

II

THE BIBLE knows man as no other book in history knows him. "And God saw that the wickedness of man was great in the earth, and that every imagination of the thoughts of his heart was only evil continually." That is the great realism, in comparison with which Hobbes, or Dreiser, or Dean Swift, or any modern like Hemingway, is as insipid as thin pea-soup five days old.

And yet this great book is equally true to the nobility of man. Here is love such as only the great can know: "And Jacob served seven years for Rachel; and they seemed to him but a few days, for the love he had for her." Great also is the character of the Joseph who was as if buried, first in the dry well and then in exile in Egypt; yet who remained loyal and loving to his father, and his people, and even to his brothers who had betrayed him: "I am Joseph your brother, whom you sold into Egypt. Now therefore be not grieved, nor angry with yourselves, that ye sold me hither: for God did send me before you to preserve life."

Great also the seer as hero, the Moses who led his people away from the fleshpots of Egypt (for which, in their forty years in the wilderness, they repined!); who had to see his people dancing before the Golden Calf; who had to die before he himself had entered the Promised Land . . . .

And here is the David who slew the giant Goliath with only five smooth stones; the great Daniel, unharmed in the den of lions; the Jael who drove the tent-peg through the head of the sleeping Sisera in such a fashion that:

> When she had pierced and stricken through his temples,
> At her feet he bowed, he fell, he lay down;
> At her feet he bowed, he fell:
> Where he bowed, there he fell down dead.

Splendor of the great deed, savagery noble and unashamed, fulfillment of the stars in their courses that fought against Sisera!

And also, to balance this with tenderness and mercy, God rebukes the petulant Jonah who grieved that Nineveh was not destroyed: "And should not I spare Nineveh, that great city, wherein are more than sixscore thousand persons that cannot discern between their right hand and their left hand; *and also much cattle?*" The supreme pity, the noble mercy, the embracing love of God, who would not destroy the innocent beasts of the field — loving not only men, but all His creatures.

And how deep and true the grief of David, even for his rebellious son: "O my son Absalom, my son, my son!" And how wonderfully readable the words of Ezekiel in the Valley of Dry Bones! — "Then said he unto me, 'Prophesy into the wind, prophesy, Son of Man, and say to the wind, "Thus saith the Lord God, 'Come from the four winds, O breath, and breathe upon these slain, that they may live.' " ' " How perfect for the Valley of Dry Bones that is our world today, the prayer that the great four winds may blow, and that the dead bones may at last, and once again, live!

Of course, the *poetry* of the Bible is magnificent. Remember the Psalms, those poems of might and majesty:

> Who coverest thyself with light as with a garment;
> Who stretchest out the heavens like a curtain;
> Who layeth the beams of his chambers in the waters;
> Who maketh the clouds his chariot;
> Who walketh upon the wings of the wind;
> Who maketh his angels spirits,
> His ministers a flaming fire . . . .

Here *is* the living God, from whom man may not flee though he takes the wings of the morning, or ascends into Heaven, or makes his bed in Hell. And here, too, is the human lyric of exile and nostalgia:

> By the rivers of Babylon,
> There we sat down, yea, we wept,
> When we remembered Zion.

Here is the absolute and eternal sense of the eternal and absolute; here is life essential and sheer:

> Thou understandest my thought afar off.
> Thou compasseth my path and my lying down,
> And art acquainted with all my ways.
> For there is not a word in my tongue,
> But lo, O Lord, thou knowest it altogether.

Here is the realization of *reality*, without which nations and individuals wither like the grass of the field, but with which they stand tall and great in their own splendid humility. And there is also that marvel among love poems, "The Song of Songs":

> Set me as a seal upon thine heart, as a seal upon thine arm;
> For love is strong as death;
> Jealousy is cruel as the grave;
> The flashes thereof are flashes of fire,
> A very flame of the Lord.
> Many waters cannot quench love,
> Neither can the floods drown it;
> If a man would give all the substance of his house for love,
> He would utterly be contemned.

Here is — a poem! Here is — love! Set in comparison with it, all the "scrannel pipes" of the sex-mongers are like the chirping of spavined crickets compared with a symphony by Beethoven. Here is passion, here is love with all its delights —

> Awake, O north wind; and come, thou south;
> Blow upon my garden, that the spices thereof may flow out.
> Let my beloved come into his garden,
> And eat his precious fruits.

Here is poetry to read, here is poetry to live; here is the sheer essential being of love. Here, too, in the earlier books, is the great Song of Deborah (from which I have already quoted), a lyric of victory and the destruction of one's enemy. And there are also poems here and poems there, of the depth of being and the essence of life, poems of the spectrum of being, poems that indicate colors below red and above violet.

One great and most readable book is *Ecclesiastes*. This is a book which we perhaps most need today — the critique of time by Eternity. Its basic affirmation is that God has set Eternity in man's heart, *but man has sought out "many inventions."* Today, in our humanistic sentimental optimism, and equally in our God-deprived humanistic panic pessimism, we need *Ecclesiastes* as a bitter and noble tonic, as the searching rays of the sun that can kill and yet without which we die. Its style is so magnificent that it is like the rhythm of great surf upon a shore of black basalt; like the music of *Dies Irae* played by a great organist:

One generation goeth, and another generation cometh; and the earth abideth forever. The sun also ariseth, and the sun goeth down, and hasteth to the place where he ariseth. The wind goeth toward the south, and turneth about unto the north; it turneth about continually in its course, and the wind returneth again to its circuits. All the rivers run into the sea, yet the sea is not full; unto the place whither the rivers go, thither they go again . . . .

* * *

That which has been is that which shall be; and that which hath been done is that which shall be done: and there is no new thing whereof men say, "See, this is new"? It hath been already, in the ages which were before us.

If only college students had been given this tonic of Eternity's skepticism of time, we would have been spared all the lies of Communism, and the Welfare State, and humanism. Even today it can be the soul's insulin to counteract our intellectual diabetes.

No one is truly educated for living until he has read and assimilated the wisdom of the essay (or poem) on time and timing:

> To everything there is a season,
> And a time to every purpose under the heaven:
> A time to be born, and a time to die;
> A time to plant, and a time to pluck up that which is planted;
> A time to kill, and a time to heal . . . .

He who knows this, has entered the enchanted Land of Wisdom; he can safely absorb even knowledge, for he is no albino academic Ph.D. The whole book is a classic of wisdom, a masterpiece of reality. Nor does it negate life, but only the lies of life; it strengthens us to run nobly the race that is set before us. It should be vocal in our pulpits; it should be resonant upon our campuses. *It is not* – and so . . . .

And how readable is *Job*, that great book that Thomas Carlyle so loved. It is the closest to drama in the Bible: the drama . . . or the epic . . . of the inner life. It deals, as Aeschylus and Shakespeare and Goethe and all the greatest seek to deal, with the Problem of Evil. Here is the fundamental cry of man's heart, "O that I but knew where I might find Him!" Here is the good man – not a mask of good, but a true and noble heart – on whom unmerited disaster falls, desolation on desolation, catastrophe on catastrophe, till his very wife in pity bids him curse God and die. But Job will not. To the end, against all the moralistic arguments of his "friends," he maintains his innocence of evil, and still he says: "Though He slay me, yet will I trust in Him."

Typical "moderns" like the late H.G. Wells (who knew the "outline of history" but never the essence of life) have never understood this book. Typical Wee Ones like Archibald MacLeish have tried to rewrite it — and perpetrated bathos. Wells supposed that the answer given is that God is represented as irrational power, before which man must bow in dumb submission. That is not what the book says! If you read the great torrent of terrible and beautiful words, which cascade like an upward Niagara of creation, you know better. God is He who makes the rain to fall upon the dry land, who gives the young lions their food, who guides the stars in their courses — who is the beneficent Lord of Life. His merciful power is so vast — a *potentia qua* of essential Life — that we cannot see His limits or comprehend His diversity; but what we do see and know indicates, even where we cannot see or know, His mercy, His loving-kindness, His power to sustain sun or planet, to feed the young lions, to water the thirsty land. And therefore, even when He slays us, we can trust in Him. This side of the New Testament, there is no answer more profound and true.

For poetry, for depth, for grandeur, here is a book that is like Jacob's Ladder descending out of Heaven, and the wrestling of God with Jacob the wanderer till the light of dawn!

And there are the readable prophets — from the Jeremiah who sees doom, to the Second Isaiah who sees destiny:

> Even the youths shall faint and be weary,
> And the young men shall utterly fall:
> But they that wait upon the Lord shall renew their strength;
> They shall mount up with wings as eagles;
> They shall run, and not be weary;
> And they shall walk, and not faint.

Here is truth become beauty, here are words that you can read and not be weary, here a book like bread for the hungry and water for the thirsty mouth! And the greatness of the thought (which is always the foundation of beauty) contradicts the "Liberal" churchmen of the little day in which we live. They suppose that the

Prophets were revolutionists, looking forward to some utopian future. Rather, the Prophets looked outside time — neither to past *nor* future, but to the eternal absolutes of truth and reality that simply *are*. They judged the present because it had *fallen away* from the Eden of God, because it had betrayed the timeless Word, because it had forgotten and fallen and failed. The great life, to them, lay not in "revolution," but in return; its nature was a recovery and a conservation of the affirmation of God which men had betrayed. All the prophets are great because they are *the conservatives of God*.

As we read this fascinating and magnificent Literature of Power, we know anew that "the status quo" is always a revolution away from the *potentia qua*. The Establishment is always a revolution against the Holy Spirit.

And how much more there is in the Bible! The beautiful story of Ruth, for example, is a joy forever:

And Ruth said, "Intreat me not to leave thee, or to return from following after thee: for whither thou goest, I will go; and where thou lodgest, I will lodge: thy people shall be my people, and thy God my God: where thou diest, will I die, and there will I be buried: the Lord do so to me, and more also, if aught but death part thee and me."

Is it any wonder that a book so great — and so readable — has been, and is, and ever shall be, the best seller among the books of the world. The Bible is the Book of Books, world without end!

III

EQUALLY readable, and equally great as literature, is the New Testament.

In all great ancient cultures there were the great Mysteries. And what is more readable by man than a Mystery? But here was the essential Mystery of God's being, of God's relationship to man, of the interplay of time and Eternity. And here is the deepest, the greatest, the central Mystery of all literature — the Incarnation, the Word become flesh, the very God becoming very man. The strangest and the greatest Mystery in all the world!

The greatest of tragedies is here, too, the Divine Tragedy, that is also in Dante's sense the Divine *Comedy*. And the wonder and the majesty and the beauty of it is that in this Biography of God as man, the humble authors rise to the height of the great argument, and present Him who "spake as never man spake." And so: "Heaven and earth shall pass away, but my words shall not pass away . . . . I go to prepare a place for you. In my Father's house are many mansions . . . . Before Abraham was I am . . . ."

And here are parables and images unequalled in all other literature; here is insight into Eternity that transcends all other human wisdom; here is the Word that does not "teach" or "preach," but tells it "like it is." Nowhere else in literature can you equal Christ's answer to jesting Pilate and his flippant "What is truth?" — the answer He had already given to doubting Thomas: *"I* am the way, the truth, and the life." The meaning of Christ is that truth is an I Am, an authenticity of being, a Word become flesh.

The magnificent and terrible drama of that Life in itself is the greatest drama in the world. And from it, in its sunlit course, arise aspects of wisdom and beauty unequalled elsewhere in the world's literature. The appreciation of the lilies of the field (would that the pseudo "flower children" would read and heed!), the miracles that rolled back the darkness of the blind and the mortality of the dead, the affirmation of the Kingdom that is not of this world, the Lord's prayer that is the great poem-of-prayer . . . all these are the Word become flesh in a literature that reveals the Mystery of Mysteries.

How readable, also, the great letters of the Saul who became Paul, wakened by the great Light on the road to Damascus. A "poet"-of-putty, like the late Edgar Lee Masters, wrote in silly ignorance: "Along came a man called Paul/ And spoiled it all." As if God would *allow* anyone to "spoil" His own drama! Paul was formerly a great intellectual, who was saved from that fate by becoming a great spiritual. His greatest words probe the Mystery and illuminate the power and the glory so that men may know God more fully through the words of mere man. And how readable his great Epistles!

Nor must we forget that tremendous and beautiful book, *Revelation.* The seer on Patmos, seeing clearly that the end of the world — of *this* world — was upon him and upon all men, did not despair like the modern "Liberal" cringing before the atom bomb; he saw this world and this life in terms of Eternity:

I am Alpha and Omega, the beginning and the end, the first and the last.

Here is "the bright and morning star," here the "pure river of the water of life, clear as crystal," here "the holy city, new Jerusalem, coming down from God out of Heaven, prepared as a bride adorned for her husband." And here are the strange prophecies and outlines of the eternal war of good with evil that shall end in the supernatural victory of good.

Underlying all the Bible, in the Old Testament and the New Testament, is the theme that pervades and unifies all: "In the beginning God . . . ." In the beginning — and in the end — God! "I am Alpha and Omega . . . ."

And always there is literature. It is never dull, never tedious (save in some genealogies), never abstract and tortured and dull like the style of John Dewey or Herbert Marcuse; it is a book for the humble tinker, John Bunyan, and for the noble modern Irishman, Lord Dunsany, and for Mr. Everyman. It is the Book of God, and therefore the Book for man. It is not a book — but a library, a universe, a cosmos of literature; a Book of Books. It is a pure river of the water of life, clear as crystal, where all the sons of men may drink.

Here is genius, here is the splendor and the essence of life, here is the work of the Holy Spirit. If, out of all the literature of the world, one could preserve only one book, that book should be the Bible. I love the literatures of Greece and Rome, of Europe and America and China; but if I had to choose one book — which God in His infinite mercy forbid! — I would choose the Bible.

Here, let us never forget, is the pure literature of the power and glory of the living word, of aesthetic *joy*. Here is life "immense in passion, pulse, and power"; here is Keats' "An endless fountain of immortal drink,/ Pouring unto us from the heaven's brink."

We should never read it as a duty, as dogma or instruction, as something merely "good" for us. Here is no mere "teaching" or "preaching." Christ, for example, was no "teacher" — He was far too great for that — He was a great artist. Was He not the human incarnation of the artist who created the cosmos?

Here is the music of the Morning Stars; here is the dance of the waves under the baton of the moon; here is the innocent joy of children playing on the beaches of the world where the mighty waters are "rolling evermore." Here is the mode of God, who gives us the bonus of color and not only the usefulness of line; who adds the joy of passion to the use of love; who flies the clouds like kites in a sky made beautiful with azure. God is no college professor, but a poet — no sociologist, but an artist — who, when He was made flesh and dwelt among men as a man, made His words to gleam like lustrous pearls or dance like lambent lightnings. Here is a book that speaks to our condition with the power and the glory, and which we read because we *love* it.

Let us read the Bible as it should be read, and the meaning will take care of itself. To paraphrase Walt Whitman: Whoso touches this Book, touches God!

Afterword

ROBERT BROWNING wrote, in "One Word More":

There they are, my fifty men and women
Naming me the fifty poems finished!

I have no "fifty men and women"; I have only perhaps fifty hints that I have shot like arrows toward a vision which I believe men have had in a nobler time, and which we may approach even today. I hope that, at least, they may have raised our aim in the high trajectory of the soul.

What have I seen? What have I tried to say? I say a firm No to the conformities and complacences of today, the platitudes, the super-stitions. I say No to the "Liberal" Yes that results in a Servile State, I say No to the contemporary creed of private man being crushed into public mass. I say No to the defeatism of the degenerate sons of Thomas Jefferson, George Washington, and Patrick Henry, who would surrender liberty even for survival. I say No to the *Insiders* who lust for One World, like a very fat goose with its single neck fast within their very greedy teeth. I say No to the secularism that is based upon a temporal (and I think a temporary) dogma of a naturalistic interpretation of the cosmos, in terms of omnipotent matter and the universally absurd.

But even more important, I say Yes to what is today the Forbidden Faith, to the heretical orthodoxy, to a sense of the beneficent mystery that surrounds our little life and our partial world. I say Yes to God, and hail Him again risen from the tomb, the stone again rolled away. I would restore God, and the values that flow from God — truth, beauty, good — to their rightful place in the hierarchy of the mind. Of course, God and these values are always there. They never ceased to be there. They have only been lost by the errant minds of fallible men, in the smog of our temporal illusions.

295

Truth is like a bell. We strike it, and then the beautiful resonance of sound fades into silence. So we must strike it again . . . and yet again . . . and yet again. We cannot attain truth by any revolutionary smashing of the bell, or by the substitution of a siren, or a fog horn, or a saxophone. We reach truth by a return and a renewal, as we reach spring, or summer, or autumn, or winter, by a renewal of the seasons that can change only because they never change. Of this I am sure. And so I have said it, though many of the men of my time may mock and deride me.

One thing helps to confirm me in my anti-conformity. It is this. I have received a deep and wide and understanding response from many thousands of men and women, even in this day when collectivism and secularism are the idols of most men's idolatry. I have found that they, too, beneath and above the political and the social, are concerned with the philosophical, the aesthetic, the spiritual. And I have received deep understanding and a glowing response from many, many young people. The youth that our conventional media of communication lust to present as only "revolutionary" (that is, conformist to our contemporary platitudes), are hungry for the bread of reality and thirsty for the waters of life. I know this by firsthand experience. They have written me, they have spoken to me, they understand me. This gives me a renewal of hope and a strengthening of faith. And in the outer and the inner world, by many strange and beneficent confirmations, I have felt the presence and the power of God. Henry David Thoreau somewhere speaks of suddenly coming into a woodland glade and feeling the assurance that some living presence had just been there and was even now almost there still. I know what he meant. I think I know even more. The strange and haunting presence is still there when I come into the glade; I have seen it, I have known it.

I know only too well the insuperable powers that have usurped the megaphone of communication in the outer world today. I know the pervading "Liberal" hypnosis that holds formidable majorities of good, intelligent Americans fast in a psychological trap. Perhaps we shall need the drastic courage of muskrat or beaver, till we gnaw a foot off to be free. I would not be an easy optimist, a sentimentalist of hope. I am a sad optimist — but a gay pessimist. I do not predicate an easy victory or an early reversal of tide and trend. If I believed only in man, only in this world, I would despair. But as a spiritual — as a fundamental Christian — I believe that the invisible is greater than the visible, that the things unseen eventually rule the things seen. Who would have wagered his life, or even a few sesterces, upon Christ versus Caesar, upon the strange gospel of the Galilean against the Roman Empire? We live (perhaps) in a new decline and fall; we must endure (perhaps) a new Dark Age. But we have a sense of Eternity; a knowledge of Him who said, "Before Abraham was I am."

Thomas Carlyle once wrote: "Our religion is not yet a horrible restless doubt . . . ; but a great heaven-high Unquestionability, encompassing, interpenetrating the whole of Life . . . ." (He was writing of the Twelfth Century.) Men, he said, then believed that this "Earthly Life and *its* riches and possessions, and good and evil hap, are not intrinsically a reality at all, but are a shadow of realities eternal and infinite; that this Time-world, as an air-image, fearfully emblematic, plays and flickers in the grand still mirror of Eternity; and man's little Life has duties that are great, that are alone great, and go up to Heaven and down to Hell."

I know that our modern age ridicules such a vision and no longer believes it. I know also that without such a vision this modern age stumbles and falls, or sinks ever deeper into a quicksand. The more secular the world becomes, the sadder and more hopeless the predicament of man. The more man is given cake to eat, the less he appreciates even bread. The TV jingle assures us, accompanied by the usual sinuous writhings, "You've come a long way, Baby!" But it does not tell us whether it is a long way from Heaven. The steadfast laurel that we seek does not grow on earthly hills. This I know.

Just because it does not grow on earthly hills, I have hope for this earth. We have perhaps reached a culmination of techniques of applied science in our marvellous and dramatic flights to the moon. Maybe, as Whittaker Chambers once said, earth is now the shore of space. We may yet voyage to the planets; we may yet win passage to other habitable earths. I do not say No to this hope; but I think our greater hope lies in far more distant worlds — that are far nearer. If Columbus transferred the unhappiness and pride and greed of Europe to a New World, was the world really — *new*? The Kingdom of Heaven lies not in space, but in spirit. What man is, and even where man goes, depends upon his character and his consciousness. Wherever he goes, he reaches only himself — and God, who was with him when he set out. So the most important question is not where he goes, but what self he takes with him, and the God he finds no more fully just by shuttling through space. Modern man should be in search of a soul, and not just of a passage to the moon. If only man can realize that, and know that it does not profit us to win all the planets unless we know what to do with them (as we do not yet know what to do with the earth), and our great need is to bring the dark side of the moon of ourselves (our subconscious) into union with the light side of the moon of ourselves (our consciousness), man may become at last the astronaut of Heaven. I have hope that man may yet see this. I have hope because there is much in man yet to be explored, and to be born.

And I have faith. I have faith just because of man's unhappiness in his secular cities. I have faith because man, having had his fling of wild oats with the harlot called "Liberal" humanism, is quite disillusioned with her. Man has made a mess of man. Therefore I have faith, because I believe that the spirit of man can reach out and touch God, and so may yet transcend humanism and man.

And so I believe that man will yet turn from the hive and the heap — the ways that insects tried, and found a dead end — and seek the life more abundant. I believe that man, awakened, will yet turn from loveless sex, from lightless knowledge, from the poverty of affluence. I believe that he will yet seek William Blake's "Auguries of Innocence" —

> To see a World in a Grain of Sand
> And a Heaven in a Wild Flower,
> Hold Infinity in the palm of your hand
> And Eternity in an hour.

I hold that faith. I also hold my own determination — come wind, come weather — to live for, and affirm, that faith and the sort of life to which it leads. I shall never reach it here and now, in this world and life. That is why I keep the faith. Browning knew:

> Ah, but a man's reach should exceed his grasp,
> Or what's a Heaven for?

And even here and now, on this beautiful and precious earth, in this mysterious and wondrous life, we can do much. We can be centers of life, centers of light, like the ebullient stars that we call suns. We may create little groups or clusters of men like stars. Around us, not shut in by the iron curtain of the coercive State (which Nietzsche rightly called "That coldest of all cold monsters"), but in the free development and enrichment of groups and independent nations and private men into units of the local and the different, we may create *from within* a living and beloved community. It may be impossible. But how shall we know until we fail — or succeed? At least, here is a faith, a hope, and a love to keep us warm . . . and alive and joyous. Most men today, not possessing a faith, a hope and a love, are neither joyous nor alive. But we may be joyous and alive again if we dream the steadfast dream, saying with Don Quixote, "The road is always better than the inn."

The wheel of the world contains many fruitful tensions and many creative opposites. The conservative does not wish to censor them or suppress them; he would keep them alive — but keep them natural and have them keep their place and proportion. The puma and the deer; the bovine creatures that eat the grass — and fertilize it; the night and the day, life and death, are coherent parts of an orbed integrity. We believe that only such integral diversity can give us one world, and we would conserve it. We would not be "Liberal" or collectivist planners, who would shoot all the pumas, and then see the deer die of a weakened stock and an over-grazed food supply. But we do wish to preserve the proportion and balance of Nature, so that when there is a flying flood of grasshoppers devouring the grass and denuding the trees of leaves, we act to restore proportion and harmony. We do not, as in India, reverence life indiscriminately, so that we coddle sacred cows that contribute nothing in milk or meat or hides, and predatory rats that eat more grain in a year than can be sent in from other lands. We wish balance, harmony, wholeness.

I am not overly fond of the late Anatole France. But I remember with delight one image of his. In one of his books, a monk is shown a great wheel full of, and vivid with, the many colors of the world; and he is told that only where or when he sees *white*, will he see truth and reality. But nowhere does he see white, only the rich diversity of the many colors. Then his teacher grasps and turns a crank, faster and faster; and as the Wheel turns and spins, the many separate and diverse colors merge and blend and become one; and, as they blend, the wheel of the world becomes a single dazzling purity of white.

That, I hope, has been my vision in these pages. I do not tolerate excesses — the flying blight of grasshoppers, the sentimental reverence for sacred cows and rats. Nor do I seek to paint arbitrarily over all the various colors of the world with white lead. I am not an egalitarian. I reverence natural diversity, and I find sufficient unity in God's natural turning of the wheel of the world.

I believe that this is what all men today subconsciously desire. I believe that if they realize this consciously, and unite their conscious thought with their subconscious desire, we may indeed have less government, more individual responsibility, and a far, far better world. That, I think, is the patriot's steadfast dream. I have sought it in these pages. And, as Robert Frost says, "You come, too!"

About the author

E. MERRILL ROOT was graduated *Phi Beta Kappa* from Amherst College and did graduate work in English and theology at the University of Missouri, Andover Theological Seminary, and Harvard. He soon became Professor of English at Earlham College, where he lectured to enthusiastic and crowded classes for forty years.

Professor Root authored twelve major volumes of poetry, rated by Robert Frost, Max Eastman, and Taylor Caldwell as among America's very best. His poems have appeared in more than forty anthologies and texts, and his essays in many more. He spoke before countless audiences. He also wrote four important volumes of prose, and contributed articles to such Conservative journals as *American Opinion, The Review Of The News, Human Events, Christian Economics, The Freeman*, and *National Review*.

Prior to his death in 1973, Professor Root lived close to the rugged Maine coast at Kennebunkport. He was an Associate Editor of *American Opinion* magazine, in which these essays originally appeared.

Merrill Root was a man who saw and said what is there, who knew the timbre and pungency and feel of life because he was in tune with it. He was a scholar, gathering and saving and growing in the savor of the giants: Goethe and Cervantes, Homer and Aristotle, Dante and Shakespeare, Milton and St. Thomas Aquinas. And he remained a teacher, lighting lamps and charging souls, and preserving by transmitting his wisdom and insight and knowledge and love of the great, the real, the true, and the beautiful. Merrill Root's character was worthy of his genius, and to the day of his death at seventy-eight he never ceased to do and say greatly what he believed to be right and true.